AMERICA'S BOARDWALKS

RUTGERS UNIVERSITY PRESS

NEW BRUNSWICK, NEW JERSEY, AND LONDON

AMERICA'S BOARDWALKS

⊸ From Coney Island to California ⊷

JAMES LILLIEFORS

LIBRARY OF CONGRESS CATALOGING-IN-PUBLICATION DATA

Lilliefors, Jim

America's boardwalks : from Coney Island to California / James Lilliefors.

p. cm.

Includes bibliographical references.

ISBN-13: 978–0–8135–3805–1 (hardcover : alk. paper)

1. Recreation—United States—Anecdotes. 2. Boardwalks—United States—Anecdotes. 3. Lilliefors, Jim—Travel—United States.
4. United States—Description and travel. I. Title.

GV53.L54 2006   917.30022′2—dc22

2005024665

A British Cataloging-in-Publication record for this book is available
from the British Library.

Manufactured in China

For D.O.D.,

who has always enjoyed walking on the boards

Contents

All photographs are by the author
except where otherwise credited.

OCEAN CITY, MD.

The Great and Strange Parade

THE SEASIDE boardwalk was invented for utilitarian reasons, so that beachgoers could stroll along the shore in their evening wear without tracking sand into train cars or hotel lobbies. But it wasn't long before the imagination of a country just becoming acquainted with the concept of leisure time transformed the boardwalk into something more: bright, alluring, loud, lucrative—and very American.

Early boardwalk towns promoted themselves as "health" resorts, masking their sensuous, and sometimes sensual, appeal with a promise of increased well-being. Physicians of the day claimed that salt air and seawater had medicinal value, and the public readily bought into it. For the expanding urban working class, resorts such as Atlantic City, where the country's first boardwalk was built in 1870, offered an escape from the heat, factory fumes, and diseases of the city.

The boardwalk's fundamental lure was more than just fresh air, though. In a time of Victorian values—long before play became serious business—the seashore resort represented an intoxicating alternative to urban American life. As boardwalks evolved, they increasingly offered products and pleasures that people could not find at home, from foot-long hot dogs and saltwater taffy to roller coasters, funhouses, and Ferris wheels.

So many city dwellers flocked to the shore for these cheap, exotic attractions that the people themselves became part of the entertainment. With no admission gate, boardwalks were democratic, inviting visitors from all social and economic strata to join the same parade. Wealthy landowners

(OPPOSITE) A throng of summer visitors crowds the Boardwalk in Ocean City, Maryland, in the 1940s. (Courtesy of the Ocean City Life-Saving Station Museum.)

mingled with shopkeepers and immigrant factory workers in this always changing real-life procession. Boardwalk benches often faced the parade, not the ocean, facilitating the idle-time sport of people-watching.

Born at a time when the country was busy rebuilding and reinventing itself as an industrial and economic power, boardwalks seemed to herald a new American Dream, one of leisure, recreation, and middle-class prosperity. As the nation grew more clumsily daring and optimistic in the twentieth century, boardwalks kept pace, becoming a showcase for inventions and oddities. On Atlantic City's boardwalk and piers, you could find a "home of the future," as well as diving horses, kangaroo boxing, the world's largest typewriter (nearly two thousand times standard size), and a "dramatic reenactment" of the Johnstown flood.

Boardwalks were the forerunners of theme parks, mega shopping malls, and other latter-day attractions, but they were never replaced by them, in the way that drive-in theaters and urban movie palaces gave way to multiscreen cinemas or that strip centers and shopping malls closed the doors on Main Street. The tale of America's boardwalks is therefore something of a mystery story: What accounts for their longevity? And what does this longevity (they are now more than half as old as the United States itself) tell us about ourselves and our country?

It isn't a serious mystery—because boardwalks are mostly about having fun—but it can be an enchanting one, solved unexpectedly on summer evenings when the sea breeze is just right and the spinning lights of pier rides pulse with a sud-

den clarity above the ocean. The key may be a whiff of frying funnel cakes or the touch of warm wood on bare feet, the faint rumble of Skee-Balls or the remembered taste of frozen custard. You may gaze at the fire of sunset above an arcade's pink neon letters and hear in the pitch of teenage voices the forgotten music of your own youth.

Most people who grew up within a few hours of the mid-Atlantic coast know the visceral come-on of the boardwalk at night—a siren song intimately tied to childhood. As an Atlantic City historian noted, a little wistfully, "The Boardwalk after dark is a great place to be young." When I was a boy in the suburbs of Washington, D.C., it seemed incredible that we could drive two and a half hours, through the corn and soybean fields of Maryland's Eastern Shore, and arrive at a place as wondrous as the Ocean City Boardwalk, with its riot of lights and sounds and smells and people. Our family trips to the shore seemed like journeys to Oz. Even the climate was different—always cooler and windier than at home—and the people were clearly less inhibited. Later, as teenagers, many of us went to the Boardwalk for our first solo vacations and found a different sort of Oz: high school without parents.

Once we outgrow the novelty of these early experiences, it is sometimes surprising to find that the boardwalk's siren song is a kind of universal music to the young, continuing to lure new generations. Even more surprising is the spell it can cast on those who aren't so young—parents, for instance, who return with their children. The boardwalk bewitches us with lost scents and sounds, reminders of why we went in the first place: to belong, to escape, to watch the parade, to feast, to fall in love.

But boardwalks have a value beyond nostalgia, it turns out. In such coastal towns as Asbury Park, Daytona Beach, Myrtle Beach, and Wildwood, the boardwalk has become the centerpiece of ambitious economic revitalization and redevelopment plans—plans that in some cases have caused contentious debates about what the boardwalk is, and should be. As more and more Americans choose to live near the coast, saltwater property values have soared, and the fate of the boardwalk is increasingly subject to political tugs-of-war.

During the summer, fall, and winter of 2004, I journeyed along the edges of the country to twelve American boardwalks—not "the best" but a cross-section that seemed to tell the tale of American boardwalks most effectively. As I talked with business owners, historians, planners, and strollers, I was often struck by the vitality of the boardwalk as an idea, rather than just a place. Boardwalks are, in a sense, living monuments—to American enterprise, to American hooey, to American stubbornness. They are a last frontier, testaments to the power of individuality in an increasingly homogenized world. People still go there for products and pleasures they can't find at home—for Thrasher's french fries, Mack's pizza, or Nathan's hot dogs, rather than for McDonald's or Wendy's.

In this sense, the boardwalk is what it's always been: an exotic and sensuous alternative to everyday life. We go to escape, to belong, to watch the parade. Because it reminds us of who we are.

The story of America's boardwalks tells a larger tale, in other words. But it also tells hundreds of smaller stories, about the people who, in various ways, have kept this great and strange parade going. You will find some of these stories—told through words and pictures—in *America's Boardwalks*.

AMERICA'S BOARDWALKS

CHAPTER ONE

ATLANTIC CITY, NEW JERSEY

America's Playground

AT ABOUT an hour past daybreak, John Paxton leaves his home at Grammercy Place in the Inlet section of Atlantic City and climbs on his bicycle. It's still cool out, but as Paxton pedals south—boardwalk planks rattling beneath his wheels—the air warms with the day's first trace of summer heat.

Paxton, a retired postal worker, takes this same two-mile route each morning, pedaling past streets he has traveled all his life—although most bear little resemblance to what they looked like when he was growing up. Occasionally another bicyclist or morning stroller will nod hello, but they are not people Paxton recognizes. He rides by the giant casinos that form the Boardwalk skyline—Trump's Moorish Taj Mahal; the towering mirrored Resorts, which seems to blend with the brightening sky; Bally's, with its Wild West theme park façade—arriving finally at Billy's Food Court on Bellevue Avenue, a small Boardwalk eatery with a handful of outdoor tables. Several men call to Paxton as he parks his bicycle.

In a city perpetually in transition, the dozen men who gather here each morning are an anomaly. They meet at Billy's for breakfast the way that old-timers gather at small-town diners or general stores—to exchange stories and to banter, to feel the texture of something permanent. These are men

Fig. 1. (OPPOSITE) The heyday of the Atlantic City Boardwalk, in 1921, looking north from Maryland Avenue. Garden Pier is on the right while the tall hotel is the Saint Charles. (From the collection of Atlantic City historian Allen "Boo" Pergament.)

who were born in Atlantic City, who went to school here, who raised their families here, who retired here. One of them describes the meetings at Billy's as "our daily high school reunion."

The men are an anomaly because they represent permanence in a city where nothing feels permanent, not even the people. After breakfast, the men sit on Boardwalk benches, and Paxton points out things that most visitors to Atlantic City don't notice. The empty lot next to Billy's, for example. Two decades ago, the twenty-three-story Playboy Casino stood there. With its giant black bunny ears, Playboy was the Boardwalk's most distinctive building, but it existed for only three years before Playboy lost its license. After the bunny ears came down, the property was rechristened the Atlantis, but the Atlantis had serious problems. Then Donald Trump took over, eventually renaming it the World's Fair; by the time he closed it a few years ago, the casino was losing millions of dollars a year. Now it's gone.

Paxton, a tall, affable man, nods toward a handsome hotel-apartment building just to the south. "That used to be the Ritz," he says. "The last of the great hotels." Back in the late 1920s, mobster Meyer Lansky honeymooned there, in the Presidential Suite. Farther down was the grand Ambassador Hotel, largest on the Boardwalk, where Warren Harding vacationed, and where Lansky, Al Capone, Dutch Schultz, Lucky Luciano, and others held a three-day organized crime convention. Several blocks from where we're sitting, on Missouri Avenue, was the 500 Club; that's where Dean Martin and Jerry Lewis first performed together, Paxton says. A little north of that is the Kentucky Avenue nightclub district, where all the top African American performers of the fifties played: Nat Cole,

Fig. 2. An aerial view of the Boardwalk in the late 1960s. With its fortunes at low ebb, the city was about to wager its future on casino gambling. In the foreground is the Steel Pier, followed by Steeplechase Pier, Central Pier, and the Million Dollar Pier. (From the collection of Atlantic City historian Allen "Boo" Pergament.)

Sammy Davis Jr., Sarah Vaughan, lots of others. "Back in those days, there were movie theaters all over town. It seemed like there was one on every block," Paxton says.

There are no clubs anymore on Kentucky and Missouri avenues. There are no movie theaters anywhere in the city. The grand hotels are gone. But Atlantic City is thriving again in other ways. You can feel it here on the Boardwalk, in the gathering crowds of people who come out as the day heats up and patches of sunlight sparkle like sequins out on the ocean.

Although its fortunes sometimes seem as fluid as a night at the craps tables, Atlantic City has a singular, sustaining allure. Visitors arrive beneath signs welcoming them to "America's Favorite Playground," a slogan that has been in use, with slight variations, for more than a century. "Playground," of course, has meant different things over the years—from health resort to amusements mecca to gambling town—but a tradition links these incarnations. Atlantic City was created as a tonic for urban life, an exotic, sensuous getaway where the rules of behavior were a little more relaxed than they were back home. In various ways, Atlantic City helped to define the American concept of vacation, giving us many of our leisure-time traditions, among them the boardwalk.

Fig. 3. John Paxton on the Atlantic City Boardwalk in 2005. (Photo courtesy of John Paxton.)

Paxton, who was born in Atlantic City sixty-eight years ago, says, "We've had good times and bad. But there's something about Atlantic City, an idea that other towns don't have. Somehow it always seems to turn out all right."

"Bathing Village"

The "idea" that first gave rise to Atlantic City was a rail shuttle from the nation's newly industrialized cities to the seashore. The person behind the idea was Jonathan Pitney, a medical doctor who lived in Absecon, across the bay and marshlands from what would become Atlantic City. An ambitious, civic-minded man who hailed from nearby Mendham, Pitney led the fight to carve Atlantic County out of Gloucester County and later served as the new county's delegate to the state constitutional convention. Pitney's most important contribution, though, was his proposal for a rail line to what was then known as Absecon Island.

In 1851, when Pitney began to sell his idea, the future Atlantic City was a remote, heavily forested barrier island infested with mosquitoes and blacksnakes. Even so, Pitney correctly sensed its potential, envisioning what he called "a bathing village and health resort . . . where salt water and sea air would provide therapy to all who are ill from city living."

It was not unusual at the time for physicians to prescribe seashore cures for a variety of elusive ailments, some of which we no longer recognize today—among them consumption, Bright's disease, and dropsy. A day or two of inhaling sea air, along with regular ocean bathing (it wasn't yet called swimming), could have remarkable curative effects, people believed. Even if the seashore prescription had no actual medicinal value, there were clear psychological benefits. Pitney imagined building a city—or at least a resort—around this idea.

The problem with Pitney's plan was getting people there. The only way to Absecon Island from Philadelphia in 1851 was by stagecoach, a journey that took about twelve hours. But the burgeoning railroad industry was rapidly changing the country, bridging the distances between cities. Steam-powered locomotives, pioneered in England at the start of the nineteenth century, began operating in the United States in 1830. In the 1840s, short-line railroads appeared all over the country; by 1850, nine thousand miles of track had been laid. The railroad was rapidly shrinking the country, revolutionizing business and travel.

Pitney had the foresight to understand that the railroad would soon revolutionize the way Americans lived their lives as well. He pitched his plan to area merchants, property owners, railroad men, and potential investors. The Absecon rail line, originating in Camden, New Jersey—twelve miles outside Philadelphia—would not only turn a profit, he told them, it would also create a land and business boom that would transform Atlantic County. A number of investors lined up behind the plan, while critics dubbed Pitney's railway the "road to nowhere."

After extensive lobbying, Pitney was granted a railroad charter by the state legislature on March 19, 1852. In June of that year, seven men met to form the Camden & Atlantic Railroad Company, the group that would build the sixty-mile railway line. A land company was incorporated the following spring and began to acquire the property that would make Pitney's dream a reality. On Absecon Island, the company bought up oceanfront lots for $17.50 an acre (land that had been purchased for forty cents an acre in 1804). Construction of the rail line began in September 1852.

One of the men who proved instrumental in the establishment of Atlantic City was Philadelphia railroad engineer Richard Osborne. It was Osborne who surveyed the train route, laid out the streets, and gave the city its name. The naming of the streets—and the city—indicates the lofty ambition behind Atlantic City. Pitney and his group envisioned the island as a new sort of American destination, built around the lure of relaxation. At first, Atlantic City would draw its visitors mostly from Philadelphia, but Pitney saw it evolving into a kind of capital of East Coast health resorts—a National Resort. ("National Resort" would become one of Atlantic City's nicknames several decades later.) Other cities gave their streets the names of presidents or war heroes; Atlantic City named streets for the United States themselves—Florida Avenue, Georgia Avenue, Mississippi Avenue, Missouri Avenue, etc. Many streets that ran parallel to the beach were named for international bodies of water—Arctic Avenue, Atlantic Avenue, Baltic Avenue, Pacific Avenue, etc. On the map he gave the land company late in 1853, Osborne penciled in the name "Atlantic City."

By the time Atlantic City was incorporated, on March 3, 1854, construction of hotels, rooming houses, and bathhouses was well under way, anticipating the influx of visitors. On July 1, six hundred invited guests boarded the nine-car Camden & Atlantic Railroad train for the two-and-a-half-hour ride to Atlantic City. Three days later, on the Fourth of July, the "road to nowhere" opened to the public.

The railroad quickly transformed the island—and the island, more gradually, transformed American notions about rest and relaxation. The middle-class vacation, a staple of post–World War II American life, did not exist at the time Atlantic City was created, but the idea of leisure—a day, or hours, spent unwinding from the workweek—did. Many of Philadelphia's factory workers labored Monday through Saturday and rested on Sunday. Often they spent part of their free day on family outings. With the advent of Pitney's rail line, families could enjoy a seashore excursion in a single day. Businesses opened near the Atlantic City train station catering to these day travelers. In addition to renting bathhouses, where visitors could change into bathing suits, merchants sold beer, fresh seafood, sandwiches, and medicinal "tonics." At the same time, several grand wooden hotels were built by the shore, encouraging longer stays. The largest of these, the United States Hotel, which took up an entire block between Maryland and Delaware avenues, was under construction when the first train rolled into town. Its name is another reflection of the nationalistic hubris that went into the making of Atlantic City.

There were other beach resorts in the country at the time—notably Newport and Cape May—but they catered to a wealthier clientele. Atlantic City helped to create the idea of the middle-class and working-class vacation. It gave people an attractive destination for their leisure-time urges. Although promoted as a health resort, Atlantic City's secret lure was, and is, its intoxicating atmosphere of freedom and pleasure. It was a place where people could go to loosen their inhibitions. Much of the city's commercial growth was based on this idea. Atlantic City's taverns, for instance, were open on Sunday, when Philadelphia's were closed. Atlantic City offered a taste of a more exciting life. To perpetuate this illusion, it increasingly offered—and invented—attractions that people could not find at home.

WITH SO MANY PEOPLE taking the train to Atlantic City, it was perhaps inevitable that a pedestrian thoroughfare would eventually be built along the beach. Surprisingly, though, the original proposal for a seaside boardwalk was not an ambitious one. Its original purpose was simply to keep sand out of train cars and hotel lobbies.

The boardwalk idea came from a Camden & Atlantic Railroad engineer named Alexander Boardman, whose coach floors were covered with sand each evening after the return trips from Atlantic City. Boardman suggested an elevated foot-walk of wooden planks on the beach, spaced a quarter-inch apart, so that walking on them would shake the sand from people's feet into the cracks in the walk. Boardman shared his idea with Henry Bonsall, editor of the *Camden Republic* newspaper, who wrote an editorial in the spring of 1870 suggesting the foot-walk. Atlantic City hotel owners, frustrated by all the sand in their carpets and upholstery, backed the idea. On April 25, a petition was brought before the city council calling for a wooden walk along the beach. It was adopted by the council on May 9, 1870. The boardwalk resolution read, in part, like this: "That the city build a board walk along the beach from Congress Hall [Massachusetts and Pacific] to the Excursion House [between Missouri and Mississippi]. That said walk be ten

feet wide; that the boards be laid lengthwise; that the Committee be instructed to proceed with the erection of the walk immediately; that the Ordinance Committee be instructed to draft an ordinance prohibiting erection of any bathhouse or building of any kind within thirty feet of the walk; and none on the ocean side except by permission of the Council."

Fig. 4. Atlantic City's Boardwalk in the 1880s. (From the collection of Atlantic City historian Allen "Boo" Pergament.)

The first Boardwalk, which opened on June 26, 1870, was ten feet wide and about a mile long, made of one-and-a-half-inch-thick yellow pine planks. It was built at a cost of approximately five thousand dollars, paid for by city property taxes. For its first ten years, the Boardwalk was a temporary structure, which was taken apart and stored during the winter.

Although the Boardwalk's commercial attractions came later, Atlantic City's emphasis on leisure made it a magnet for a variety of entrepreneurs. During the same summer the Boardwalk was built, a Philadelphia cabinetmaker named Gustav Dentzel brought a European-style horse-drawn carousel to the beach and set it up near the Boardwalk. The success of his ride soon led to others. In 1872, William Somers introduced his Observation Roundabout. (In 1893, George Washington Ferris copied Somers's idea and called it the Ferris wheel; Atlantic City historians say the famous ride should rightfully be called the Somers wheel.) Electric lights came to the island in 1882, helping to transform the Boardwalk into a nighttime attraction.

Much as Atlantic City was conceived as a health resort but became something very different, the Boardwalk soon had a purpose beyond keeping sand out of train cars: It became a stage, a place where people could see and be seen. On sunny afternoons, hotel guests would dress up and walk along the seashore, shielding their skin from the sun with hats and parasols. The Boardwalk was the place to be, not unlike a crowded city street—except that it bore no traffic other than people, and the air was cool and fresh, not polluted with factory smoke.

The Boardwalk helped Atlantic City grow—literally and in terms of reputation. Word-of-mouth interest spread rapidly in the 1870s. In 1874, President Ulysses S. Grant stayed at the United States Hotel, becoming the first president to stroll the Boardwalk. Two years later, the Boardwalk hosted an Easter Parade, the first of many shoulder-season attractions. By the end of the decade, there were several hundred boardinghouses and hotels in the city.

When a second, larger Boardwalk was built in the spring of 1880, the laws were changed, allowing commercial buildings within ten feet of the promenade. The Boardwalk soon became a bustling business street, precursor to the shopping mall, and the word "boardwalk" a part of Atlantic City culture. The resort's population grew with the walk: At the time of the first Boardwalk, it was 1,043; by the second, in 1880, 5,477; the third Boardwalk, in 1883, it was 7,942; the fourth Boardwalk, in 1890, 13,055. By 1910, with the Boardwalk a national attraction, the population was up to 46,150—more than it is today.

In the early 1880s, another Boardwalk tradition was born: the ocean pier. The first commercial pier was built by a Baltimore entrepreneur named George Howard, who understood the visceral appeal of being able to walk out over the water. Howard's Pier, which extended 650 feet into the ocean, featured a covered pavilion at its end for concerts and dances. Applegate's Pier followed, with sunbathing pavilions and a giant freshwater drinking fountain that consumed three thousand pounds of ice a day. John Young bought Applegate's Pier in 1891 and added amusement rides, an enclosed ballroom, and an electric trolley. The double-decked Steel Pier, which would become Atlantic City's most famous, opened in 1898. In 1906, Young built the Million Dollar Pier, which included a theater, a ballroom, an aquarium, and his own three-story, twelve-room private villa. Two years later, Coney Island amusements pioneer George Tilyou opened Steeplechase Pier, filling it with rides, games, and the world's largest electric sign: 27,000 lightbulbs advertising Chesterfield cigarettes. The Garden Pier, opened in 1913, featured beautifully landscaped gardens and presented entertainment geared to an upscale audience.

Like any successful venture, the Atlantic City boardwalk and entertainment piers soon had imitators, becoming the model for boardwalks in other New Jersey coastal resorts, including Wildwood, Ocean City, and Asbury Park. But for decades Atlantic City remained, true to Pitney's vision, the capital of Atlantic coast resort towns.

Fig. 5. City of eccentrics: Young's Million Dollar Pier, circa 1910. The structure halfway out is Young's three-story private villa. (From the collection of Atlantic City historian Allen "Boo" Pergament.)

Vicious Ideas

By 1886, when Atlantic City's fifth and final Boardwalk was built, the walk had become Atlantic City's major attraction, more popular, it seemed, than the beach itself. Crowded with tens of thousands of people every day, the now forty-foot-wide Boardwalk and the amusement piers gave entrepreneurs a ready-made audience. The only limits to what the Boardwalk could be were human imagination and the law.

Early in the twentieth century, Boardwalk strollers could enjoy theatrical productions, amusement rides, freak shows, fortunetellers, daredevil stunts, and an assortment of confections. The Boardwalk was a showcase for inventions and oddities, and every day there was a new audience, anxious for new attractions. On the Steel Pier, young bathing beauties rode "diving horses" forty feet into a twelve-foot pool of water. From the Million Dollar Pier, a shackled Harry Houdini jumped into the ocean and rose to the surface unchained. Many entertainers got their starts in Atlantic City, including W. C. Fields, who performed as "the Tramp Juggler" in a Boardwalk arcade in the 1890s. Moving pictures also appeared on the Boardwalk in that decade, as did the first "air-conditioned" theater. Rolling chairs were introduced to transport guests from one attraction to another. For several decades, Atlantic City was the main tryout town for Broadway shows. In 1910, a dirigible called *America* took off for a transatlantic flight from Atlantic City (captain and crew were rescued in waters near Cape Hatteras, North Carolina). Twenty-one years later, the "rocket glider" was launched from the Steel Pier; it soared about one thousand feet before nose-diving into the ocean.

In 1921, hoteliers came up with the idea of a fall festival on the Boardwalk, featuring a "National Beauty Tournament." A local newspaperman, Herb Test, is credited with calling the winner "Miss America." It was the beginning of the motion picture era, and Hollywood talent scouts came to the pageant, some promising contestants roles in movies or stage shows. The first winner, sixteen-year-old Margaret Gorman of Washington, D.C., resembled film star Mary Pickford. The judges in those days were illustrators, who captured the spectacle for magazines and newspapers.

The contest drew some strong criticism from the beginning. Complained the Trenton YWCA: "It was noticed by competent observers that the outlook in life of girls who participated was completely changed. Before the competition, they were splendid examples of innocent and pure womanhood. Afterward, their heads were filled with vicious ideas." The *New York Times* called the contest "a reprehensible way to advertise Atlantic City."

As the pageant became increasingly successful—and, some charged, decadent—criticism mounted, and from 1927 to 1932, and again in 1934, it was suspended. Revived in 1935, the pageant was "reformed" so that talent was considered along with beauty. Guidelines from 1938 made talent 25 percent of a contestant's score. The rest of the criteria: attractiveness of face, 25 percent; figure, 25 percent; personality, 15 percent; and grace of carriage, 10 percent.

The Miss America Pageant was typical of the grandiose schemes that have fed Atlantic City for decades. Others—some far more ambitious—were less successful. In 1926, for example, the lavish $5 million President Hotel opened on the Boardwalk with a top floor designed to be a "Summer White House," but President Calvin Coolidge turned down several invitations to stay there, and the hotel never lived up to its name. Twenty years later, the city lobbied the United Nations to make its headquarters in Atlantic City. The UN politely declined.

Better results came with the Atlantic City Convention Hall, built on the Boardwalk in 1929 at a cost of $15 million. For years, it was the largest and most successful convention facility in the world. Recently renovated, the building still bears the dedication inscribed in concrete back in 1929: "A permanent monument, conceived as a tribute to the ideals of Atlantic City, built by its citizens and dedicated to recreation, social progress and industrial achievements."

Fig. 6. Contestants in the first Miss America contest, on the Boardwalk in Atlantic City. The winner, sixteen-year-old Margaret Gorman, is pictured at left. (From the collection of Atlantic City historian Allen "Boo" Pergament.)

Grandiosity was part of the "idea" behind Atlantic City, an idea as large as the American Dream—but only part of it. From early on, there were two distinct and seemingly incompatible sides to the city and its boardwalk. Because it required no admission and had no standard of entry, the Boardwalk attracted working-class visitors seeking cheap, exotic fun. At the same time, it targeted wealthy visitors who wanted to dress up and enjoy the natural charms of the seashore (it was only in the 1950s that people began "dressing down" to walk the boards). These two elements—highbrow and lowbrow, in broad terms—have somehow managed to coexist and survive.

Atlantic City historian and native Allen "Boo" Pergament recalls that what made an evening on the Boardwalk so enchanting was that it didn't have to cost a penny. "You could walk from one end to the other and be entertained just by all the people and the signs and the architecture. You could stop and watch the sand artists, the auction galleries, the saltwater taffy machines, the DuPont exhibit's products of the future, the live cooking demonstrations. It was always exciting, a sight to behold."

Saving History

Several blocks from where John Paxton's breakfast club meets each morning, Robert Ruffolo sits in his crowded antiques shop on Atlantic Avenue. The faded sign out front reads WE BUY ANYTHING OLD.

Ruffolo is a collector of history. The colorful stories of Atlantic City's past can be glimpsed in the hundreds of black-and-white photographs that he owns, along with a wealth of Atlantic City memorabilia. He displays, for example, a book of autographs collected in 1939, signed by all the performers who appeared on the Steel Pier that summer. There's a Bob Hope signature on one page, dated July 15. Ruffolo flips to another page, signed by members of the Harry James Orchestra on July 31. One of the signatures is that of Frank Sinatra, the orchestra's singer. Underneath it, the book's original owner wrote this reminder in parentheses: *Singer.*

Atlantic City has played host to presidents, entertainers, business leaders, and gangsters, but it seems oddly uninterested in promoting or preserving its history. Ruffolo, head of the city's historic society, says, "Trying to do something with history is an uphill battle."

For historic preservation to gain ground, he says, "you have to have multi-generational families living in the town, and Atlantic City doesn't have that. The few families that have been here that long are not in control of things. The ones who made money didn't stay here. The ones making the big bucks today aren't living in Atlantic City. We lose a little history each day."

Atlantic City business and political leaders acknowledge that the city does little to promote its history. What's distressing about that, Ruffolo says, is, "You don't just lose history, but you lose the reasons that made the history happen. You forget the things that made Atlantic City great."

Ruffolo moved to Atlantic City in 1972, six years ahead of the casinos. Originally from North Carolina, he came for the summer and "fell in love with the beach, the Boardwalk, and the girls. I've been here ever since. I still love going up there and hearing the ocean and the seagulls, smelling the salt air, seeing the people. That hasn't changed."

Other things have, though. While the casinos have brought the city billions of dollars in revenue—and help attract about thirty million tourists a year—they are self-contained entities, Ruffolo says. "They bring people to the city, but just into their boxes. It's like catching fish. Once they're there, they don't have to leave the casinos. They have restaurants, shopping, everything right there."

Ruffolo is one of several local people who are quietly working to preserve the history of Atlantic City, to make sure people know what made it the capital of East Coast resorts. Still, he acknowledges what drives the town. "It's real-life Monopoly," he says, referring to the famous board game based on the streets of Atlantic City. "Buying and selling property. It's a new game every day. Unfortunately, history can't compete with that."

A World's Fair Every Day

Lorenzo Langford, a third-generation Atlantic City native, worked for thirteen years in the Boardwalk casinos, first at Caesar's when it opened in 1979, then at Playboy/Atlantis, and finally at Taj Mahal. He started out as a dealer and became a floor supervisor and later a pit boss. Then, at the urging of friends and colleagues, he decided to enter politics. In the summer of 2004, Langford is the mayor of Atlantic City.

Fig. 7. Historian Robert Ruffolo, paging through a book of autographs collected at the Steel Pier in 1939. "We lose a little history each day," he says.

He is sympathetic to the concerns of people such as Ruffolo, in part because of his own Boardwalk memories. Langford speaks in a measured, thoughtful manner, but when he talks of the Boardwalk, his tone relaxes, becoming at times almost childlike.

"I would have to say that the Steel Pier was probably the greatest entertainment venue in the history of the world," he says, sitting in his seventh-floor office on Tennessee Avenue. "Really. We used to have the General Motors exhibit open to the public at no charge, and you could go there and see the cars of the future. I remember the first time I went in there and sat in a car, pushed a button, and the windows came up. It was like you were on

Mars. The technology was brand-new, and you got it here first. It was like the World's Fair up there every day.

"When you paid your dollar ninety-nine, you could go on the Steel Pier for the whole day. Everything was one admission. They had three movie theaters, showing first-run movies, all kinds of amusements and games of chance. At the end of the pier, there was a water circus act, with diving horses. There was a 'Stars of Tomorrow' show, which was like *Star Search*, and another show that was like *American Bandstand*. Then you had the main venue, which had acts like the Four Tops or the Temptations. There was so much to do you couldn't get it all done in a single day. It was amazing."

Fig. 8. *The Steel Pier in the 1930s: "It was like you were on Mars." (From the collection of Atlantic City historian Allen "Boo" Pergament.)*

The city is moving in a good direction again, Langford says, "but Atlantic City has lost something. I've always thought we sort of shot ourselves in the foot by defining ourselves as a gambling town. The true secret of our success will be in our ability to diversify our product. We have to remember what we had and why, and understand that we can have that again."

When Langford walks the Boardwalk—which he tries to do once a week—"I think about what we need to do," he says. "I think people are starting to realize that we need to spend more time and energy promoting our beach and our Boardwalk. And we have been. The city's been working to find its way back." He cites the recent $100 million beach replenishment project, the establishment of beach bars across from the casinos, and improved lighting.

"I think we need to complement the new by bringing back some of the old, meaning amusement piers and nongaming attractions like roller-skating rinks, movie theaters, bowling alleys. I think the two can peacefully co-exist. I mean, I remember there used to be sixteen different movie theaters in town; now we have none."

Langford doesn't gamble but says the casinos "fit the mystique of what Atlantic City is. Atlantic City has always been a place where certain vices were courted. That's part of who we are. I mean, Atlantic City was founded by aristocrats from Philadelphia who wanted a place to go and let their hair down. Every town has its own character. That's part of the character of this town. We need to remember that and keep improving in other areas, combining the old and the new. That's the key. The Boardwalk is still the busiest pedestrian thoroughfare in America. Thirty-four million people a year walk on that Boardwalk. That's an awesome distinction."

Sea Air in Every Box

People bring their own invisible histories to Atlantic City. They come to feel the freedom of walking barefoot on sun-warmed wood; to rediscover lost desires that the salt air and Boardwalk lights once seemed to encourage; to hear the echoes of forgotten friends. For some people, the Boardwalk's poetry is a taste—of cheap culinary delights that can be found nowhere else. All boardwalks have such traditions. In Wildwood, there is Mack's Pizza and Douglass Fudge; in Ocean City, Maryland, Thrasher's french fries; in Rehoboth Beach, Dolle's caramel corn and Grotto Pizza. Often these businesses enhance their mystique by calling themselves "world-famous" or "the original."

One tradition that has survived all the changes in Atlantic City is salt-water taffy, which was invented here in the early 1880s. Two of Atlantic City's earliest taffy businesses, Fralinger's and James Brothers, are still operating, with several Boardwalk locations.

"Saltwater taffy is one of the things people have always associated with Atlantic City," says Frank Glaser, who owns both taffy businesses. "I try to create an atmosphere in the stores that accentuates that reputation, giving them an old-fashioned flavor."

His stores are fun, with vintage advertising posters on the walls (SEA AIR AND SUNSHINE SEALED IN EVERY BOX, reads one) and free samples. Glaser, who works out of an office above a James candy store on the Boardwalk, says that he never has to go out and sell taffy. "People come to us," he says. "When they visit the seashore, they want an experience that's different from what they're going to get at home, and saltwater taffy has always been part of that. It's one of the memories people take home with them."

There are several recorded origins of the term "saltwater taffy," the most popular being that it originated with a Boardwalk candy seller named David Bradley. One day in 1883, the story goes, stormy seas flooded Bradley's store; rather than ruin his taffy, the saltwater gave it a distinctive flavor. Historians say the more likely explanation is that the phrase simply had a nice ring to it.

Joseph Fralinger is the man credited with popularizing saltwater taffy. Fralinger and his wife came to Atlantic City in 1884 to open a cigar store and lemonade stand after running unsuccessful businesses in Philadelphia. A year later, he took over an existing taffy business next to his lemonade stand, offering molasses-, vanilla-, and chocolate-flavored taffy. Eventually he sold twenty-five varieties. Fralinger was the first to sell saltwater taffy in one-pound souvenir boxes, still the most popular size.

In the 1880s, before the invention of the taffy puller, the corn syrup, sugar, and molasses candy was cooked in copper kettles over open coal fires, then cooled on marble slabs and stretched out five or six feet, to add air to the confection. The "taffy pull" was a regular Saturday night Boardwalk attraction.

Around 1900, a midwestern candy maker named Enoch James came to Atlantic City and opened a Boardwalk taffy business not far from Fralinger's. James claimed to have been making saltwater taffy for years and called his product "the original" saltwater taffy. He also advertised his candy as "Cut to fit the mouth."

In 1923, a taffy merchant named John Edmiston was given a trademark (No. 172,016) for the name "saltwater taffy." It did not sit well with the established taffy firms such as Fralinger's and James Brothers. The James company brought suit against Edmiston and the case ended up before the U.S. Supreme Court.

The high court finally ruled against Edmiston. "Saltwater taffy," it wrote, "is born of the ocean and summer resorts and other ingredients that are the common property of all men everywhere."

Under the Boardwalk

Seated on a ledge beside the Korean War memorial, Ed the Clarinetist is playing a slow, occasionally squeaky version of "Take Me Out to the Ball Game." His eyes are closed; a look of serene concentration fills his face. An American flag, a can for contributions, and a sign saying GOD BLESS YOU are on the Boardwalk in front of him. People pass by without stopping or even seeming to notice.

During a break between songs, Ed talks, reluctantly at first, about why he performs on the Boardwalk each day. "This is my faith," he explains. "I'm God's personal musician. I'm doing this for God. This is my church out here."

He tells the story of a despondent man who was walking down the Boardwalk late one night several years ago when he heard Ed playing "Somewhere over the Rainbow" on his clarinet. "He told me that it literally saved his life, hearing that. If I hadn't been here, he'd have killed himself. That's why I do this."

There are other Boardwalk performers who always draw a crowd—the statue man, for instance, who is a favorite among children, and the Michael Jackson impersonator who dances the moonwalk to a tape of "Billie Jean." Ed says he is not interested in making money or attracting attention. "That's about ego," he says. "That's not what I do."

As Ed continues to talk, the conversation turns a little odd. "I'll tell you what I'm really concerned about. It isn't the Boardwalk, it's under the Boardwalk. I've got a plan where I'm going to try to get the rights for under the Boardwalk. I'm going up to Trenton and secure the rights. That's my dream, to control under the Boardwalk. I'm going to clean it up. There's a whole culture under there—drugs, prostitution, you name it—that I would like to clean up."

"UNDER THE BOARDWALK" SOMETIMES has a less than romantic meaning in Atlantic City. Because of its reputation as an end-of-the-road destination, a Wild East town by the sea, the city attracts its share of "characters" and people at loose ends, along with the casino high rollers. The city estimates that thirty to fifty people sleep under the Boardwalk each night. Most of them are addicted to alcohol or drugs or are mentally ill. Some are young runaways. A few are gamblers who have lost all their money. They sleep in cardboard boxes or huddled under old blankets. William Southrey, president of the Atlantic City Rescue Mission, goes under the Boardwalk every week during the season and tries to encourage them to seek help. The mission's pink art deco building provides 130 beds, spaghetti meals, group prayer sessions, and a free medical clinic. "We try to establish a relationship and build a trust and eventually give them a reason to hope again," says Southrey. Last year, 3,027 homeless people came into the shelter.

The homeless are a blight on a city that is trying to remake itself as a class act, some officials say—"the other side of the allure of Atlantic City," according to one. At times, the smell of human waste drifts up through the boardwalk slats. There have been homicides, rapes, and fires under the Boardwalk, police say; several years ago, a man burned to death there. Officials say the homeless problem has improved in the past several years, but as Southrey notes: "It's not something that goes away. Most of these people have been homeless for a long time. It's a way of life before they come here. So it's difficult changing them."

A FEW BLOCKS FROM where Ed the Clarinetist is playing, rolling-chair operators sit in a row waiting for customers. At least two of them are asleep. There are far more rolling chairs this summer than there are people who want to ride in them.

"I think part of it is, they've been gambling, they lose money, they come out here and they don't want to spend more money," one of the operators says.

A father and son walk by rapidly, the boy trying unsuccessfully to repeat "She sells seashells by the seashore."

"I mean, they've just lost everything in the casinos," the operator continues. "They don't have enough for a soda and a hot dog. I know what that's like. I go in there and lose all my money, too, but I make sure I have ten dollars or twenty dollars left, so I can get drunk."

Two couples walk over and inquire about the cost, which is about a dollar per block for one rider. The operator smiles and assumes a businesslike manner.

"How far is it to Resorts?" a heavyset woman asks.

"It's about eight blocks."

All four people look north and squint.

"How far is it really?" she says. "Four?"

"From here? It's six blocks. Normally I charge ten dollars for two people, but I'll take all four of you for ten dollars."

They look at one another and squint toward Resorts some more. Finally the woman makes up their minds. "We'll walk."

"Eight?"

"No."

"All right, how about seven?"

The Gamble

Atlantic City flew so high in its early decades that the fall to earth in the 1960s and 1970s should not have been unexpected. Beginning with Pitney's vision of a national health resort, Atlantic City has always depended on the trick of perception. People came here because it felt exotic and exhilarating. They got caught up in the glamour and honky-tonk excitement of the Boardwalk and spent money, perpetuating the illusion of Atlantic City as America's Playground. (A postcard from 1923 shows a winking bathing beauty saying, "Gee, but ain't money slippery in Atlantic City.")

But by the 1960s, the illusion was no longer working. The concept of the middle-class vacation, which Atlantic City helped to pioneer, had changed over the years, becoming more diverse and sophisticated. Air travel enabled people to visit far-flung places, while a culture of automobile travel, with motels and fast-food restaurants, made it easier to discover new destinations. Atlantic City's cheap thrills and celebrations of American ingenuity seemed archaic, reflecting a country

Fig. 9. Giant Monopoly deeds along the Boardwalk tell Atlantic City's history. The famous board game was based on the streets of Atlantic City.

that no longer existed. Time had taken away its allure. People stopped visiting; businesses closed; residents moved away; unemployment rose; infrastructure crumbled; neighborhoods turned to slums.

The world saw all of this in 1964, when Atlantic City, still trying to flex the muscles of its reputation, hosted the Democratic National Convention. Because there was little news surrounding the event itself—Lyndon Johnson was a shoo-in for the nomination—many journalists wrote about the setting instead. What they saw, and wrote, wasn't pretty. "That was kind of our death blow," Mayor Langford says.

Fig. 10. Resorts, the first of Atlantic City's Boardwalk casinos, reflects the summer sky.

Forces of change and tradition have long contended in Atlantic City. Then again, perhaps the city's salient tradition is that of reimagining and remaking itself. After 1964, Atlantic City needed a new face. It found one a decade later with typical daring, becoming the first city outside Nevada to legalize casino gambling. In doing so, Atlantic City was providing America with a glimpse of the future. Today, eleven states allow commercial casinos, twenty-eight states offer Indian casinos, forty states have created lotteries, and online gambling is a burgeoning industry. Once considered a vice, gambling has become a national pastime.

Casinos gave Atlantic City instant national recognition again. Prosperity was a little longer in coming. During the first five years of casino gambling, the resort's household median income—about half the state average—remained unchanged. Population declined. Unemployment and crime rose.

Things improved after the state legislature created the Casino Reinvestment Development Authority, requiring casinos to pay 1.25 percent of their gross gaming revenues—now about $350 million a year—to an independent state agency. The agency, which funds development projects, has razed old row houses and replaced them with suburban-style homes and duplexes. Atlantic City is now undergoing its biggest building boom in a quarter century, including several large noncasino projects, which will include entertainment, shopping, and dining. In 2003, the billion-dollar Borgata, the city's grandest casino, opened; it was the first new casino property since 1990.

Atlantic City still has problems, including high unemployment and lots of boarded-up buildings, but people don't talk about them as much as they used to. Most residents seem at peace with casino gambling. Business leaders say that if the gaming market can grow to $5 billion—from its current $4.4 billion—and the business community continues to diversify, Atlantic City will soon be a booming resort again, maybe even a national one.

Meanwhile, Atlantic City retains its storied reputation along with a surprising, elusive beauty. Go out to the end of the Steel Pier just before sunset on a summer night and you may catch a glimpse—in the long, silent flow of people back and forth or the dreamy interplay of the sky's colors with the casino lights. Atlantic City remains a place of high ideals and considerable contradictions, much like the country it tries to represent. It is a great experiment that has at times gone wrong; a funhouse for adults; real-life Monopoly. And as anyone who has played Monopoly knows, the most valuable property in the game is the Boardwalk.

CHAPTER TWO

CONEY ISLAND, NEW YORK

Shadows of a Spectacle

OR A BRIEF TIME, early in the twentieth century, Coney Island was the most dazzling spectacle in the world—a wonderland of light, imagination, and ingenuity that seemed to herald an emerging nation's promise at the dawn of the century it would come to dominate. Coney Island's three great amusement parks—Steeplechase, Luna Park, and Dreamland—took guests not on rides but on journeys: under the sea and around the world, to the past, to the future, to outer space, to inner space. Luna Park, the world's first theme park, glittered with a quarter million lightbulbs on playfully ornamented palaces and Oriental towers, at a time when electricity was still a novelty. At Dreamland, where the themes were life, death, and morality, rides included the Creation, Hell Gate, and the End of the World.

The news about Coney Island traveled quickly, and visitors came from all over to see for themselves. Some arriving by boat thought New York was on fire when they first saw its blazing forest of lights. The Soviet writer Maxim Gorky wrote, of his visit in 1907: "With the advent of night a fantastic city of fire suddenly rises from the ocean into the sky. . . . Fabulous beyond conceiving, ineffably beautiful, is this fiery scintillation. . . . The visitor is stunned; his consciousness is withered."

Fig.11. (OPPOSITE) The lights of Luna Park, considered the first theme park, circa 1904. (Courtesy of the Brooklyn Historical Society.)

The Coney Island that Maxim Gorky discovered may not be the Coney Island that people see when they visit today, but Coney Island in summer is still a spectacle, carrying the burdens and blessings of what it was: an American symbol, now in the midst of renaissance. Go on a crowded evening and you may hear its seductive, gritty language; you may see glimpses of an earlier American civilization. For Coney Island is history now, too—birthplace of the amusement park and the roller coaster (and, some say, the hot dog), a place where people of all ages could experience life in a way that the rest of the world seemed to discourage: with wonder.

United Nations by the Seas

"Everywhere I go, when I say the words 'Coney Island,' people's faces light up," says Carol Hill Albert. "They associate it with some time in their lives when they were very happy, and often have a story to tell. Even if they haven't been here, they are intrigued by what they have heard about Coney Island."

Albert is in her second-story office at Astroland, the largest of Coney Island's two remaining amusement parks. Across West Tenth Street, a chorus of screams rises from the 1927 Cyclone coaster as it plunges eighty-five feet on wooden tracks. The late-morning breeze is tart with salt and rich with a blend of Coney Island smells—Italian sausage, french fries, beef on a spit, pizza, fried shrimp. Albert, who has just come in from a walk through the park, is pleased and surprised by the crowds. "It's astonishing, really, what is coming back here," she says.

Albert worked for years in Manhattan as a vice president at the publishing firm of Harcourt Brace Jovanovich. She wrote novels, too, and once judged the National Book Awards. But she quit publishing several years ago to run Astroland, which was founded in 1963 by her father-in-law, Dewey Albert. "This is more fun," she says. "I don't think there's anyplace else you'll find the variety of people you do here."

Although Astroland is teeming on this particular summer morning, July is, in a sense, the off-season for Albert. "The winter is when all the work and the planning goes on," she says. "By the time we open, it's like opening a Broadway show. Everyone knows their lines, you hope all the equipment is operating properly, and you're the director; you sit back and observe how it's going.

"Have you seen the Top Spin yet?" she asks, turning to watch the ride just outside her window—a row of seats that flips in upside-down loops before falling through a fountain of water.

Albert, who lives in Manhattan and drives into Brooklyn each day, is a true believer in Coney Island. Discussing its troubled past and the ongoing comeback, she is thoughtful and philosophical. "I think anyone who's been in business here for any period of time can't help but be impressed by what I call the iconic power of Coney Island," she says. "It becomes in some ways a paradigm of what's going on in the larger society. During the sixties, when racial issues were dividing the country, there were a lot of racial incidents in Coney Island, and it generated a lot of fear. I don't know if it's because people want to think of a 'Playground by the Sea' as one of the most innocent of places, but it seemed to have more of an impact here than it might have had elsewhere.

Fig. 12. Park-goers are entranced by the new Top Spin ride.

It took a long time to get over that. I think it was the equivalent of tourist places that had to get over the SARS virus. Places in Canada are still recovering. Then, in the last ten years, there has been a real revitalization, a lot of it even without much institutional support. People have gone back to what made Coney Island great, and one of the things that made it great—and unique—was that it is this incredible melting pot. Walk down the Boardwalk and you see all these different cultures—Russians, Asians, African Americans, Hasidic Jews, Spanish, Middle Eastern. Coney Island is a little United Nations by the sea, a gathering of every race, every religion, every country.

"Coney Island has always represented freedom and tolerance," she continues. "I think it gave us a true example of a democratic culture. One of the reasons sideshows developed here is it's the type of theater that works even if you don't speak English, if you're a recent immigrant. You can be entertained by someone eating fire or hammering a nail in his head even if you don't know what he's saying."

The revitalization of Coney Island has so far included $18 million in Boardwalk renovations, the $280 million remaking of the Stillwell Avenue subway station—the largest in the world—and the 2001 opening of Key-Span Park, a 7,500-seat stadium that is home to the Brooklyn Cyclones, the

New York Mets' farm club. These are just beginnings. In 2003, New York mayor Michael Bloomberg formed the Coney Island Development Corporation, carrying on the pledge of his predecessor, Rudolph Giuliani, to invest millions of dollars in rejuvenating Coney Island. The thirteen-member Coney Island Development Corporation is currently drawing up plans to develop vacant property, strengthen the area's existing commercial base, and market Coney Island as a year-round at-

Fig. 13. Coney Island coming back: the crowds at Astroland on a summer afternoon.

traction. Giuliani likened the neighborhood to Times Square, which shed its seedy image to become an international tourist attraction.

On a summer morning in 2004, as the throngs of people passing Albert's office window thicken, Coney Island feels vital again, crowded and safe. But, as Albert notes, the challenge for Coney Island will be to preserve its "iconic" quality in the tide of revitalization. "What we don't want is for it to become some slick, Disneyfied version of what it used to be," she says. "That's happening all over. Nobody wants a mall here. So while it needs to be architecturally enhanced, we need to preserve the spirit that has always been central to Coney Island. We need to keep its character intact."

"All Is Bizarre and Fantastic"

The harvest of Coney Island's heyday can be traced to the seeds of corruption planted by one man: the community's most powerful early politician, John McKane. When McKane and his family moved here from Ireland in 1841, the region was blanketed with forest and sparsely populated, with just a few tobacco, corn, and cattle farms. Coney—supposedly named by early Dutch settlers for the rabbits, or *konijn*, that once ran free—was accessible then only by boat or by carriage along the Shell Road, a mile-long oyster-shell toll road constructed in 1823 from the town of Gravesend. Although a hotel was built at Coney Island in 1829, it wasn't until after the Civil War that Coney Island became a resort.

The first steam-powered railroad arrived at Coney Island in 1866, the year that John McKane started his construction business in nearby Sheepshead Bay. McKane knew that Coney Island was on the verge of a building boom, and he sensed that many of the Gravesend townspeople and nearby farmers did not understand how valuable their land would soon be. Over the next several years, McKane became Coney Island's most prolific builder—and its most influential politician, winning election in 1867 as Gravesend constable and the next year as one of three commissioners for what was known as Coney Island's "common lands." As commissioner, McKane regularly received kickbacks for awarding leases to the common lands; as a builder, he won lucrative contracts from those developing the property. In the 1870s, with big money pouring into Coney Island, McKane solidified his power base, aligning himself with Brooklyn political boss Hugh McLaughlin and offering leases to his business cronies and political allies. He was elected town supervisor of Gravesend in 1876. Five years later, McKane formed his own police force and named himself chief, which gave him virtual control over Coney Island. "Houses of prostitution are a necessity on Coney Island," McKane once said. "After all, this ain't no Sunday school." The *New York Times* referred to Coney Island as "Sodom by the Sea."

But Coney Island also became known during this time for its innovative amusements industry. The industrial age was in full flower, and Coney Island displayed something new: Besides creating products that could improve efficiency and quality of life, the machine age could also provide entertainment and escape. In 1876, the resort's first carousel was built by a Brooklyn furniture maker named Charles I. D. Looff. (In 1870, when he immigrated to this country from Denmark, Looff was told he needed a middle name for his "I.D."; he didn't have one so wrote the initials "I. D.") Looff, who carved the carousel horses from leftover wood at his furniture shop, went on to become the most important and influential carousel maker in the country. His horses, known as the "Coney Island style," were characterized by their dramatic poses, flaring nostrils, glass jewels, and bright colors. He later moved his business from Brooklyn to Rhode Island and then to California, where he operated carousels in Santa Cruz, Santa Monica, and San Francisco.

That same year, Andrew Culver, a railroad man and investor, purchased the three-hundred-foot-tall Sawyer Tower from the 1876 Philadelphia Exposition and moved it to Coney Island. Culver, who operated the Prospect Park & Coney Island Railroad (which brought passengers to Coney Island for thirty-five cents), renamed it the Iron Tower and sold steam elevator rides to the top, where guests could enjoy the "Grand View of 50 Miles." Eight years later, in 1884, LaMarcus Thompson built the Gravity Pleasure Switchback Railway on Tenth Street, the country's first roller coaster. George Tilyou, a real estate developer, brought the Ferris wheel to Coney in 1894 (advertising it as the "world's largest," although it was considerably smaller than the one he had seen on display at the Chicago Exposition the year before).

In 1893, McKane's reign came to an end when he was convicted of contempt and election fraud and sentenced to six years in state prison. He was released for good behavior in 1898—the year Brooklyn was annexed as part of New York City—and died the following year.

McKane's tolerance of illegal activity in Coney Island led, at least indirectly, to the invention of the amusement park. The first enclosed park was created by a world-traveling adventurer named Paul Boyton in 1895. Boyton leased a parcel of land on West Twelfth Street and Neptune Avenue and loaded it with rides, games, circus performers, and trained sea lions. To keep out Coney Island's riffraff, he surrounded his amusements with a ten-foot-tall fence and charged ten cents admission. He called his business Sea Lion Park.

Two years later, George Tilyou fenced in his amusements at West Sixteenth Street and also charged a dime for admission. The main attraction at Tilyou's park was a mechanical horse race from England featuring eight double-saddled wooden horses that patrons could ride for half a mile along an undulating track. Other attractions included the Human Roulette Wheel, the Barrel of Love, and the Blowhole Theater. Tilyou named his park Steeplechase Park, after the horse race, but the park's enduring symbol was the leering clown face that greeted guests—an image that would be replicated at boardwalks and amusement parks all over the country. Tilyou, a skilled self-promoter who called himself "the first impresario of controlled chaos," proposed to a Brooklyn newspaper in 1897 that a 1,500-foot-long boardwalk be built along the beach, similar to the one in Atlantic City, as a way of linking the amusements and the beach, but it was not built during his lifetime.

The great amusement parks of Coney Island competed fiercely with one another, each seeming to redefine the boundaries of what an amusement park could be. In 1903, Frederick Thompson and Elmer Dundy, who had operated Trip to the Moon and other rides at Steeplechase, decided to create their own park. They leased Boyton's Sea Lion Park, moved Trip to the Moon there, and expanded the park to adjacent land. Luna Park, which opened on May 16, 1903, was unlike anything seen before, with more than 250,000 electric lights and whimsical architecture that fantastically and haphazardly blended styles—Renaissance, art nouveau, Moorish, Oriental. Live camels and elephants walked the grounds. The idea, according to Thompson, was to create "emotional excitement in the very air." In a 1904 magazine article, he wrote: "Everything must be different from ordinary experience. . . . When a stranger arrives at Coney Island . . . his eyes tell him he is in a different world—a dream world, perhaps a nightmare world, where all is bizarre and fantastic."

The success of Steeplechase and Luna inspired William Reynolds, a real estate speculator and former state senator, to try for something even grander. Reynolds formed a company called Wonderland Associates in 1904, which bought up sixty acres of land on two adjoining properties and built Dreamland. The most ambitious of Coney Island's three parks, Dreamland was conceived as an amusement park of the imagination. Its design was more refined than the other parks', its attractions more thought-provoking—although it called attention to itself with the tallest structure in Coney Island, the 375-foot Beacon Tower. Among other attractions at Dreamland were a biblical Creation exhibition, a village populated by three hundred midgets, a wild animal pavilion, and a boat ride called Hell Gate. At night, a million lights glittered in Dreamland, according to Reynolds. The electric bill to keep it going was said to be four thousand dollars a week.

By 1905, Coney Island was no longer considered Sodom by the Sea. It was a spectacle, a magnet for the middle class, magnificent proof that we need never outgrow our capacity for wonder. A story in *Cosmopolitan* magazine that year stated: "Coney Island is the Tom-Tom of America. Every nation . . . has needs of orgiastic escape from . . . the world of what-we-have-to-do into the world of what-we-would-like-to-do, from the world of duty that endures forever into a world of joy that is permitted only for the moment."

Fig. 14. A Coney Island landmark: the 1920 Wonder Wheel.

Coney Island provided something people could not find anywhere else. It granted them access to a side of themselves that yearned to retreat from adult strictures into a domain where they could be like children again, dazzled by the size of life's promise, by the scope of its possibilities.

But the heyday of Coney Island was short-lived—only about ten years. On opening day of Dreamland's 1911 season, a fire started in the Hell Gate ride, and the park burned to the ground. It was never rebuilt. Luna Park, which had earned Thompson and Dundy $600,000 in their first year of operation, filed for bankruptcy that year, largely because of Thompson's personal problems. (Dundy had died of pneumonia in 1907.) Luna was taken over by creditors and never regained its glory, finally closing in 1946 after a series of fires. George Tilyou, the visionary behind Steeplechase Park, died in 1913.

The boardwalk that Tilyou had envisioned was finally built in 1923, at a cost of $3 million, but by this time Coney Island was a very different place. The extension of the subway line from Manhattan to Surf and Stillwell avenues in 1920 dramatically changed Coney Island. Suddenly, millions of the city's poor and working-class residents could visit the seashore for a nickel. Coney Island became known as the "Nickel Empire" and as the "poor man's paradise." Whereas a quarter million people visited Coney Island twenty years earlier, nearly a million were now traveling to its beach on hot summer afternoons. Coney Island's amusements industry reflected this change. The emphasis was now on cheap fun—thrill rides and carnival games— rather than exotic architecture or imaginative rides with a message. During the 1920s and into the 1930s, Coney Island was a mecca for roller coasters and "gravity" rides. In 1927, Jack and Irving Rosenthal commissioned the Cyclone, at a cost of $175,000. Charles Lindbergh, an early rider, was quoted as saying that riding the Cyclone was scarier than flying across the Atlantic Ocean.

By the late 1930s, Coney Island had eleven roller coasters, twenty shooting galleries, two wax museums, three freak shows, and seventy ball games. On the Fourth of July 1938, 1.3 million people visited, *Fortune* magazine reported. Two years later, the Tilyou family brought the Parachute Jump to Coney Island from the New York World's Fair. The 262-foot ride, originally developed by the United States military to train paratroopers for combat, became a new landmark.

Fig. 15. The Cyclone, one of the country's iconic roller coasters, first opened in 1927.

The long decline of Coney Island began in the late 1930s when Robert Moses and the city Parks Department took over control of its beach and boardwalk, with a goal of "improving" the waterfront. "There is no use bemoaning the end of the old Coney Island fabled in song and story," Moses wrote in a report to Mayor Fiorello La Guardia. "The important thing is not to proceed in the mistaken belief that it can be revived." He proposed that most of the "mechanical noise-making and amusement devices and side shows" be replaced with residential development. For the next thirty years, he pushed this agenda, seizing property and turning it over to private developers for urban renewal projects.

In the 1950s, the twenty-acre Luna Park site was declared a Title I urban renewal zone, reducing Coney Island's amusement district by a third. Rather than "improve" Coney Island, the renewal efforts created a mood of uncertainty and unease in the business community. Many people abandoned Coney Island in those years. Stores and homes were replaced by welfare offices and drug treatment centers. It wasn't until the 1980s that preservationists and hard-core believers in Coney Island began to turn the image around and the real "improvement" began.

A New World Record

On July Fourth, the crowds arrive early at the corner of Stillwell and Surf avenues to stake out spots for Coney Island's best-known event, the annual Nathan's Famous International Hot Dog Eating Contest. Several thousand people pack the streets for the contest each year. Most are curious onlookers, but some of the world's top eaters—or "gurgitators," as they are called—are also on hand. "It's a veritable who's who of competitive eaters," says George Shea, founder of the Competitive Eating Federation, which sanctions the event. These include the world burrito-eating champion, the world ice-cream-eating champion, the world hard-boiled-egg-eating champion, and many others. All have come to Stillwell and Surf for what is considered by some the Super Bowl of eating contests.

As the 12:40 starting time approaches, competitors talk to reporters in a tent next to the staging area. All have had to qualify for this championship through a series of tournaments over the past year. Ed "Cookie" Jarvis explains that it's important to keep eating in the hours before the competition: "If you fast, it shrinks the stomach." Eating brownies, says Jarvis, not only keeps the stomach its proper size but also prevents nausea. Eric "Badlands" Booker, who, like Jarvis, weighs about four hundred

Fig. 16. The old Parachute Jump tower rises above the Boardwalk.

pounds, says it's important to bring the championship Mustard Yellow International Belt back to America. "With the exception of 1999, it's been in Japan," he says. "A lot of people would like to see it back here, where it belongs."

For the past three years, the hot dog competition has been won by Takeru Kobayashi, a 130-pound Japanese man who in 2001 stunned the competitive eating world by consuming fifty hot dogs and buns in twelve minutes—nearly doubling the previous world record of twenty-five and a half. In the rarified realm of hot dog eating, size is not as important as technique. The year before, former NFL player William "the Refrigerator" Perry started the contest but had to drop out after eating just four hot dogs.

The introduction of contestants begins before noon and continues for more than half an hour. Contestants come in all sizes and shapes—and from everywhere. The defending female champion, Sonia "the Black Widow" Thomas, is a hundred-pound Korean-born resident of Alexandria, Virginia. Introduced last is Kobayashi, who is carried to the stage on a hot-dog-shaped throne.

Minutes before 12:40, the twenty contestants are seated at a long table in the warm Coney Island sun. The breeze is salty; it smells of hot dogs. The judges are sworn in, and the rules are read, all with a seriousness of purpose that elicits giggles from the crowd. "Eat! Eat! Eat! Eat!" people chant raucously as competition begins.

George Shea announces the action as if it were a championship prizefight: "I have never seen the likes of this. . . . We are three minutes into the contest and if it continues at this pace you will see history made here today. . . . We have a dogfight. . . . The Americans are the three horsemen of the esophagus . . . but Kobayashi is rewriting the rules of our universe here today. . . . If I don't miss my mark, and I rarely do, we are going to see a new world record."

The dogfight does not last long. Kobayashi, who has a technique of breaking his hot dogs and buns in half before ingesting them—it is known, in competitive eating circles, as the "Solomon technique"—soon pulls away from the other gurgitators. At the halfway point, he has consumed thirty-three hot dogs.

Fig. 17. Takeru Kobayashi, with his Mustard Yellow International Belt, after eating fifty-three and a half hot dogs in twelve minutes on July 4, 2004.

"This is nothing short of an emotional journey!" shouts Shea. "A journey into what it means to be a human, the very essence of competitive eating, symbolizing the very essence of humanity, our struggle to survive!"

Kobayashi slows in the second half—as competitive eaters normally do—but still beats his own world record, eating fifty-three and a half hot dogs in twelve minutes. The twelve-minute standard is said to date to 1916, when the first, impromptu hot-dog-eating contest took place here at Nathan's.

Once the results become official, Kobayashi is mobbed like a rock star. Onlookers jockey to stand next to him, to get his photograph and autograph. He is treated as a true champion, which he is: someone who has just accomplished what no one else on earth can do (and most wouldn't want to try). The International Hot Dog Eating Contest has been called a grotesque display of America at its worst—a celebration of excess and consumption, of cheap food and obesity, of our country's "toxic environment"—but it can also be interpreted as a satire of our obsession with competition, of our notions of "bigger is better" and instant celebrity. The fact that a skinny Japanese man dominates the event each year adds a humorous twist of irony. Most who gather here for this annual street happening don't take it so seriously, of course. The hot dog contest is fun—and well suited for Coney Island, both because it celebrates the weird and because it furthers a cherished local legend: that the hot dog was invented here.

Fig. 18. The women's champion, Sonia "the Black Widow" Thomas, who ate thirty-two hot dogs.

A CONEY ISLAND BUSINESSMAN named Charles Feltman is often credited with inventing the hot dog. What Feltman sold—first from a pushcart in the 1860s, and later in his restaurant—was not called a hot dog, though; it was a "dachshund" sausage sandwich, a food probably invented in Germany several centuries earlier. (In 1987, the German city of Frankfurt promoted the five hundredth anniversary celebration of the frankfurter.) The term "hot dog" first turned up in magazine articles from the mid-1890s.

In 1915, a Polish immigrant named Nathan Handwerker took a job at Feltman's restaurant in Coney Island, which was then operated by Feltman's sons. After working there a year and saving three hundred dollars, Handwerker leased a store at Stillwell and Surf avenues and opened his own business, selling hot dogs for five cents apiece—half the price Feltman's was charging. Handwerker cooked his hot dogs on a twelve-foot grill and sold them "to go"; Feltman's restaurant was a sit-down. Handwerker also used aggressive marketing techniques, including paying men to wear doctors' uniforms and stand around his counter, then mounting a sign that read IF DOCTORS EAT OUR HOT DOGS, YOU KNOW THEY'RE GOOD! Today Feltman's restaurant is long gone and Nathan's is, to some, as much a symbol of Coney Island as the Parachute Jump and the Cyclone and the Wonder Wheel.

AFTER THIS YEAR'S CONTEST, Kobayashi sits in front of a plate of fifty-three and a half hot dogs—the amount he has just eaten—and, through an interpreter, conducts a brief press conference.

When will you eat next?

"Tomorrow."

Do you have anything special planned for tonight?

"He's going to see Lyle Lovett in concert," says the interpreter.

He is asked his age and—*I know the ladies will want to know this*—his marital status.

Kobayashi is twenty-six. "He demurs to the second part of that question."

Will you be back?

"Yes. He will definitely be back. Next year. He says he plans to break the record again."

Freak Show

Sideshows by the Seashore, a few blocks from Nathan's on West Twelfth Street, is the last traditional ten-in-one circus sideshow in the world, according to Dick Zigun, who runs it out of a 1917 building that was once home to the Wonderland Circus Sideshows. For a five-dollar admission, you can see such performers as Insectivora the female fire eater, Ravi the Indian rubber boy, and Eek the Geek, an illustrated man who makes himself the filling for a bed-of-nails sandwich.

Zigun, who came to Coney Island in 1979, has played a significant role in keeping the wild and weird sides of the resort healthy. "I grew up in P. T. Barnum's hometown of Bridgeport, Connecticut," he explains, sitting in the Freak Bar next to the sideshow. "I've always been interested in vaudeville sideshows, amusement parks. As with anyone who has a degree in theater, I was drawn to New York, but instead of aspiring to Broadway, I was inspired by Coney Island. I saw Coney Island as the stage for what I wanted to do. . . . Coney Island is different from every place in the world, and I'm committed to keeping it that way."

Fig. 19. Dick Zigun, at Sideshows by the Seashore. Zigun puts on Coney Island's annual Mermaid Parade.

Besides the sideshow, Zigun's nonprofit Coney Island USA, which he founded in 1980, runs the Coney Island Museum and presents the annual Mermaid Parade, a Mardi Gras–style celebration held in June. Other events include a film program, a Coney Island history lecture series, and an annual tattoo and motorcycle show.

Zigun, who lives in a room above the sideshow, is wearing a shirt that says FREAK SHOW. " 'Freak,' " he explains, "means being different. It's a positive thing. It's cool to be a freak." Sideshows, which were popularized in this country by Barnum in the nineteenth century, are a Coney Island tradition. The most famous was the Dreamland Sideshow, which operated for twenty years on the site of the old Dreamland amusement park; many of the performers in Tod Browning's controversial 1933 film *Freaks* worked there.

"At one point there were as many as two hundred sideshows touring the United States," Zigun says. "Mostly for financial reasons, rather than political correctness, they died out. Sideshows just don't turn a profit. They're labor intensive. People in show business won't do it because it's not good business. Things change. But it's Coney Island. It's something you won't see anywhere else.

"So we're carrying on something. In a sense we're a throwback, but we're not a museum piece. It's not re-creating the way sideshows were in the 1950s.

It's pretending they never died out. And if you wonder what a sideshow would be like in New York City in 2004, well, you just saw it."

Cyclones

Stan Fox is having a slice of pizza and a soda at Peter Pizza as the crowds funnel out of KeySpan Park, where the Brooklyn Cyclones have just finished a noon game against the Williamsport Crosscutters.

"Hey! Did we win?" Fox asks.

"Yep, Cyclones won."

"All right!"

"Four to three!" shouts a woman passing by.

The Cyclones, named for Coney Island's famous roller coaster, play thirty-eight home games this season at KeySpan Park and are now in first place in the New York–Penn League. When Fox grew up here—several blocks away, on Mermaid Avenue—KeySpan Park was Steeplechase Park and still full of amusements. It may have been past its prime, but not in his recollections.

"It was a great park," he says. "Great place. You'd go in for one dollar and get a brown ticket, good for fifteen rides during the week. Every time you went on a ride they'd punch a hole in the ticket, and a lot of times you could stand around the gate and people who were leaving, adults in particular, maybe didn't use all their rides, so you'd say, 'Hey, mister, can I have what's left on your ticket?' You'd get a lot of free rides that way. It was a great place."

Fox has worked in the amusements business most of his life, starting as a change boy in his brother's penny arcade. Today he's an importer of European equipment and an amusement park consultant. "My mother grew up in Newark," he says, "and moved to Coney Island in 1940. She ran a rooming house down here, and then she met my father and got married. I was born in 1944. My mother used to work in the arcade in the summer, giving out change. My father never did. In summer, he was a waiter in several restaurants here that are empty lots now.

"My brother started working in a popcorn stand here, but it was so hot that after two days he couldn't take it. So he quit that job and went to work in a penny arcade as a change boy, and he was in that business for the rest of his life. He started working there in 1939 and wound up buying it in 1957, and my family ran it until 1977, when we sold it. The arcade closed in the early eighties."

AFTER LUNCH, FOX WALKS the streets of Coney Island, talking about the good days and the bad, mostly the good. He stops occasionally to chat with merchants and police officers.

"There's the arcade there," he says, pointing to a boarded-up building. "My brother's original arcade was where those red doors are." A few minutes later, he says: "My public school, it was right behind that church. It's been demolished. My junior high is still here, Mark Twain, and Abraham Lincoln High School. A lot of famous people went to Abraham Lincoln: Arthur Miller, the playwright; Lou Gossett Jr.; Neil Sedaka; Marv Albert, the sportscaster. They all grew up in Coney Island."

Fox walks down Mermaid Avenue, the street he grew up on, although his old home is gone. "A lot of the area where I grew up became run-down. Most of it was rebuilt. For a while, Coney Island was in a depression."

The worst years were in the 1960s and 1970s, he says. There were lots of reasons. One was television: "People didn't need to go out so much to be entertained, so they stayed at home." There were also serious problems plaguing the area—crime, drugs, racial tension, arson—that kept people away.

In 1964, the last of Coney Island's great amusement parks closed. Steeplechase was sold by the Tilyou family to developer Fred Trump (Donald Trump's father) for $2.2 million. Trump wanted to build condos on the land but could only do so if the city rezoned it. Trump ending up selling the property back to the city, which today owns KeySpan Park.

"Fortunately, the city wouldn't change the zoning," Fox says. "That would have ruined Coney Island. Instead, this is what has brought Coney Island back from its long Rip Van Winkle slumber. The ballpark has been the linchpin of everything that's about to happen. That park is what has saved us."

Fox indicates where, a hundred years ago, Coney Island's other two great parks operated. Luna Park is housing now; Dreamland is the New York Aquarium.

"This is a great place again," he says. "There are fifteen million people within an hour or an hour and a half of here by subway or car. Nowhere else do you have that. But you have to give them a reason to come here. For a long time, we didn't do that. The administrations we had in office didn't care. Now they do. And this is a great place again."

Walking down the Bowery, past rows of arcade games, Fox exchanges pleasantries with a couple of police officers. The air is smoky with summer food smells. Barkers shout: "Pick your prize. Any prize. Need two more players. Pick any prize." Several booths away, another calls to him. "Hey! Pick your prize. Any prize. Need two more players. Pick any prize."

Fox nods a hello.

Jimmy Prince

If you want to know the history of Coney Island, you can go around to Jimmy Prince's Major Markets Prime Meats on Mermaid Avenue, a couple of blocks from the beach. There's no bookstore in Coney Island, but Major Prime Meats sells copies of Charles Denham's *Coney Island Lost and Found,* considered by many here the definitive history.

A butcher shop may seem an unlikely place to buy a history book, but the store itself has the feel of a historic site. There are old Coney photos in the window, sawdust on the floor, and a talking bench where on this summer afternoon a couple of men seem to be sleeping. Outdoor loudspeakers pipe Ella Fitzgerald and Frank Sinatra to the street.

Fig. 20. *Jimmy Prince, behind the counter at Major Markets Prime Meats on Mermaid Avenue.*

"We've sold more than nine hundred copies of the book," says Prince, a kind-seeming man with an infectious smile, who has worked in this store for fifty-five years.

"We just always operated as a neighborhood store," he says when asked about its longevity, "and the best thing you can do is be friendly to people. We have always been known for the best-quality meats. We go out of our way to give our customers the best."

Prince is also known for giving free pieces of bologna or candy to children and for keeping the same clientele for decades, even as the area went through rough times. Major Prime Meats is the oldest store on Mermaid Avenue. Recently, *New York* magazine rated it New York City's best butcher shop.

"Coney Island is a place I love, and this butcher shop is one of the things people associate with it. Sometimes people come in here who haven't been to Coney Island for years, and they see it hasn't changed, and they say it makes them feel like children again.

"Have you seen my sign?"

He holds out the hanging sign above his meat counter, which seems a sort of mirror, reflecting the personality of Jimmy Prince:

> *May the sun shine all day long,*
> *everything go right and nothing go wrong.*
> *May those you love bring love back to you*
> *and may all the wishes you wish come true!*

Intangibles

There is a hidden language in Coney Island, spoken with many accents, in unexpected ways and places. No one comes to Coney Island alone; people always bring with them what they have heard or what they remember or what they expect. Sometimes, these notions become part of the larger concept of Coney Island; more often, they disappear once the vocabulary of the resort is understood. If Coney Island once represented the optimism of the American Dream, it today seems more tattered, but also more real. The hidden language of Coney Island says what first impressions often don't; it is a discordant music—beautiful, ugly, and real, full of surprising rhythms.

At a Boardwalk pavilion, dozens of Hispanic people dance to Latino music in the warm summer drizzle. A group of elderly women talking in Russian walks past. Teenage African American boys chase one another out onto the sand; several white girls giggle at them. To the north, amusement lights brighten like a promise against the tenements. The trash cans are all overflowing. Coney Island is crowded and safe tonight, a destination in the imagination, but a real destination as well, a place to become lost; the perfect, permanent American carnival.

IN THE MORNING, DENNIS Vourderis, co-owner of Deno's Wonder Wheel Amusement Park, is hosing down the pavement at his Boardwalk park, thirty-five minutes before it opens. The Wonder Wheel, built in 1920, is a 150-foot-tall Ferris wheel with sixteen swinging passenger cars and eight stationary cars, all of which offer remarkable views of the Atlantic Ocean and Coney Island. The ride was named a New York City Landmark in 1989.

"It's the same ride that was here in 1920," Vourderis says, "except we've made some modern additions to bring it up to code. It's our busiest ride, our diamond in the rough. We spend a lot of time on the maintenance of it."

Deno's is named for Dennis's father, Denos, who immigrated to the United States at age fourteen and eventually went into business as a hot dog vendor on Coney Island. Vourderis says he was nine years old when his father got his first Coney Island concession. "He and I worked side by side, scooping Italian ice. I grew up on the Boardwalk here, behind the counter at the restaurant."

Denos Vourderis used to tell his wife Lula that someday he would buy the Wonder Wheel, one of Coney's Island's two most famous rides. In 1983, he did. A few years later, he added other attractions and made them a single amusement park.

"It was a funny time to do that," says Vourderis, "because we were still going through the dark ages then. Those were tough times for people here. But my father hung in there. He always had faith in Coney Island, because he knew what it *had been*."

Denos passed away in 1994, just as Coney Island was beginning to come back. These days, the park is run by his sons Dennis and Steve.

"My father poured hundreds of thousands of dollars into his business at a time when it was unheard of. Everyone was running away, and my father was putting all this money into improving the park.

"I used to say, 'Are you sure you want to do this?'

"He'd say to me, 'Are you nuts? You analyze too much. If I had your brains, I'd never be where I am now.'

"He didn't see what other people saw. He always said, 'I know this place will be better. It has to be.' And you know what? He was right."

CHAPTER THREE

ASBURY PARK, NEW JERSEY

The Currency of Memory

F OR YEARS, people have come to Asbury Park from around the world to look for things that no longer exist. They park their cars and walk the run-down, eerily deserted beachfront streets; they photograph buildings that have been boarded up for decades; they stroll a decaying mile-long Boardwalk where nothing is open.

Others talk of a place that gave them hard-to-imagine riches of memory, a city by the sea that once pulsed with its own music and glowed with carnival lights, where innocence and decadence mingled deliciously in the breeze. It is difficult to reconcile these memories with what Asbury Park has become. Many longtime residents lament the fact that those who grew up here during the past quarter century know the waterfront only as dilapidated and abandoned. David Dorfman, who was raised nearby, says he used to take his children here and try to explain it. "They couldn't understand. Why did people talk about the Boardwalk all the time?" Dorfman started a Web site a few years ago for people to share their memories of Asbury Park. "It seemed like something nobody was doing much about. People were losing that."

No other boardwalk town has fallen quite so far as Asbury Park, which in the 1990s was nicknamed "Beirut by the Sea." Perhaps because of this, it

Fig. 21. (OPPOSITE) Crowds mob the Asbury Park Boardwalk for an 1890s baby parade. (Photo courtesy of the Asbury Park Press.)

is a place where the potency of memory is felt more keenly than in other sea-side resorts. When returning to the good places of our youth, one former resident said, we expect to find a few poignant reminders along with the in-evitable changes—but this doesn't happen in Asbury Park.

The stories people tell of Asbury Park are a kind of sentimental ar-chaeology, allowing glimpses of a lost, mostly transient culture, of a board-walk once considered among the Shore's most vital. They tell of rituals and rites of passage, of hanging out on rainy summer nights at the Casino, of days on the beach and nights on the rides, of cruising "the circuit" for hours, of favorite foods—Miramar Grill french fries, Mrs. Jay's hot dogs, warm Belgian waffles with ice cream, Criterion candy—of bumper cars and crane machines and wheels of chance, of the om-inous flashing clown faces at Palace Amusements and the classic brass-ring carousel, of walking the beach and mak-ing out under the Boardwalk, of discovering Bruce Spring-steen at a club called the Stu-dent Prince, of meeting and making friends on a Boardwalk so crowded at night that it became impassable.

Fig. 22. The once-majestic Casino building at the Boardwalk's south-ern end.

Most of the old businesses that anchor these memories are gone now. In the summer of 2004, Palace Amusements, with its 1888 carousel build-ing, was demolished. The fifty-six acres of beachfront property in Asbury Park are now controlled by a single developer, Asbury Partners LLC, which has long-term plans to rebuild and revitalize the oceanfront. At the same time, a number of smaller investors, including an increasing gay population, have been buying up rooming houses and transforming them into attrac-tive homes.

This isn't the first time that Asbury Park has been poised for a comeback, but Asbury Partners, a joint venture of M. D. Sass Municipal Financial Partners III and Ocean Front Acquisitions—investment groups based in New York City and Lakewood, New Jersey—appears to have deep pockets and a deep commitment. And the oceanfront has started to come back.

Over the winter of 2003–2004, the firm rebuilt the resort's broken Boardwalk at a cost of $5.8 million. It was a first step. Still, on a recent prime summer weekend, most of the buildings along the new Boardwalk were shuttered. Many were boarded up and decorated with graffiti. Only one commercial venture was open at lunchtime, a food stand selling pizza and sodas. There were no customers.

Fig. 23. The Asbury Park Boardwalk, summer of 2004.

Ghost Town

"This place is full of ghosts, man," says Charles "Chico" Rouse, looking south down the empty Boardwalk from Asbury Park's Convention Hall. "So many people have been here. So much has happened. They say the city has a curse. I don't believe that."

Rouse's father was Charles Rouse, a noted saxophonist who played with Thelonious Monk from 1969 to 1973 and worked with Miles Davis, Dizzy Gillespie, and others. His mother was a dancer in New York City's Cotton Club.

Rouse, who went to grammar school and high school in Asbury Park, talks with free-flowing enthusiasm about the city and its musical heritage, pausing occasionally to smoke his pipe. "It's ironic, this town is known all over the world for its music history, but most of the stories you hear about the Asbury Park music scene are from the 1960s to the present," he says. "If you want the real meat and potatoes, you have to go back to the thirties and forties. I mean, a lot of people don't realize it, but Asbury Park was the most happening town on the Shore besides Atlantic City. All of the music legends came here. Every one—Tommy Dorsey, Count Basie, Dizzy Gillespie, Sarah Vaughan, Frank Sinatra, Benny Goodman."

Chico has worked in the music business much of his life, playing in jazz bands and managing theaters and hotel venues on the Jersey Shore. He's now executive director of special events for Asbury Partners, charged with bringing concerts and other events to the beach and to Asbury Park's two architectural jewels, the Paramount Theatre and Convention Hall.

"These buildings have so much history," he says, walking into the grand arcade that connects the two. The buildings were designed in the 1920s by the firm of Whitney Warren and Charles Wetmore, which also designed Grand Central Station and the Ritz-Carlton hotels in New York City and Atlantic City. Although in need of repair and refurbishing, they retain an ornate elegance, with elements of French and Italian architecture. Both are on the National Register of Historic Places and owned by Asbury Partners, which plans extensive renovations.

"It's like going into a tomb sometimes, coming in here," Rouse says, stepping into the cavernous Convention Hall, which seats 3,600. The echo of footsteps in the old empty hall is a little unsettling. "Thinking about all the people who have played here—the Beatles, Sinatra, you name it. The Convention Hall was once one of the bigger venues in the country, but the whole business is different now. It got bigger. This is now considered small or midrange in terms of capacity. But there's no building like this anywhere."

Chico steps out from the darkness onto the Boardwalk. Bright clouds boil up behind the crumbling Casino building; a carpet of shadow covers the beach. "It's still strange sometimes, seeing that Boardwalk with no one on it," he says. "When I was growing up, I'd come out here and never want to leave. Everything was here. Rides, amusement games, miniature golf. I used to stay out here all day, just going from one place to another."

Across the street, a car is parked. Two girls cross the road, stopping to take a picture of Madam Marie's fortune-telling booth. Closed for years, Madam Marie's is still known because of a reference to it in a Springsteen song from thirty years ago.

"I grew up here, went to school here, graduated from here, came back here," Rouse says. "I walk along this Boardwalk and I think: 'You can't kill this animal, man. It's too strong. Wound it, okay. But you can't kill it.' I wouldn't be here if I believed that."

"There Will Never Be Another"

Unlike Coney Island, with its early history of tolerance and corruption, Asbury Park was conceived as a model of Christian piety. Its founder, a moralist businessman named James Bradley, sought to establish an upright community that would be a good neighbor to the Methodist camp he had discovered just to the south in Ocean Grove. Bradley, who had built a thriving brush-making business in New York City, purchased the five hundred acres of forest land that would become Asbury Park for about ninety thousand dollars in January 1871. He named his community after Bishop Francis Asbury, the founder of Methodism in the United States.

Bradley wanted Asbury Park to be different from other East Coast resorts—clean, wholesome, beautiful, religious. His plans called for generous amounts of open space, including parklands and manicured gardens, with boulevard-sized streets that would flare at the oceanfront, acting as funnels for sea air. "There will never be another seaside town on the Atlantic Coast from Sandy Hook to Barnegat Inlet with as wide streets and open spaces as Asbury Park," he wrote in his diary. "Future generations will have opportunities to ornament the town by statuary, vases, gardens and fountains."

Bradley, who would later be elected to the state senate on a temperance and antigambling platform, donated land in his new community for the construction of churches, while large residential lots were earmarked for Victorian-style summer homes. In 1873, the city's first hotel opened; others soon followed, including, in 1877, the block-long Coleman House. Although the railroad did not stop in Asbury Park until 1875, Bradley provided horse-drawn coaches to shuttle visitors from the train depot in Long Branch. Asbury Park became known as a lovely and charming seaside resort, the first on the Shore to offer electricity. An 1878 New Jersey atlas referred to it as "the magic place." By the early 1880s, the assessed value of the community was $1.5 million.

For several decades, Bradley's vision of a morally upstanding, health-enhancing resort prevailed. Alcohol was banned in Asbury Park. Female visitors rented swimsuits made of heavy flannel with sleeves to the wrists and pants to the ankles (they were nicknamed the "Bradley Bag"). Signs posted in Asbury Park bathhouses read: MODESTY OF APPAREL IS AS BECOMING TO A LADY IN A BATHING SUIT AS IT IS TO A LADY DRESSED IN SILK AND SATIN. A WORD TO THE WISE IS SUFFICIENT. (The novelist Stephen Crane, who spent summers in Asbury Park, parodied Bradley's morality policing in local newspaper columns, once creating this imaginary Bradley sign: "Don't go in the water attired merely in a tranquil smile.")

Bradley built Asbury Park's first oceanfront boardwalk, a narrow walkway, in 1878. It was expanded into a full, promenade-style boardwalk in 1880—more than a thousand feet long and from sixteen to thirty-two feet wide, with benches every ten feet on either side. The Boardwalk furthered Bradley's vision of the resort. It was intended for restorative walks, Monday through Saturday. Amusements and commercial ventures were banned.

Asbury Park, despite its success, was not unaware of the growing competition from other resorts, particularly nearby Long Branch, or of the need for self-promotion. One such promotion was the Asbury Park Baby Parade, which debuted in 1890, when 165 babies were paraded down the Boardwalk in carriages and strollers. The city also began calling itself the "Venice of the Seashore," offering visitors gondola rides on its lakes in boats steered by men dressed as Italian gondoliers. Bradley made the Boardwalk more enticing for children by placing old boats and fire engines beside it. Meanwhile, Asbury Park businessman Ernest Schnitzler developed more sophisticated amusements on the west side of Ocean Avenue, including a Ferris wheel–like observation wheel and platform tower and the Palace Merry-Go-Round.

Asbury Park was incorporated in 1897, separating from Ocean Township, and Bradley's influence began to wane. City hall, sensing the potential to vastly boost municipal coffers, decided to allow amusements and other commercial enterprises along the Boardwalk. In 1903, after the legality of Bradley's ownership was challenged in court, he was forced into selling his holdings to the city for a mere $100,000.

Wrested from Bradley's vision, Asbury Park became a more carefree resort—and it continued to grow. By 1904, there were eight hundred hotels in the city and more than 4,500 bathhouses. Bradley, dividing his time between New York City and Asbury Park, would sometimes take out newspaper advertisements criticizing the town for its willy-nilly growth. Before he died in 1921, at age ninety-one, he reportedly said, "I would have been much happier in my old age had I never heard of [Asbury Park]." A month after his death, a statue of Bradley was unveiled in Asbury Park; it still stands today, across the lawn from Convention Hall.

The decade after Bradley's death saw enormous prosperity in Asbury Park, including the building of Convention Hall, the Paramount Theatre, and the new Casino, all designed by Warren and Wetmore. The Paramount's opening in July 1930 featured the Marx Brothers and Ginger Rogers. As Chico Rouse points out, Asbury Park was for years one of the Jersey Shore's top entertainment venues.

With the opening of the Garden State Parkway in the 1950s and changes in travel trends, the city lost some of its vacation business, but it developed its own unique flavor. In the 1960s and 1970s, thousands of young people would migrate to Asbury Park on summer evenings to cruise "the circuit," a loop that took them down Ocean Avenue to Kingsley Avenue, then south on Kingsley back to Ocean. Along the circuit were Palace Amusements and a dozen rock clubs where musicians such as Springsteen, Jon Bon Jovi, and Southside Johnny and the Asbury Jukes got their starts. Some who cruised the circuit considered those decades to be Asbury Park's best days, but many residents disagree, saying the clubs and the cruising brought an undesirable element to Asbury Park. "I never wanted my children going down there to the Palace or to those clubs," one city official says.

On July 4, 1970, race riots broke out in downtown Asbury Park. Publicity about the riots, which continued for four days and led to $5 million in damage to the city, kept many tourists away for the rest of the summer;

Fig. 24. The Boardwalk in 1977 was a playground of rides and games. (Photo courtesy of the Asbury Park Press.*)*

some say they never really came back. Others attribute the city's decline to increased tourist competition, unresponsive leadership, and various financial and social problems.

Ironically, as Asbury Park was fading, Bruce Springsteen began to romanticize the resort in his music, winning a national audience for his songs about working-class life on the Jersey Shore. His 1973 debut was titled *Greetings from Asbury Park, N.J.*, and its postcard-style cover featured various Boardwalk and beach scenes. "Fourth of July, Asbury Park (Sandy)," from his second album, painted a fanciful picture of Boardwalk characters such as Madam Marie, "the wizards . . . down on pinball way," and "the boys from the Casino, who dance with their shirts open, like Latin lovers along the shore." Asbury Park was not mentioned by name on Springsteen's third album, 1975's *Born to Run*, but was referred to several times. The album—a breakthrough that landed Springsteen on the covers of *Time* and *Newsweek*—conjured up a Jersey Shore version of *West Side Story*, full of energy, drama, and poetry ("Man, there's an opera out on the turnpike/ There's a ballet being fought out in the alley"). His 2002 album *The Rising* reflected a more sobering, contemporary view of Asbury Park, in a song titled "My City's in Ruins."

Fig. 25. *Stairway decoration in the old Paramount Theatre.*

During the 1980s, a series of mysterious fires, an influx of mentally ill patients who had been released from state institutions, and corruption in the city government deepened Asbury Park's troubles. Businesses closed, investors went elsewhere. Panhandlers and drug dealers frequented the Boardwalk.

In 1986, with the city sliding toward bankruptcy, rights for waterfront redevelopment were sold to a Connecticut developer named Joseph Carabetta, who had grand plans for reviving Asbury Park. Carabetta began construction of a 160-unit condominium building across the street from the Boardwalk, but he was forced to halt the project in 1989 as he ran out of funds. He filed for bankruptcy in Connecticut in 1992, and his case in effect tied up the Asbury Park oceanfront for ten years. The girdered frame of his proposed condo building stood unfinished for fifteen years, a monument to all that had gone wrong in Asbury Park. Finally, in 2004, it was taken down.

"When It's Gone, It's Gone"

Local history books line a shelf at Don Stine's Antic Hay bookshop in downtown Asbury Park. Stine, who grew up here and worked his first jobs on the Boardwalk, is heartened by what's happening to the city's waterfront. "Fourth of July was nice to see," he says. "The Boardwalk was new. People were out, like the old days. It was a good feeling."

But he's also concerned.

Earlier this year, Asbury Partners tore down the old Palace Amusements building to make room for a hotel/retail/restaurant complex. Within the Palace was an 1888 carousel building. Stine, a trustee of the Asbury Park Historical Society and president of the Merchants Guild of Asbury Park, says it may have been the oldest amusements site in the country.

"When that Palace carousel building got knocked down, it was a wake-up call for us. We got behind the eight ball on that. There was a great potential for that building that the developers didn't understand.

"Historic preservation is a relatively new idea in this town. The historical society is just a couple of years old," says Stine, looking out the store's front window at the traffic. "It hasn't been a concern before. The Casino building on the Boardwalk is the way it is because a past city council voted decades ago to sell the copper roof and put up a tarpaper and plywood roof. No one said anything about it. They had a party in there to celebrate, and it rained and the roof started leaking. That's why that building is in such sad shape. Because a city council thought it was better to sell the roof for money than to repair it the way it should have been repaired."

Fig. 26. The Stone Pony club, made famous by Bruce Springsteen. In the background is the skeleton of Joseph Carabetta's never-completed 160-unit condo building, a monument to failed dreams.

Stine is also president of Save the Stone Pony, a group of residents concerned about the fate of the famous rock 'n' roll club, which is now also owned by Asbury Partners. "The Stone Pony needs to be rebuilt. The building is in poor shape," Stine says. "But if you rebuild it, are you really rebuilding it or are you building something new? I think you can keep the façade similar and restore the interior exactly as it was. People want to sit at the bar and see the memorabilia. That's an important part of what Asbury Park is. The worry many people have is that the future of the Stone Pony is in the hands of people who don't want it there."

Stine and others believe the waterfront redevelopment plans are too focused on retail and residential use and not enough on entertainment. "It's never going to be like it was, granted, with the rides and the Skee-Ball," Stine admits, "but I've always advocated an entertainment district by the Boardwalk, in keeping with what has historically been there. There are other things you can do—a rock 'n' roll museum, amphitheater, IMAX, open-air bandshell concerts.

"But if you're going to have an entertainment district, you don't want to rip up stuff like the Palace carousel. It would have been a great draw to be able to say, 'You can come here and see the oldest amusements site in the entire nation.' . . . The sad part is we had that opportunity, and we lost it. When it's gone, it's gone."

Saving Tillie

For eighteen years, Bob Crane worked in Washington, D.C., as chief of staff to four members of the U.S. Congress. He grew up in Oregon and now makes his home in the Washington suburb of Silver Spring, Maryland. He has never lived in Asbury Park but has felt a connection with the city much of his life.

In July 1998, Crane was browsing the *Asbury Park Press* online when he read that the Palace Amusements building was going to be demolished in two weeks. "There was nothing in the story that mentioned opposition or anything about a preservation effort. Nothing. It drove me nuts," he recalls. "Here's this place that every time you go to Asbury Park you see people stopping in front of it and taking photos. If you spend any time standing outside the Palace, you can meet people from all over the world who know about it.

"I figured two weeks wasn't enough time but I thought somebody needed to do something, or try to do something. So I e-mailed five of my friends that day, all of whom said they would help out, and we became the original six members of Save Tillie."

With its aqua cinder-block façade, adorned with a mural featuring looping funhouse letters and two leering clown faces—nicknamed "Tillie" because they are based on the face from George Tilyou's old Steeplechase Park in Coney Island—the Palace was an Asbury Park landmark. But it hadn't been open since 1989, and city officials said it was structurally unsound.

Crane soon learned a lesson about the workings of Asbury Park politics, he says.

"What we discovered was that the two-week threat was part of a long, ongoing battle between the city of Asbury Park and the bankrupt developer, each trying to force the other to pay for the demolition. Once we realized what was going on, then we knew that those two forces had basically stalemated and neither was going to win. Neither was going to go to court."

The stalemate, he says, gave the group time to organize and come up with a plan. The nonprofit Save Tillie organization set up a Web site and launched a campaign, which became successful, to win the Palace designation as a state and national historic site. Membership in Save Tillie eventually reached about a thousand, with members in twenty-seven states and sixteen countries.

The Tillie campaign began as a hobby for Crane, but a few years into it, he quit his congressional position to work full-time on saving Tillie from the wrecker's ball. "I found myself thinking about it all the time, and I no longer had my heart in my work in Washington," he says. His wife and daughter, he adds, understand the value of historic preservation and have been supportive.

Crane's group initially wanted to save the whole Palace Amusements complex (the oldest part was constructed in 1888 to house a Looff carousel; the Tillie clown faces were painted by Leslie Thomas in 1956 on the outside of a new building) but decided to focus on Tillie because it was "the most identifiable image in Asbury Park."

As Save Tillie garnered media attention, both locally and nationally, it became a thorn in the side of the new waterfront developers, Asbury Partners, who wanted to tear the building down. Asbury Partners "are not preservationists," Crane says. "They have told us many times that they saw no future for the building at all." Save Tillie also drew fire from some residents who called the Palace an eyesore and complained that the Save Tillie movement was being spearheaded by an outsider who didn't understand the workings of the city. At times, Crane said, the Save Tillie fight became "a battle for the soul of Asbury Park."

At one point, to stem the controversy, Asbury Partners offered to sell the building. Save Tillie advertised the Palace on eBay, but there were no takers at the asking price of $2.5 million ("a ridiculous price," Crane says). Eventually, a compromise of sorts was reached: Save Tillie and the Asbury Park Historical Society worked together to salvage 125 items from inside the Palace, including parts of rides

Fig. 27. The landmark Palace Amusements building. It was demolished in the summer of 2004.

and games, signs, and murals. Then on June 11, 2004, Tillie itself was saved—or, rather, one of the two Tillie faces. The rescue plan was devised by a steel fabricator contractor and Save Tillie member named Gary Loveland. Using equipment from his firm, Universal Fabricators, Loveland cut through the cinder-block wall and inserted a steel frame around the sixteen-by-fourteen-foot mural. A crane then lifted Tillie and lowered the ten-ton piece of wall onto the back of a flatbed truck. The two hundred people on hand cheered as Tillie was driven down Ocean Avenue for storage, past other still-standing Asbury Park landmarks: the Casino, the Stone Pony, Madam Marie's, Convention Hall.

Crane and others in Save Tillie acknowledge that their "victory" was a small, if symbolic, one. The larger issue is the value of Asbury Park's musical history, Crane says. He cites the example of Liverpool, England, where music tourism has become a $25 million industry in recent years. "Liverpool did the same thing. They turned their back on it. They imploded the Cavern Club. Where were the Beatles fans when they did that? Finally, they realized what they had and embraced Beatles history. It started with a small group of people giving tours, and as it picked up the city realized it had made a mistake. They redid the Cavern Club, preserved John and Paul's homes. Maybe music tourism will never be a $25 million industry in Asbury Park. It's hard to put a dollar figure on it. But it's a natural resource that is being ignored."

Springsteen himself has increasingly lent a hand to the Asbury Park revitalization efforts, including benefit concerts and a recent book signing at Stine's store. In 2001, just after the Palace was recognized on the National Register of Historic Places, Springsteen contacted the Save Tillie organization. "He heard about it on the radio in New York," Crane recalls. "He called one of our founders, Debbie Robinson, and said he'd like to meet with us. We went up for a show. I'm proud that we didn't act like fans and make fools of ourselves. We mostly talked about architecture and sense of place and what it takes for communities to survive. He talked about the *Tom Joad* tour and how he liked playing the classic old downtown theaters, how it brought people back into the downtowns and how we needed more of that sort of preservation in the country."

Asbury Partners plans to build a hotel complex on the site where the Palace stood. The developers say it will have "an amusements theme" and include some artifacts salvaged from inside the original Palace building. Save Tillie will exist at least until the new building is opened, Crane says.

"Music is a powerful force that reaches deep into people and affects them emotionally," he says. "You can't underestimate that. People come to Asbury Park because it deepens their appreciation of the music, particularly when you can see the places from the songs in concrete and brick."

Solving the Problems

On a bright summer afternoon, Larry Fishman is sitting in the windowless conference room of Asbury Partners' Boardwalk offices, explaining what the new Asbury Park will look like. The offices are appropriately unassuming, tucked among the shuttered oceanfront buildings, with only a small sign on the door announcing their existence.

Fishman, a genial, sometimes guarded man, runs Asbury Partners with his brother Glen. In 2001, Asbury Partners bought Carabetta's tax liens, acquired Asbury Park's oceanfront property, and won the redevelopment rights.

One of the first stages in their $2.1 billion redevelopment project was rebuilding the Boardwalk. Next will be retail shops and Boardwalk pavilions. "Right now, there are six stores open on the Boardwalk. By the end of this summer, there will be fifteen stores. Next summer, it will be a much different experience," Fishman says.

Three thousand new residential units are planned along Ocean Avenue, he says, the first few hundred of which are now under construction. Plans also call for 450,000 square feet of commercial development including shops, restaurants, and hotels.

"A lot of this will be driven by residential," Fishman says. "Homes are always first. We have a number of hotels we've talked to. No one is currently willing to jump in until the residential component is in place. Until you get a critical mass of approximately five hundred homes, we don't expect the hotels to start construction."

Unlike in the 1980s, Fishman maintains, the Asbury Park waterfront is ripe for revitalization. "Circumstances have changed considerably. It now has a responsible government. That, along with changes in the interest rate, which affected the residential home market, have made the city much more attractive to development."

If the redevelopment goes forward as planned, the new Asbury Park will be, in some ways, starkly at odds with the old. Fishman acknowledges this, and the criticism that Asbury Partners' plans all but leave out amusements. "The fact is, the times have changed," he says. "People no longer spend the amount of time coming to the shore for amusements. They choose alternate sites such as Six Flags or Hersheypark, which are much larger. That's a fact. The country's changed. We looked at that very closely, and it was determined that the Asbury Park redevelopment would take on more of a lifestyle appearance. The bulk of the Boardwalk experience here will be the unique retail environment, coupled with the beach, ocean, and restaurants."

He defends the controversial demolition of the Palace. "If someone had the notion that the building should be saved, they should have come here with that idea thirty years ago. You don't wait until the building is crumbling to the ground to decide to restore it. What we are planning to do is to incorporate that valuable piece of real estate into a hotel/retail establishment and still keep the imagery of the Palace in the development. As we see it, that solves all of the problems."

Fishman says he understands those who feel strongly about Asbury Park's music history. "I spent summers at the Shore. I probably spent more time here than 90 percent of the people you're talking to. The history is extremely important, I appreciate that, especially the music history. It's a great hook. 'Come on down, and while you're here, have a drink in the Stone Pony, where Bruce got started.' But you also need a nice restaurant. You need a place to buy a beach chair, and you need a store to buy suntan lotion. So you have to incorporate all the different elements. We plan to absorb rather than eliminate [the past],' he says.

Fishman steps outside, onto Asbury Park's brand-new Boardwalk, which was completed the month before. The southern yellow pine wood still smells fresh in the afternoon sun. A year ago, you couldn't ride a bike on the Boardwalk, he notes, because much of it was caving in. When NBC's *Today* show came here a couple of years ago to film a Springsteen concert at Convention Hall, officials had to place plywood on top of sections of the Boardwalk so crew members wouldn't fall through.

"Asbury Partners was able to build this mile-long stretch in a little under nine months," Fishman says, pointing out that an earlier six-hundred-foot section took the city two years to complete. Walking south toward the old Casino, Fishman talks about the Boardwalk project and what it means for Asbury Park.

"This was important, to see this Boardwalk rebuilt. It's one part of a complicated equation. There are many moving parts. Not everybody recognizes that," he says. "Asbury Park is a city that has been in decay for quite a while, remember. There are certain buildings that need attention—the Paramount Theatre, Convention Hall, the power plant, the carousel building. But everything can't stay just the way it was.

"We can't keep dwelling on things that were failures and somehow think that bringing back all the failures is going to be the salvation of Asbury

Park. The reason things fail is they don't work. If you look at the history of Asbury Park since the 1890s, it has consistently modified and reinvented itself to be a tourist destination, and that's what we're doing. That's how it historically survived: It reinvented itself. The Asbury Park of 1910 was different from the Asbury Park of 1930 and 1960.

"Unfortunately, after 1970, with urban unrest and decay, Asbury Park did not reinvent itself, and it hasn't done so since then," Fishman continues. "It stopped reinventing itself for thirty years, and therein lies the overall problem. It has not been able to evolve. And this is what we're trying to work with the city to do: take the best components of SoHo, South Beach, and Inner Harbor and have a successful beach and boardwalk again."

The Bad Guys

Asbury Partners aren't the only ones working to resuscitate Asbury Park. On a summer Sunday morning, Kate Mellina drives into the east side of town pointing out all of the old homes that were recently refurbished. Many display gay-pride rainbow flags on their porches. Over the past several years, an influx of gay residents and investors has helped raise property values and expectations for the future.

Mellina, a city councilwoman, moved to town with her husband in the late 1980s. After taking a buyout from Bell Labs, she purchased a retail space downtown and opened an art gallery in 1996. She also helped launch a grassroots homeowners association, heading its committee to improve quality of life.

"We had ideas about an arts district, about improving downtown, but at the time you couldn't get anybody at city hall to help you or listen to you," Mellina says. "It was very frustrating. People were angry, and basically what we were saying was 'Help! Please, please, please, you've got to help us because nothing's being done.' So we put together a petition that we circulated to the governor and our elected and state officials, asking them for help." To attract media attention, homeowners posted sos signs on their lawns and tied yellow ribbons around trees.

At the time, Asbury Park's waterfront was stalled in bankruptcy proceedings, and city hall was mired in contentious infighting and corruption.

"There was a widespread feeling that things weren't kosher," Mellina recalls. "People started coming to us with stories about bid rigging, about concessions at city hall being handled in cash, corruption in the police department, the school board, in elections. All sorts of things. We weren't savvy enough to really know what to do with all of these allegations, but I used my old Bell Labs expertise and put together a three-inch binder where I collected all of them, which we ended up showing to the prosecutor's office."

Their efforts eventually led to a federal raid on city hall and to the indictments of the city manager, the mayor, the mayor's top advisor, and others. But for several years, she says, she didn't know if their campaign would do any good. "It was scary because as soon as the word got out that we were working on this thing, I started getting calls. 'Oh, it would be a shame if your house burned down.' That went on for a long time. It was a living hell. I mean I was scared out of my frigging mind. The bad guys were so ingrained here, it seemed like we weren't making any progress at all."

At the end of 2000, she closed the art gallery, which she says couldn't survive in the mostly empty downtown. Friends convinced her to run for city council in the May 2001 election. "The last thing I wanted was to run for office," she says, driving past a downtown restaurant called Moonstruck, where people are lined up waiting for a table. "All I had ever done was hand out campaign literature for McGovern once. I did not want to do this. But I wasn't sure what to do with my career, so I decided, 'I'll run, and if I'm supposed to win, I'll win.' So I ran at the last minute, and I lost."

Mellina came in eleventh among twenty candidates vying for five seats. "I thought, *Thank God*." The next month, however, a recount gave her 167 extra votes, enough to win her a seat. "They had undercut me in two districts, putting the wrong numbers down. They cheat on everything here. You name it, they do it. But it never occurred to us that they were writing down the numbers off of the machine wrong. Nobody had ever thought of that possibility. I was the first person in the history of the county to lose an election because the numbers were copied down from the machine wrong."

The city was at a new low ebb when Mellina came into office on July 1, she says. "We were about to be taken over by the state. One of the first things that happened was that we got called down to Trenton and were told that Asbury Park is five million dollars in the hole. 'You have all these problems, we're coming in to take over.' But we said, 'No, we just started here.' We managed to hold them off for a couple of months and put together a five-year plan. We immediately negotiated on the beachfront because if you can't do something to show you're making progress there, they're going to take over."

Although she does not endorse all of the Asbury Partners' redevelopment plans, Mellina has faith their efforts will succeed. "If I thought the oceanfront redevelopment might go awry again, I think I'd have killed myself by now. If it does, we've set ourselves back another ten or twenty years. I think we *have* to make sure it works."

She is driving along Ocean Avenue now, past the

Fig. 28. *The eyes of Tillie look out from the city storage site where he resides temporarily.*

husk of Carabetta's unfinished condominium project. "This is an important time. The bad men are still out there, and now, with a lot of money coming in for development, some of the people with the bucks behind the people who got arrested are going to be out in force again." She parks across the street from Convention Hall and walks toward the Boardwalk. "But I've been fighting the bad guys eight years now, and I think we're gaining on them for the first time. So many new residents are moving in, it's going to be harder for them to play the game the way it was. I don't know if I want to run again, but I feel good about where things are."

Six months later, Mellina will give up her council seat with several months remaining in her term. When the next elections are held in the spring, she will run again but will not win.

Later that day, walking down the Boardwalk, still a city councilwoman, she laughs. "Sometimes, it seems funny being so serious about all of this. People complain about Tillie; they say it's just a chunk of concrete with paint on it. That's true, but you could also say that those love letters you have tucked away are just paper with ink on them.

"The Boardwalk was the magic part of summer. Meeting your friends up there, eating pizza and ice cream, the silly amusements. You'd always feel sort of free up there on the Boardwalk. It was a different world. Asbury Park doesn't have that now, but you can just feel how important it is to people, and you're just dying for it to come back and have personality again.

"Things go in cycles," she adds. "People who moved from here twenty-five or thirty years ago would be horrified by what it has become, that's true. But those who left five years ago are so excited by the direction it's going. Things that might look ugly to you look great to me."

CHAPTER FOUR

WILDWOOD, NEW JERSEY

Every Night Is Saturday Night

O N A breezy summer night in Wildwood, three teenage girls sit on a Boardwalk bench, watching the people, smoking cigarettes, talking on cell phones, waiting for something. An elderly couple steps up to the counter at Giovanni's Pizza and orders two slices of cheese. A family of five passes, the father carrying a giant toy giraffe. A few blocks later, the tallest of the children stops, becoming part of a small crowd gathered at the entrance to the country's only boardwalk chapel. "Watch the tram car, please!" cautions an automated voice, and the crowd reluctantly parts.

The excitement of Wildwood is its incongruities. The Boardwalk's quirky traditions quietly seem to vie for space each evening along its two-mile length. In his 1963 song "Wildwood Days," Bobby Rydell sang of a resort where "Every day's a holiday and every night is Saturday night"; it's a sentiment that still rings true. The Boardwalk here is wild and whimsical, with more amusement rides than any other boardwalk in the country, most of them packed on three ocean piers, giving the evening parade a perpetual carnival backdrop.

In the mid-1990s, Steven Izenour, the late architect and author, visited Wildwood and called it "one of the last really down and dirty, Tacky with a capital *T*, beach resorts." This, Izenour insisted, was a good thing. "What

Fig. 29. (OPPOSITE) Prizewinners on a summer night in Wildwood.

you need to do is take Tacky to new heights. In an increasingly homogenized commercial world, it's the perfect counterpunch strategy, and given the years of ad hoc evolution it took to make it what it is, nobody, not even Disney, could beat you at your game."

The game on Wildwood's Boardwalk is "more is more." There is so much going on here that it's nearly impossible to focus on any one thing. But that's the point: The Wildwood walk is not a place to think, or to savor; it is a place to experience the sensory storm of sea breeze and fried foods, colored lights and colorful people, win-a-prize games and pizza parlors, music that blares for a moment and then folds into the sound of another music—although, on summer evenings such as this one, the true music of Wildwood is a dazzling static.

What Survives

Robert Scully's grandfather moved to Wildwood from Atlantic City in 1902, two years after Wildwood's first Boardwalk was built. Originally from Philadelphia, he married an Atlantic City girl and came to Wildwood to build houses. Scully's father, Joseph, constructed the city's first convention hall and the Boardwalk's Cedar Avenue connection.

Scully was a builder, too, who built some twenty stores on the Boardwalk during the 1960s, 1970s, and 1980s. Today he's curator of the Wildwood Historical Society.

In a closet-sized office at the historical society's museum on Pacific Avenue, Scully pages through photographs showing what Wildwood used to be. Its history, he says, is not unlike those of other Jersey Shore boardwalk towns—Asbury Park, Seaside Heights, Ocean City—even though each has developed a distinct identity. "Atlantic City set the example. People came to the seashore because the doctor said it was good for you. Then Atlantic City built a boardwalk, and it was successful, so other resorts followed."

The man considered the "father" of Wildwood was Philip Baker, a hotel operator and investor from Vineland who, with his two brothers, bought up a hundred acres of shorefront property in 1885 for nine thousand dollars. The Bakers imagined a cottage colony by the sea, which tourists would visit to breathe the sea air and bathe in the salt water. They named their development Wildwood because of the area's dense growths of trees, many of which had twisted limbs and trunks.

Four years later, the railroad reached Wildwood, spawning the first development boom. Wildwood then consisted of four dirt roads; its main attractions were a sixty-foot observation tower and an excursion pavilion used for dances. But with the railroad came boardinghouses and grand hotels—first the Hotel Wildwood, then the elegant, four-story Hotel Dayton, which was dedicated for the 1890 season by President Benjamin Harrison.

Foot-walks were laid along the beach in 1890, although it wasn't until 1900 that the first real Boardwalk was built—and another four years before Wildwood had a raised wooden walkway. Amusements began to appear along the beach in the 1890s, similar to those in beach resorts to the north. Wildwood's earliest amusements pioneer was Gilbert Blaker, a Philadelphia wallpaper merchant. Blaker leased the Excursion Pavilion, expanded it into Blaker's Pier, and each season offered something new—a carousel, an ice cream parlor, a dance floor, a lunchroom, an auditorium.

Wildwood was incorporated in 1895, with Latimer Baker named its first mayor. Three years later, the Bakers purchased another 110 acres, more than doubling Wildwood's size. The land to the north and south of Wildwood also developed—as Wildwood Crest, to the south, which was incorporated in 1910, and Anglesea, to the north, which was renamed North Wildwood in 1906 and incorporated in 1917—and the three cities collectively became known as the Wildwoods.

Wildwood settled into its own niche as a beach resort, never as liberal or permissive as Atlantic City nor as restrictive as Asbury Park or Ocean City. Although Wildwood had several grand-style hotels, it didn't attract the high-society crowd that went to Cape May. "Wildwood developed its own character, as more of a middle-of-the-road beach town," Scully says. "As a result, we didn't have the ups and downs that some other resorts did."

In the first decade of the twentieth century, as many as twenty thousand people arrived by train in Wildwood on summer mornings—more than visited any other beach resort except Atlantic City and Coney Island. The amusements industry flourished here during the teens and the twenties. In 1918, Edward Rhoads built the Amusement Center on Boardwalk-front property owned by Blaker; it featured a roller coaster, a Ferris wheel, and an ornate carousel. Ten years later, Sportland opened on the North Wildwood Boardwalk, with 1,600 bathhouses, a giant saltwater swimming pool, and a stage where orchestras performed "music to swim by." In the 1920s, several ocean piers competed to outdo one another with their Coney Island–style rides, dance halls, theaters, and midway games.

Most of Wildwood's early Boardwalk businesses are gone today, but a few have survived. In 1917, Charles Douglass, a candy maker from Philadelphia,

opened a small saltwater taffy store on the Boardwalk. After the war, he expanded the business and began offering fudge. Douglass Fudge is still one of the mainstays on the Wildwood Boardwalk. Earl Groff sold hot dogs on the Boardwalk beginning in 1925 and in 1928 opened a full-service restaurant, which is now a Boardwalk institution.

In the 1930s, the amusements industry was hard hit by the Depression, and a growing permissiveness on the Boardwalk began to tarnish the image of Wildwood as a family

Fig. 30. The Boardwalk in the late 1940s. (Courtesy of the Wildwood Historical Society, Inc., Robert J. Scully, Curator.)

resort. In response, Wildwood and North Wildwood tightened their laws, banning beer, carnival barkers, mind-readers, and fortunetellers.

After the Second World War, however, Wildwood entered a period of sustained prosperity. With the country's middle class enjoying new reserves of wealth and leisure time, Wildwood launched a provocative ad campaign, which included an image of attractive women in short pants and sleeveless blouses hitchhiking beneath a huge sign pointing to "Wildwood by the Sea." Families were taking to the road on automobile vacations, and motels sprang up all over the country, offering an informal, modern environment, with swimming pools, playgrounds, and recreation rooms featuring television sets and Ping-Pong tables.

Wildwood, in the mid-1950s and early 1960s, was a model for the northeastern United States motel industry. Up to a dozen new motels opened each year in Wildwood during these years, some replacing hotels and rooming houses. In 1956, the Wildwood Hotel Association changed its name to the Wildwood Hotel and Motel Association. Wildwood's motel architecture was angular, loud, and colorful; motel names often reflected the culture: the space race (Satellite, Astronaut), popular cars (Bel Air, Thunderbird), Hawaiian statehood (Aloha, Ala Kai).

Wildwood became the East Coast's blue-collar Riviera. As one longtime business owner recalled: "Back then, if you had money you got on a new thing called a jet and you went to Miami. If you didn't, you got in your car, a Bel Air convertible, and you drove over to Wildwood." For years, dozens of rock 'n' roll clubs attracted thousands of young people to the Wildwoods. After Dick Clark's *American Bandstand* debuted in 1957, he brought a live version to Wildwood's Starlight Ballroom. Wildwood in the 1950s was stylishly modern, young, and hip.

Fig. 31. The Starlight Ballroom during the big band era. (Courtesy of the Wildwood Historical Society, Inc., Robert J. Scully, Curator.)

FORTY YEARS LATER, IN mid-1996, architect Steve Izenour, author of the book *Learning from Las Vegas*, toured Wildwood and discovered that dozens of these old space-age motels were still in business. Wildwood's image had taken some hits by then, and the tourism industry was in need of fresh ideas. Izenour urged that Wildwood simply promote what it was, cashing in on its architectural heritage the way Cape May had done with Victoriana and Miami Beach with art deco. "Appreciate Wildwood for what is: The

'un-bored walk,' " he wrote. Izenour warned against "robbing future generations of a page of architectural history."

In 1997, a group of business and motel owners banded together to form
the nonprofit Doo Wop Preservation League, dubbing Wildwood's 1950s
motel architecture "Doo Wop," after the singing style popularized in that
decade. The league's mission is "to foster awareness and appreciation of the
popular culture and imagery of the 1950s and 1960s and to promote preservation of the largest collection of mid-century architecture found in the
United States."

The Doo Wop Preservation League offers narrated tram tours of Wildwood's loosely delineated Doo Wop district and a stylish, informative Web
site, which includes "Demolition News" and "Doo Wop Heroes"—the latter
listing properties that have been "saved" from demolition. "The America of
the 1950s and early 1960s was an optimistic, confident, forward-looking society," the Web site states. "The seashore architecture of this era reflected the
spirit of the people: brassy, bold and boastful. . . . Angular elements, space-
age imagery, tropical themes and colors, with spectacular neon signage turning up the volume even more, combine to form a fairyland atmosphere."

In 1999, Wildwood businessman Jack Morey, whose father built some of
the original Doo Wop motels, bought the Wingate Motel and invested $3.5
million renovating it into a delightfully exaggerated example of Doo Wop
called the Starlux. Then–New Jersey governor Christine Todd Whitman
was on hand for the motel's dedication, to "plant" a plastic palm tree. Many
businesses in the Wildwoods have since adopted the theme and signage style
of Doo Wop architecture, and Wildwood has garnered plenty of national
media attention because of it.

But Wildwood's Doo Wop campaign has increasingly hit some hard
economic hurdles. With Wildwood in the midst of a condominium boom,
there's simply more money to be made tearing down motels and replacing
them with condos than there is in refurbishing fifty-year-old buildings. Despite extensive publicity, the Doo Wop movement has not drawn significant
outside investment, and some business owners here say it has only nomi-
nally enhanced tourist traffic. "When you're offered a million dollars for a
property valued at half that amount, it's difficult to say no," says one former
motel owner. Over the past several years, Doo Wop motels have been de-

molished about as quickly as they were built in the 1950s—including some of the classic ones, such as the Satellite and the Frontier. As this continues, the idea of a Doo Wop historic district becomes less feasible. The Doo Wop Preservation League has applied for National Historic Register designation, but its application has been returned several times because the zone changes in size as more old motels are torn down to make way for condos.

IN HIS TINY OFFICE on Pacific Avenue, Robert Scully opens another book of photographs. This one's filled with photos of buildings that are gone. There are dozens and dozens of them.

"We've been able to get pictures of most of them. As a builder and a historian, I have an interest in saving records of these buildings. . . . I also understand the economics of the market," he says. "Some things survive and some don't. Four or five years ago, you could buy a little house on Second or Third Street for a hundred and fifty thousand dollars. Now the same house is going for four hundred thousand, and that's just to get the lot, for a tear-down. . . . That's the market here right now." While the Doo Wop movement was seen as a chance to brand Wildwood, many in town say the incentives were never strong enough to entice property owners to participate.

History plays only a modest role in the Wildwood beach experience, according to Scully. "We get about five thousand, six thousand people through the museum. For most people, unfortunately, it is not part of why they come here. We don't have historic sites or historic buildings in Wildwood. People are more interested in lining up at their favorite restaurants. Instead of history, they have their own traditions."

Fig. 32. The retro space age–style Starlux motel. Former governor Christine Todd Whitman was at the opening to "plant" a plastic palm tree.

Mrs. T

Amid the impermanence of a Wildwood evening is a handful of businesses that seemingly never change. You step off the Boardwalk into a long, dim entryway and, settling on a squeaky stool at the end of the counter, begin to feel that you have somehow found your way to an earlier time.

You may recognize the manager here, a friendly, plain-speaking woman known as Mrs. T, who has worked the Wildwood Boardwalk fifty-three summers.

"Be with you in a second," she says when you catch her eye. The oven doors open and close; a warm, mouth-watering aroma of pizza crust and tomato sauce slowly fills the room. Outside, neon lights brighten in the evening sky.

Mrs. T sits for a moment, on the only available stool. The Boardwalk, she says, "is my fountain of youth. It keeps me young. I like the action." Mrs. T's real name is Rose Tata. She's eighty-four years old and has worked at Mack's for thirty-two years. She moved here from Philadelphia with her husband. "I was going to retire," she says, "when one of the Mack boys came up to me and said, 'Why don't you come up and work for me a couple of days.' I've been here ever since then. They're good people."

Fig.33. Rose Tata, Mrs. T, at Mack's: "Life changes, but we don't change."

The Mack boys are Joe and Duke Mack, who started the restaurant in the late 1950s.

"We have a lot more pizza places now than we did then," Mrs. T says, looking out at the action and the gathering dusk. "But Mack's has nothing to worry about because they have generations of people who come down here for the pizza. It's a taste that they never forget. You should have been here last night—there wasn't enough space for everyone.

"People will come all the way here from Philadelphia sometimes to pick up three or four pies. A man told me yesterday that he drove four hours for a Mack's pizza. I said to him, 'You're a damn fool.' I was kidding. That's how people are about Mack's pizza."

Mack's does have a distinctive taste: It's the crispy crust. Or is it the tomato sauce? Mrs. T says she "can't reveal" what makes this pizza special, except that "they use the very best ingredients. And they cook it a little different."

After a moment, she gets up to tend to someone at the Boardwalk end of the counter.

Sitting at a table against the wall is Anne Robbins, who is visiting Wildwood with her two daughters. Robbins grew up in the Philadelphia suburbs and says Mrs. T waited on her when she came to Wildwood with friends as a teenager. "It's the first thing we do when we come here. To me, it's as essential as the beach. We come in here for lunch and have a pizza pie and some days come back for dinner. Now my children are the same way."

Mrs. T returns and sits down. After Anne Robbins and her daughters say good-bye, she asks, "You see that? Mack's could probably change, but people always say they're happy it never does. We're one of the reasons people keep coming back. Life changes, but we don't change."

Summer Main Street

The pillar of the Wildwood Boardwalk has for years been the Morey Organization, which owns and operates the three amusement piers that give the resort its identity. Morey's Piers encompass about a million square feet of wood and concrete and nearly a hundred rides, which the organization classifies as Mild Thrill ("expected movements and anticipated thrills"), Moderate Thrill ("may contain unanticipated thrills"), and High Thrill ("high speeds with extremely unusual and stressful physical forces . . . startling and unexpected thrills").

The Morey amusements empire, which employs more than 1,500 people in summer, was started modestly in 1968 by two Wildwood brothers, Bill and Will Morey. Bill was a Boardwalk concessions operator; Will was a developer who had built a number of the Doo Wop motels. During a 1968 vacation to Florida, the brothers saw a huge, twelve-lane fiberglass slide in a Fort Lauderdale parking lot and decided to buy one for Wildwood. They purchased two lots on the beach to accommodate the slide, which was known as the Wipe Out, and opened it for the 1969 season at the new Morey's Surfside Pier. The slide was an instant hit, and the Moreys began adding rides and amusements to the site, including the popular King Kong ride in 1971 and a haunted house the following year. In 1974, they purchased a lot separating their two properties and expanded the amusements complex by eighty thousand square feet, renaming it Morey's Pier.

Wildwood was still a competitive amusements market in the 1970s, with five separate operators. The Moreys strengthened their position by offering elaborate modern rides found nowhere else on the Jersey Shore. These included the Poseidon Adventure in 1974, Planet of the Apes in 1975, and the Jumbo Jet roller coaster, which they bought in Germany for $400,000 and opened in 1976. The largest amusement park in Wildwood at the time was also the oldest, the Marine Pier and Playland, which first opened as the Amusement Center in 1918. After the 1976 season, the Moreys purchased the five-hundred-foot Marine Pier, and invested $1.5 million in renovations and new rides. They gave their new pier a nautical theme, calling it Mariner's Landing. In 1978, both piers were enlarged and a water park complex was added. A larger, $5 million expansion in 1985 included a two-and-a-half-acre water park called Raging Waters. In 1984, the Moreys purchased the Fun Pier, which they redeveloped as an "adventure" pier featuring go-cart tracks, bungee jumping, and helicopter rides.

By the late 1980s, the Morey Organization was simultaneously operating three major amusement piers, something no other amusements operator in any other boardwalk town had ever done. Expansions and additions continued through the 1990s, among them the $6 million Great Nor'easter, a 2,150-foot-long steel roller coaster that suspended riders below the tracks, and a double monorail ride that circled Mariner's Landing and Raging Waters.

The Moreys' dedication to high-quality, leading-edge amusements helped sustain Wildwood as a family attraction during the 1970s and 1980s—a time when many Jersey Shore towns were in decline.

"It's funny, for a while we watched as boardwalks to the north of us were going by the wayside, and we started wondering if it was a bad algae heading south," says Jack Morey, who today runs the Morey Organization with his brother Will (they are the sons of Will and Bill Morey). "At the same time, theme parks began to use 'boardwalk' as a theme. And we finally decided that maybe we ought to celebrate that we have this historic boardwalk and that we are one of the few remaining ones in the country."

It was Jack Morey, the main force behind the Doo Wop preservation movement, who brought Izenour to Wildwood in 1996. Although Izenour is often associated with Wildwood's 1950s motels, Morey says the piers and the Boardwalk were "equally if not more fascinating" to him. "What he really enjoyed was the whole chaos of it all."

Morey, whose office is on the Boardwalk at the Schellenger Avenue Pier, is well respected in the region for his forward-thinking efforts to better market Wildwood. Most of his ideas these days have to do with anticipating the future of tourism and, he says, "working with others to reinvent the Boardwalk/beach experience. With increased competition, we need to look at new ways to position ourselves. I see loyal crowds continuing to come to this boardwalk, but for shorter periods of time. That's the trend. It used to be people would come to the beach for two weeks. Then it went to one week. Now it's a few days."

Although the amusements business is healthy in Wildwood, it is not expanding, he says. The Morey company owns a fourth pier, which it uses as a maintenance shop; there are no plans to install rides.

"What we need to do, and what we are trying to do, is look at the whole beach/Boardwalk combination—take what's good about it, what's unique, and what's bad, and see how we can make it work even better." The good things about the Boardwalk are its traditions and its "supercharged atmosphere," Morey says. "You don't want to lose any of that. But you can also have other attractions that appeal to a different market."

Morey's vision is that the Boardwalk will become "a summer main street": "What that means is you still have the sensory overload that people expect, it's still a place to walk and watch people do crazy things, but you can also have a decent dinner at an outdoor café, with beer and wine, and visit some nice shops. And once that development takes place, it's my belief that the area above the stores will become prime residential."

Morey and others would also like to see a transformation of Wildwood's beach, which is the widest on the East Coast. While other boardwalk towns have spent millions of dollars pumping sand onto eroded oceanfronts, the

Wildwoods' beaches, thanks to a configuration that allows them to trap sand, have actually grown over the years and are now well over a thousand feet wide in some places. Wildwood should take advantage of this, planners say, by developing recreation areas and perhaps a bike path like the one in Venice Beach, California.

The key to reinventing Wildwood, Morey says, will be a single tourism vision. That's quite a challenge when three separate municipalities and thousands of business and property owners are involved, but the Wildwoods Chamber of Commerce—which represents all three cities—and many business leaders support early plans for enhancing what is already one of the most distinctive beach/boardwalk combinations in the country.

Fig. 34. In the morning, bikes dominate the Boardwalk. City leaders are exploring a plan to create a separate bike path along the beach.

Still, changing the beach and the Boardwalk won't necessarily change public perceptions. A recent study, unveiled at a "Summit on the Shore" tourism conference in Wildwood, shows that the public still harbors negative notions about the Jersey Shore, associating it with urban blight, discarded hypodermic needles, and *The Sopranos*. The $270,000 study included surveys of about seven thousand people.

Morey acknowledges that image must be an important component of the Wildwood plan. "We don't want to create something that is completely new and lose the flavor of Wildwood," he says. "We've got to blend the old and the new, and to make the old seem new again. It goes back to what Steve Izenour said. We begin with what's already here and make that a theme, so that people who come here every year with their families are not going to be disappointed. But then we might also get a hip, newer crowd that comes here and says, 'That's the wackiest place I've ever seen. We should come back here at least once a year.'"

Planting Seeds

On a breezy summer night, the curious stand in clusters in front of an old wood-frame building on the Boardwalk, watching as five young people sing Christian hymns to an accompaniment of folk guitar, fiddle, and tambourine. Later, as a minister talks of the "God-shaped hole we are all born with," a scruffy, barefoot passerby shouts, "Preach it, brother! Praise the Lord!" His tone is mocking, but the sermon doesn't miss a beat.

Of all the oddities on the Wildwood walk, the Boardwalk Chapel is in some ways the oddest. Not the chapel itself, which is a modest and charming orthodox Presbyterian church, but the fact that it's here at all—and has been for nearly sixty years—wedged among the cheap thrills and sweet confections.

Jon Stevenson, director of the chapel for the past twenty-seven summers, explains it this way: "Jesus said go where the people are. There are throngs of people here, even if many walk by and don't pay attention. The Bible told us to go to remote parts of the earth. In a way, Wildwood is a remote part of the earth. . . . Jesus urged people to take the gospel to places that are unusual. That's what Leslie Dunn did here."

Fig. 35. *The Boardwalk Chapel, where services are held nightly at* 8:00 P.M.

Reverend Leslie Dunn was the chapel's founder—a New Jersey preacher who stood on the Wildwood beach one morning in 1944 and had a vision: to reach out to the millions of people who visit here each summer and to save as many of them as possible. Dunn scraped together $2,995 to buy a piece of Boardwalk property at a tax auction and created the chapel, originally called the Gospel Pavilion, for the 1945 season. He delivered the first sermon here in July. Nowadays, services are held every night at 8:00 P.M. from Easter to Labor Day and include songs, sketches, and a sermon.

The Boardwalk ministry also furthers Dunn's vision by reaching out to Wildwood's summer visitors. The chapel's mostly volunteer staff has a goal of talking to two thousand people each season and handing out thirty thousand Christian pamphlets. But if preaching on the Boardwalk is a numbers game, Stevenson acknowledges that the percentages aren't good.

"Humanly speaking, I'm sometimes discouraged. But it isn't by my might that I do this, or by my will, it's by my faith. . . . Our role in Wildwood is to proclaim the gospel, to spread the good news. Most of the people on this Boardwalk are not part of the community. If they were, we'd follow up. Instead, what we do is plant the seeds. The watering and growing go on elsewhere."

Every summer, the Boardwalk Chapel enlists about a dozen young "volunteers," who pay $420 to work at the chapel, participating in the services and testifying on the Boardwalk. Each receives lodging and basic meals and is free to work other jobs in the Wildwoods. Occasionally volunteers will see tangible evidence that their seeds have taken root.

Fig. 36. Back to reality: "You Are Now Leaving the Boardwalk of Fame and Happiness."

"One day a man came running in all out of breath and said, 'Who's in charge here?' He wanted to let us know that he was here six years ago and shortly after that was led to Jesus. Someone else wrote us to say that she was directed to the Lord because of literature she got here. Sometimes we hear about it twenty years later, sometimes a few weeks later.

"It's nice when that happens," adds Stevenson, whose parents were missionaries and whose daughter worked at the chapel several summers ago. "But we go by faith here. We measure success by the fact that we are doing this, not by the results. Every summer, we're successful because we have planted seeds. Only the Holy Spirit can open people's hearts."

When this evening's service ends—minutes before nine thirty—the summer volunteers fan out onto the Boardwalk. Most of those they approach with pamphlets decline or else ignore them. A few listen politely.

Blocks from the chapel, two young volunteers—a man and a woman—approach three teenage girls who are sitting on a bench, smoking cigarettes, watching the parade. One of the girls turns away. She is talking on a cell phone. The other two pretend not to notice. The young man tries to sit beside them, and they scoot away several inches. Finally, one of the teenagers accepts the pamphlet; she says she would like to take it home and read it. The young man and woman move on, disappearing in the herds of people making their ways north and south.

The breeze is cool now, spiced with french fries and caramel corn. Hiphop blares from a storefront. It's a starry night, but the spinning, plummeting lights of Morey's amusements steal the sky. "Watch the tram car, please," cautions an automated voice. It's a Saturday night in Wildwood.

CHAPTER FIVE

CAPE MAY, NEW JERSEY

The Echoes of History

IN CAPE MAY, the Boardwalk is a walking place, not a commercial place. Along most of its 1.4-mile length you will find shoreline on one side and whimsical, pastel-colored Victorian houses on the other. Early in the day, Cape May's coast seems gloriously fresh, its sun-struck surface glimmering, its smooth-sand beach trespassed only by shorebirds—sandpipers, black skimmers, piping plovers, terns. In autumn, dozens of species of songbirds linger for days in Cape May before making the flight across Delaware Bay. Nature can seem magnified here—although this is actually its true size, undiminished by the noises and distractions that dominate most boardwalk towns.

Just five miles from Wildwood, Cape May seems very remote—a gracious seaside city with the largest collection of Victorian houses in the country, a resort that lives pleasantly in the past without the amusement park lights and amplified music of other Jersey Shore towns. "We are," says one Cape May business owner, "the anti-Wildwood."

The Boardwalk here is a concrete promenade built on top of a bulkhead that stretches from First Avenue to Madison Avenue. It was constructed after the March 1962 Ash Wednesday storm that tore apart the city's timber boardwalk and its foundation, along with the seaside convention center and several other structures. The concrete bulkhead, built by the Army Corps of

Fig. 37. (OPPOSITE) March 1962: Cape May's original wooden boardwalk was destroyed in the Ash Wednesday storm. (Courtesy of the Cape May Historical and Genealogical Society.)

Engineers as a buffer against future storms, extends about three feet below grade and is anchored in the sand by thirty-foot pilings. According to Cape May County county engineer Dale Foster, the bulkhead—along with an ongoing sand-renourishment program—has done its job. The bulkhead has not required any major maintenance in its forty years of existence, he says.

Virginia Beach, Myrtle Beach, Daytona Beach, and Venice Beach also have concrete walks, all known as "the Boardwalk." But in Cape May, the walk is always called "the Promenade." A handful of boardwalk-style businesses front the Promenade—small arcades, gift shops, restaurants, a fudge seller—but this is a different sort of boardwalk, which could serve as a model for other resorts looking to reinvent themselves without the honky-tonk.

Fig. 38. The Promenade: a walking place, with Victorian inns as a backdrop.

Cape May retains the original idea of boardwalk towns: It's a place to relax rather than to be entertained and stimulated. Among those who used it as a getaway in the nineteenth century were future president Abraham Lincoln and Presidents Ulysses S. Grant and Benjamin Harrison. It's a city of simple pleasures, where you can take in the historic district on a horse-drawn carriage, have lunch at a shady sidewalk café on Jackson Street, bike to view a sunset at Cape May Point, and enjoy the evening's cross-breezes on a wraparound wooden verandah.

Ruin and rebirth are intertwined in Cape May's history. When a fire destroyed the center of the resort in 1878, city leaders decided to rebuild Cape May as a more modest city, but in ornate Victorian and Gothic styles; these are the structures that give Cape May its charm today. At the time of the 1962 storm, however, the resort was embroiled in debate over the future of those buildings, many of which were in disrepair. Some developers wanted to Wildwood-ize Cape May, replacing the Victorian homes with motels, while a countermovement sought to preserve and restore them. The three-day March 1962 storm—and the need to rebuild afterward—helped crystallize the debate, eventually leading to the city's designation as a National Historic Landmark. Today Cape May is a refreshing departure from the rest of the Jersey Shore. It professes to be the "nation's oldest seashore resort"—a claim that, surprisingly, seems to be true.

The First Resort

Cape May's destiny has been shaped, in large part, by its unique location: on a cape between the Atlantic Ocean and Delaware Bay, at the southern tip of New Jersey. The area was first settled by migrant whalers in the 1600s, although the Kechemeche Indians of the Lenni-Lenape tribe had long used the cape as a hunting ground. In 1621, the Dutch West India Company sent a sea captain named Cornelius Mey to explore the region. Several years later, Dutch settlers bought land from the Indians and began to establish fishing and whaling communities. Swedish explorers also came to Cape May during this time and purchased land, as did whalers from Cape Cod and Long Island. The county and the cape came to be called May, an anglicized version of Cornelius Mey's last name. Among the early families to settle here were the Schellingers. Ken Schellinger, Cape May's assistant city engineer, traces his family's presence in Cape May to about 1690. "My ancestors were all whalers and farmers," he says. "That's what this region was built on."

Cape Island, the early name for what is now the city of Cape May, began to develop at the end of the seventeenth century, with small homes, public houses, and taverns. By the mid-1700s, Cape May had become the East Coast's first "bathing resort," advertising its natural attractions in Philadelphia newspapers.

In 1816, the year the first woodburning steamboats docked in Cape May, Thomas Hughes opened a hundred-room hotel that would come to be called Congress Hall. Even larger hotels were soon built to accommodate the crowds, which were now coming from not only Philadelphia but also Baltimore, New York, and Washington. The New Atlantic Hotel, which opened in 1842, had room for three hundred guests.

Sea-bathing in those days was a segregated activity; white flags denoted the hours that women could bathe and use the beach, while red flags indicated when it was the men's turn. Swedish novelist Frederika Bremer, who visited Cape May in 1850, described the resort's natural lure: "It is a republic among the billows," she wrote, "more equal and more fraternized than any upon dry land; because the sea, the great, mighty sea, treats all alike, roars around all and over all with such a superiority of power . . . the sea purifies them all."

Construction began in 1852 on what was to be the world's largest hotel, the four-story Mount Vernon, which was designed to host more than 3,500 guests. A major portion of the hotel opened in 1854, three years after Cape May's incorporation, but it burned down two years later.

The completion of the railroad from Philadelphia in 1863 signaled a new surge of interest in Cape May, creating the vacation cottage era, yet the expansion of the northeastern railroad industry soon took its toll on the resort. Newer coastal towns, such as Atlantic City and Asbury Park, not only offered more enticing attractions but were closer to urban population centers.

After the fire of 1878, the city decided to reposition itself in the changing resort marketplace. It rebuilt quickly, in Queen Anne, Gothic, and Victorian styles, and promoted an image as a quieter, classier alternative to Atlantic City. In 1882, John Philip Sousa led a weeklong series of concerts on the lawn of the reconstructed Congress Hall hotel, meant to symbolize the city's rebirth.

Still, Cape May struggled through much of the twentieth century. The growth of the railroad market, the rising significance of the automobile in American society, and the competitiveness of the fledgling tourism industry made Cape May's distant location a hindrance, although many loyal vacationers enjoyed its relaxed pace. In the 1950s, early preservation efforts led by Dr. Irving Tenenbaum and others resulted in old-fashioned streetlights and stirred debate about the city's Victorian heritage. When most of the Boardwalk was destroyed in 1962, city leaders suddenly faced a new, more urgent question: What are we going to do about Cape May?

Changing Character

Growing up in neighboring Wildwood, Bruce Minnix says he thought of Cape May as "dumb, dumb, dumb. There were no amusements, nothing. It was just dumb. There was no reason to go there."

Minnix, who worked for years in television, directing *Days of Our Lives, Search for Tomorrow,* and Jacqueline Kennedy's tour of the White House, among other shows, eventually changed his mind. "As I got older, I became very interested in the feel of Cape May," he says. "I've always been fascinated by the individual character of small towns. This became a place that appealed to me very much. . . . And, of course, anytime we want, we can still drive the five miles over to Wildwood and ride the roller coaster, which I love to do with my grandchildren."

Minnix, now eighty, is sitting in a rocking chair on the front porch of his Jackson Street home, a green wooden building from 1897 known as the Holly House. It's a Sunday morning, and he and his wife Corrine have just finished reading the *New York Times.* In the distance, sunlight sparkles on the Atlantic Ocean. The Minnixes bought Holly House in 1962 and operated it for many years as a bed-and-breakfast.

Fig. 39. *Former mayor Bruce Minnix, on the porch of his 1897 home. Minnix was a key figure in Cape May's Victorian preservation movement.*

"I never wanted to get into politics," says Minnix, a tall, bearded man with an urbane manner and mischievous smile. In the 1970s, a pivotal time in Cape May history, Minnix served as mayor here and was a driving force behind preservation efforts. "What happened was, one night a group of us were sitting here on this porch and we got to talking about plans to tear down the old Emlen Physick house. I don't know that we had given a lot of thought to the house before, but it seemed a shame to us that they kept tearing down these old houses. That was the trend we had seen. We didn't want the town ruined, and turned into a motel haven. So we decided that night to do something about it. The Physick Estate was the cornerstone of our efforts.

"In the 1960s, Victorian houses were not considered a big attraction. Many had not been kept up. People associated them with horror movies. But after the [1962] storm, the city had a big problem, and one of the ideas that came out of that was to try this gimmick of making the old Victorian houses a tourist attraction. When you've only got one thing to sell, that's what you sell. And all Cape May had were these old wooden houses. So they came up with a slogan: 'Our Future Is in Our Past.' That got some publicity.

But after we moved here full-time and saw what was going on, we realized that there were a lot of people in government who wanted to tear everything down. That's when we decided to get active."

The Physick Estate is an eighteen-room mansion on Washington Street. Built one year after the 1878 fire, on a four-acre lot with nine outbuildings, it was designed by Frank Furness, who also designed the Pennsylvania Academy of Fine Arts in Philadelphia. The house is considered one of the country's finest examples of "stick style" architecture, notable for its oversized features, upside-down chimneys, stick-like porch brackets, and the grid pattern of its outer walls. The interiors, too, show the distinctively ornate design patterns created by Furness.

The mansion was built for Dr. Emlen Physick and his widowed mother. "It was an odd household," says Minnix. Physick came from a wealthy Philadelphia family; his grandfather Dr. Philip Syng Physick was known as "the Father of American Surgery" and as the inventor of the stomach pump. "Emlin Physick, who never married, was an illegitimate child, who couldn't get the name or the inheritance unless he became a doctor. So he became a doctor, built this huge estate, and never practiced medicine."

The history and architecture of the estate made it interesting enough to be converted into a museum, Minnix and others believed, "but we went to the city and they wouldn't even talk to us. They said the property was too valuable. That showed how divided things were. So we decided to form a group and save it."

The group, known as the Mid-Atlantic Center for the Arts, or MAC, was born on Minnix's front porch in 1970, with a goal of saving and preserving the Physick Estate. "There was a municipal election coming up," he recalls. "We created a reform party and campaigned on preserving our architectural heritage, never specifically mentioning the Physick house."

Cape May was run by a three-member city council at the time of the 1972 elections. The reform candidates won two of the three seats that year; Minnix received the most votes, making him the mayor. "It astounded me," he says. His first official act was accepting the grants to save the Physick Estate; his last official act, in April 1976, was receiving the designation of the city as a National Historic Landmark.

Minnix credits a number of other "reformers" with carrying the torch for preservation, among them Carolyn Pitts and Ed Bramble, who helped win the town a listing on the National Register of Historic Places in 1970, and Dr. Tenenbaum. Today MAC has more than three thousand members and operates the Physick Estate as a historic house museum.

"We really worked together to change this town," Minnix says. And the city did change after winning landmark status. "It gives you publicity you could never buy. It also focuses what you want to do. So all of these elements began working together, and the result was a gigantic boom. Word got around. People wanted to come here again."

In the 1970s and 1980s, Cape May became a fashionable resort, known for its Victorian architecture, quaint shops, natural attractions, and arts community. In some

Fig. 40. The Physick Estate, built one year after the 1878 fire.

ways, though, Cape May isn't so different from what it was. Its year-round population, for instance, has hovered around four thousand for the past century (in summer, the resort attracts about thirty thousand visitors).

And the Boardwalk, although now known as the Promenade, is not unlike it was in 1961, Minnix says. He finds a photo of the old wooden walk that was there before the storm. "Most of the buildings you see there now are basically in the same places buildings were before the storm. Shops were just rebuilt, but it's the same configuration. There was a small arcade here then; there's a small arcade there now. What happened was, the city became better, not bigger or different."

Minnix recalls that when he ran for mayor in 1972, an opponent handed out campaign literature accusing him of being a Communist. "If you speak your opinions, that shouldn't mean you are a Communist," he laughs. "This country was founded on the idea of the freedom to say what you want to say. We won our freedom and created our democracy because of it."

During his years as mayor, Minnix once appeared on the television show *What's My Line?* He was introduced as "Bruce Minnix, director of the soap opera *Search for Tomorrow*." The panel tried to guess his "other line."

"They were stumped," Minnix recalls. "They all knew me, but they didn't know about my other job. I don't know that any of them had even heard of Cape May. I ended up winning the fifty dollars in prize money. . . . I guess this other job has turned out to be the more important one."

Diamonds

The reward for walking up the 199 steps of the Cape May Lighthouse's cast-iron spiral staircase is a new perspective. From the Watch Room Gallery, the view of sea and land is quietly stirring. Cape May from here is small but seductive, a painted resort benefiting again from its unique location, a wooden city once very vulnerable to fires and storms, now largely fortified against them.

The lighthouse, located in Cape May Point State Park, was constructed in 1859, after erosion forced an earlier lighthouse to be abandoned. Before it was operated by electricity, the light was fueled by whale oil, and the old oil storage rooms can still be seen on either side of the entrance hall. Over the past decade, MAC has overseen restoration of the lighthouse, including re-painting the tower light beige and the lantern red. The lighthouse is still an active navigation aid with a light visible twenty-five miles out to sea, flashing every fifteen seconds.

On the beach down below, children and their parents sift the sand for diamonds—not real diamonds, but quartz stones that are known locally as "Cape May diamonds." There are many legends about these stones, said to travel from the upper reaches of the Delaware River to their resting spot here on Cape May Point. The diamonds—found nowhere else in the world—are available in local gift and sundry shops for as little as fifty cents. Some are cut, polished, set in gold or silver, and sold as jewelry. A sign in a Promenade shop calls Abraham Lincoln "one of the first Cape May diamond collectors," but a local historian says Native Americans collected them hundreds of years ago and may have used them as currency. The term "Cape May diamond" apparently originated in the late 1800s.

Just offshore at Sunset Beach is the hulking wreck of the SS *Atlantus*, an experimental concrete ship that ran aground here in June 1926, a jutting memorial to an ill-conceived idea. The *Atlantus* was one of twelve concrete ships built during World War I; but the ships proved too heavy for sea travel and construction was abandoned.

On early maps, Cape May Point was the southern tip of New Jersey. It is still widely known for this distinction, although a Coast Guard staff officer recently noticed that on nautical charts the Cape May Point Lighthouse was not quite as far south as a portion of beach in the city of Cape May. Global positioning systems bore this out: The state's southernmost point is actually just off the Cape May Promenade, behind the convention center. In 2002, the city dedicated a buoy there, set in a bed of red rocks next to Henry's restaurant. The plaque reads: CITY OF CAPE MAY, SOUTHERNMOST POINT IN NEW JERSEY.

Cape May is not just a city; it is an alliance of natural and historic attractions. For those staying in a nineteenth-century inn near the Promenade, diamond hunting at Sunset Beach is an agreeable diversion. There are many others: a visit to the Audubon-run Cape May Bird Observatory; a walking tour of the Victorian district; a drive to Fisherman's Wharf, a working fishery that also includes a fish market, bar, and souvenir shop and the Lobster House restaurant.

Fig. 41. *The Promenade features a handful of kiddie rides, but none for adults.*

The soundtrack of Cape May is the surf; you hear it at surprising times and places, during the day and especially after dark. Cape May announces itself not with lights and music but with its subtleties—a slow series of enchantments. Cape May can be as mysterious and unpredictable as it is charming. Of course, it is not without its troubles, ranging from scarcity of parking to philosophical differences about future development, which some preservationists say could threaten the city's national landmark status—along with all the more general, and inevitable, problems that accompany success.

Hauntings

As nine o'clock approaches, a crowd of about sixty people stands on the Promenade across the street from the Hotel Macomber, awaiting the start of the Haunted Cape May Tour. It's breezy, and a nearly full moon casts Victorian shadows along Beach Drive.

The Hotel Macomber, constructed in 1911, is a four-story, wood-shingle building, which, the tour guide explains, is haunted by a former guest—a woman who visited three or four times a year in the 1940s and 1950s, always staying in Room 10. Each summer now, guests in Room 10 report being awakened by dresser drawers opening and shutting, the twist of a doorknob, or lights turning on, she says. The former guest, who died long ago, loved the place so much that she continues to visit. "The hotel often has a waiting list of people who have requested Room 10," the guide explains.

The Hotel Macomber has at least one other ghost, she says—a former waitress, known as Lily, long since deceased, whose presence is supposedly still felt, and seen, in the hotel's kitchen and dining room. Farther along on the tour, she plays a tape of a woman's voice, recorded in a tavern known as Cabanas. The voice is said to be that of a woman who committed suicide here.

Al Rauber, who started the Haunted Cape May Tour ten years ago, is a paranormal "investigator" who says he has studied thousands of hauntings since 1970. His investigations involve tape recordings, photography, electromagnetic field detectors, thermometers, and, he says, a lot of patience. Cape May has more haunted buildings than any other city he has examined, Rauber says. "There are several reasons for that. It's a very old city, so you have more history than you do in most places, and it's in a densely populated area. But it's also the nature of the history. Cape May has a very violent past, with a lot of floods and fires and, going way back, pirates. Hauntings are generally tied in with emotional activity. You also often find hauntings in houses that have been altered or renovated, and there's been a lot of that in Cape May."

Rauber, who is fifty-six, hails from Central New Jersey and now lives near Pittsburgh, where he works for a major appliance manufacturer. He says his paranormal studies started as an offshoot of his interest in history. In 1970, after earning a degree in history, he joined the Somerset County Historical Society, writing a column in its newsletter called "Tales of Old Somerset."

"I'd been interested in parapsychology since I was in high school, and when I did the column, people started telling me about their houses, about the ghosts and folklore surrounding them. And so two of my loves came together."

His interest in the paranormal led him to Cape May. "I used to go down three or four times a year, and as people got to know me, they'd tell me of some experience they had that they couldn't explain, and I'd investigate. It soon became clear that there was an inordinate amount of hauntings in Cape May. I started writing everything down, and at one point I realized that there were so many places that are haunted that I could do a tour down there if I wanted to."

The Haunted Cape May Tour advertises itself as "the only authentic walking ghost tour of Cape May," with "no folklore, no fairy tales, no fantasies." The hauntings cited on the ninety-minute tour are based on interviews with inn owners and follow-up investigations, says Rauber, who concedes that he is often unable to verify the stories he is told. "One of the problems we have is that so many of the original records have been lost or destroyed."

But Rauber, who has appeared on a number of television programs about the paranormal, including a Sci-Fi Channel show called *Sightings!*, stands behind his own studies. These include capturing electronic voice phenomena, or EVP—voices that are inaudible to the human ear but turn up on tape—and measuring electromagnetic fields using a handheld meter. "I can usually go into a house and tell by the EMF reading where the activity has taken place before the owner tells me. . . . This is the energy that someone has left in the house."

Asked about the woman who haunts the Cabanas tavern, he says: "I have never been able to verify that there actually was a woman who committed suicide. But I was investigating it, walking through . . . with a tape recorder going, and afterward we played the tape and heard a voice saying, 'She's pretty.' The only ones upstairs were myself, my partner Diane, and the manager of the place, so I assume she must be referring to my partner." Tour guides play the tape of this recording each evening.

Rauber says the purpose of the Haunted Cape May Tour is to educate people. "I don't want to scare people, I want them to learn something. I want them to consider this from a scientific standpoint."

Not surprisingly, the Haunted Cape May Tour has drawn some critics and skeptics. "I encourage skepticism," says Rauber, who conducts the tour himself a few times each summer. "People should not come to this expecting to see ghosts. They should come to this expecting to learn something.

"People ask me, 'Aren't you ever frightened?' I say, 'How can I get frightened if I'm learning something?' Nowadays there are a lot of people who are interested in being frightened. Look at your most popular movies. People love that. They decide they're going to experience something scary whether it happens or not. Something will fall in the next room and they'll get a rush out of it, they'll say it's a ghost. That gives what I do a bad name. If you want to know what frightens me, that's it: The people who really believe their walls are going to turn to blood."

Two Ways of Telling History

One of the houses on the ghost tour is the two-story Colonial House, the oldest surviving building in Cape May, dating to 1775. The tour doesn't go inside this house—or any of the other supposedly haunted buildings—but Cape May historian Jim Campbell holds the keys and opens the door.

He smiles when asked if the house is haunted. "Haunted by history," he says.

The Colonial House was built by a whaler named Memucan Hughes, and for a while it served as a tavern for whalers and fishermen. In 1806, Memucan's eldest son, Israel Hughes, married Mary Eldridge, and the six-room house became their home.

Now owned by the city of Cape May, the Colonial House is a museum and the office of the Cape May Historical Society, of which Campbell is president. The museum is open four hours a day and presents small historical exhibitions about Cape May. Campbell, an accommodating man, goes into a back room to get photographs and news clippings showing the Cape May Boardwalk early in the twentieth century. The oldest records here of a boardwalk date to 1903, although he suspects there were plank walkways on the beach much earlier. Some historians say that Cape May had a small boardwalk as early as 1868, even before Atlantic City.

The photos show a procession of arches lighting the Boardwalk, the long-gone ocean piers, and an amusement park that once stood at the Boardwalk's end. "The amusements all went north," says Campbell.

Campbell moved to Cape May from the Philadelphia area and worked for nearby Cold Spring Presbyterian Church, one of the oldest churches in the region. The church's first, wooden building was constructed in 1718; the current brick church dates to 1823. Buried in the church cemetery are more *Mayflower* descendants than in any cemetery outside of Massachusetts.

Campbell, who compiles genealogies, writes historical articles, and gives lectures (a talk this summer is entitled "Digging Up the Past—A History of Funeral Practices in America"), says he likes the pace of Cape May and the wealth of history here. But he says the lack of financial support for preserving that history is sometimes disheartening. "I guess there are two ways of telling history here," he adds: The historical society tells it the traditional way, while the restored Victorian buildings, with their period furnishings and narrated tours, tell it in a more participatory, and more popular, way.

AT THE END OF THE DAY, people are drawn to the Promenade, and it becomes clear how different this boardwalk is from others. Most American boardwalks parallel the Atlantic Ocean, running north-south, but because of Cape May's unusual location, the Promenade here leads people in an east-west direction, straight toward sunset.

Along Beach Drive, American flags ripple in the breeze. Kites fly over the Cape May beach. Young families and older couples make their way to the western end, where the sun can be seen setting near the lighthouse. On wooden porches along Beach Drive, guests sip cocktails and wait for the sunset's afterglow.

One of those out this evening is Bruce Minnix, the former mayor, who is strolling the Promenade with his wife. They're eating ice cream. "When I got to be mayor," Minnix says, "my mother was fond of saying to me, I should go sit on the rocks and just look at the water for a while. I said, 'Well, but I have all these things to do.' She said, 'No, you need to look at the water and relax and enjoy yourself. Honey, go do it.'" He laughs. "I guess I'm doing that now."

Fig. 42. The Colonial House, the oldest surviving building in Cape May, dates to 1775.

CHAPTER SIX

REHOBOTH BEACH, DELAWARE

Resistance and Charm

EHOBOTH BEACH is more citified and sophisticated than most mid-Atlantic beach resorts, but its 1.1-mile-long Boardwalk is agreeably tacky, with video arcades, rides, pizza parlors, a haunted house, souvenir sellers, and lots of benches with reversible seatbacks, giving sitters the option of people-watching or gazing at the sea.

Ninety-one-year-old Rehoboth Beach resident Jack Salin says the Rehoboth Beach Boardwalk hasn't changed much since the Second World War. "About the only change I can see is they don't have railings on it anymore. Otherwise, it's about the same. The attractions are the same. We had one amusement park then, we have one now. It's still a gathering place."

Salin, a retired engineer, remembers people meeting on the Boardwalk during World War II and looking out across the ocean toward Europe. "You couldn't see what was happening, of course, but you could imagine it, and talk about it. That's what people did. They did the same thing during World War I. . . . When they weren't looking to the ocean, they'd be looking at each another."

The city of Rehoboth Beach, on the other hand, "has changed drastically," says Salin, who lives a block and a half off the Boardwalk. "A lot of old

Fig. 43. (OPPOSITE) The Rehoboth Beach Boardwalk before the 1914 storm, which destroyed Horn's Pavilion and much of the walk. (Courtesy of the Rehoboth Beach Historical Society.)

houses are being torn down now and being replaced with new, larger ones. I don't like that much. It's not the Rehoboth Beach that we knew."

Bill Bahan, who began visiting Rehoboth in the 1960s and retired here in 1990 after a career with IBM, calls the Boardwalk "a constant." "Nobody's seen any reason to change the Boardwalk. It's been washed out by storms a few times, but it's been rebuilt about the same as it was." Bahan, who is president of the Rehoboth Beach Historical Society, walks the boards with his wife and their dog almost every day.

Rehoboth Beach lies between Cape May, New Jersey, and Ocean City, Maryland—both geographically and philosophically. It has a little of Ocean City's razzle-dazzle and some of Cape May's charm, but for the most part, Rehoboth's personality is its own. The one-square-mile city is a vibrant, low-rise resort with lots of trees, unusual shops and restaurants, and a few trendy nightclubs. During summer, free concerts are staged nightly on a Boardwalk bandstand, and the breeze is often scented with a distinctly pleasant blend of caramel popcorn, sea salt, and cut grass. The bandstand concerts range from jazz to classical to swing to Elvis and Sinatra tributes.

Traditionally, Rehoboth—which bills itself as "the Nation's Summer Capital"—has been the resort of choice for Washington-area beachgoers, while those from Baltimore prefer the more down-to-earth Ocean City. In the late 1960s and early 1970s, as Ocean City embraced high-rise development, Rehoboth leaders stood firm against tall buildings, keeping the city's height limit at forty-two feet. The result is two very different cities. Rehoboth's intimate ambience sometimes draws comparisons to New England seaside villages, while Ocean City seems more akin to the densely developed Jersey Shore resorts. Rehoboth is known for its arts community, its family-friendly atmosphere, and its substantial gay population.

Although it is Delaware's largest beach town, Rehoboth is a small-scale resort, with a year-round population of less than 1,500 and a peak summer population of about 65,000. The city never enjoyed the dramatic growth spurts of many boardwalk towns, nor the steep declines. Some longtime residents, though, say the recent leaps in land values are making Rehoboth a different, more exclusive place.

"Everything changes, I guess, and sometimes you don't like to see it," says Salin.

Everything except the Boardwalk.

Broad Places

The history of Rehoboth Beach can be found a few blocks from the Boardwalk in a two-story wooden cottage on shady Christian Street. The cottage, which dates to the 1890s, is one of the old "tent" houses built here when Rehoboth Beach was a religious camp. Today the cottage houses the Anna Hazzard Museum, a repository for hundreds of photos and artifacts charting the evolution of Rehoboth Beach from a spiritual retreat to a tolerant vacation resort.

"Rehoboth has gone through a number of phases," says Irene Simpler, the volunteer curator of the museum and a resident of Rehoboth Beach for more than fifty years, "but the Boardwalk has been there right from the beginning, when Reverend Todd came here and started the Methodist Episcopal Camp in 1873." The first Boardwalk, she notes, was an eight-foot-wide path of oak planks that stretched about a thousand feet along the beach.

The earliest visitors to the Rehoboth area were probably Native Americans, who journeyed to the beach in summer for the cool air and to fish the ocean and nearby bays. Dutch and British settlers farmed in the region beginning in the mid-seventeenth century.

But the first settlement at the beach was a religious encampment established in 1873 by Reverend Robert Todd of Saint Paul's Methodist Episcopal Church in Wilmington. Todd, inspired by a visit to the Ocean Grove Methodist camp in New Jersey the year before, purchased 414 acres of coastal land for about ten thousand dollars and created the Rehoboth Beach Camp Meeting Association of the Methodist Episcopal Church. The association received a charter from the Delaware legislature in 1873 for a "Christian seaside resort." To support its endeavor, the group also sold plots of land surrounding the camp—a move that eventually undermined Todd's dream of a Christian retreat.

The name Rehoboth came from nearby Rehoboth Bay, which was discovered and named in the seventeenth century by English explorers from the Virginia colony. The source of the name was the Bible: In Genesis 26:22, Isaac digs a well and "call[s] its name Rehoboth, saying, 'For now the Lord has made room for us, and we shall be fruitful in the land.' " In Hebrew, Rehoboth means "broad places."

The Camp Meeting Association laid out its encampment grounds in a fan-shaped design at what is today the western end of Rehoboth Avenue. The camp featured "broad places"—wide streets and parkland—and a number of small, one-room wooden cottages that were called "tents," built around a tabernacle building. The first religious assemblies were held that summer, and they grew larger for several years.

In 1878, the railroad line was extended from Lewes south to Rehoboth Beach, and suddenly outsiders who had no interest in the Methodist Episcopal camp began visiting the coast. Supply and demand dictated what happened next. Lots that Todd's group had sold to support the camp became summer cottage sites, and soon the nature

Fig. 44. The Anna Hazzard House, on Christian Street, built in the 1890s by the founder of a religious camp association. Rehoboth took its name from the Bible.

of Rehoboth Beach changed—from a religious getaway to a vacation resort. In 1879, the legislature shortened the charter name to "the Rehoboth Beach Association," removing reference to the church, and in 1881, the religious meetings were discontinued.

The influx of visitors to Rehoboth quickly created a market for commercial enterprise. Rehoboth's first amusements vendor was probably Charles S. Horn, who built a 150-foot pier and pavilion here in the 1880s. Horn later opened the city's first movie theater.

"Storms have played an important part in the history of Rehoboth Beach," says Simpler. "The first big one that we have records of was in 1914. That destroyed the pier and the pavilion and the Boardwalk." In fact, she says, much of the city's history can be marked off by natural disasters and advances in transportation. The paving in 1925 of a road from Georgetown to Rehoboth Beach, for example, created a tourism and building boom, as did the opening in 1952 of the Chesapeake Bay Bridge.

The Anna Hazzard house—named for the woman who lived in this building from 1927 until her death in 1968—was built in the 1890s by the founder of a second, short-lived religious camp association. It was moved to this address at 17 Christian Street in 1975 and turned into a museum. The house will soon be moved again, to the old Ice House property at the Canal Street entrance to the city. The Ice House, once a liquor store, will become the new, much larger historical museum, and the Hazzard House will be an artifact on the grounds. The move is part of a three-year project known as Streetscape, which is transforming the look of Rehoboth Beach by moving power lines underground, widening sidewalks, and installing old-fashioned streetlights. "I like seeing the wires down," says Simpler. "Some people aren't pleased with all of the other changes, however. They think it looks too generic, or like Ocean City. Some people liked things the way they were."

Watching the World

"The best part of my day," says Allen Fasnacht, co-owner of the Funland amusement park on the Boardwalk, "is working these kiddie rides at night. There's hardly a night goes by that a family doesn't say to me, either the father or the mother, 'I remember when you put me on this ride, now you're putting my kids on it.' And it's even to the point where I'm getting grandparents who'll say, 'You put me on this ride, now you're putting my grandchildren on it.' People like seeing the same faces year after year. I have mothers coming up and hugging me and I don't know who they are. It's kind of weird.

"Often people will ask, 'How long have you been working here?' not having any idea that I'm part of the family that owns this place. I answer with a question: 'How long have you been coming here?' "

Fasnacht first visited Rehoboth Beach in August of 1961 while vacationing with his family in nearby Bethany Beach. The Fasnachts came here from Hershey, Pennsylvania, where they ran a small picnic park used for family reunions and company barbeques. Fasnacht remembers walking down the

Rehoboth Beach Boardwalk one day and discovering the small amusement arcade then known as Sport Center.

"They had this new ride there that I'd never seen. It was a kiddie helicopter that had a bar you could push to make it go up and down. That interested me. Other kiddie rides at the time just went around in circles. This was something new. I thought it would be a nice ride to have at our park, so I went in and started talking to the kid who was running it, but I sensed right away that he was very reluctant to talk to me. Finally, he said, 'The boss doesn't like us talking to people. And he's coming out of his office now.'

"I turned and saw Mr. Dentino, the owner, coming out. He stopped at the next ride and I went over and introduced myself. And almost before I said hello, he said, 'Do you want to buy this place?' My initial reaction was 'No, we have one headache, who needs another?' I just wanted to learn about the helicopter ride. But on our way back to Bethany, where we were staying, I said to my dad, 'Pop, you know that place is for sale. What do you think?' And my dad said what I did: 'We don't need another headache.'

"But then the next morning, it was funny, he woke me up, pounding on my door, and he said, 'You know, maybe we should go back up there and take another look at it.' We had taken a couple days off before our kids had to go back to school, so we drove back and saw Mr. Dentino. This time he would hardly talk to me. The only thing he'd say was, 'You go back to Pennsylvania and think about it, and if you're still interested, we'll meet in Wilmington and talk to my additor.' He meant auditor, but he pronounced it *additor*. So that's what we did. I later learned that Mr. Dentino and his son had gotten to talking and they had decided that I was an Internal Revenue agent. That's why he didn't want to talk about business."

Jack Dentino started what is today Funland with a single concession back in 1939: a game called Spill the Milk, in which players tried to knock down a pyramid of six wooden milk bottles with a baseball. Dentino, who slept on a cot in a room behind the game, charged a nickel for three tries. Later, he added other sports-oriented games, including batting cages and miniature golf, and called his business the Sport Center. In the 1950s, he brought in kiddie rides and arcade games such as Skee-Ball. By 1961, Dentino was looking to sell the business and retire.

The Fasnacht family liked the feel of Rehoboth. It was family oriented

PLATE 1, ABOVE: The Atlantic City Boardwalk, looking south from Bellevue Avenue.

PLATE 2, LEFT: Boardwalk performer Ed the Clarinetist.

PLATE 3, ABOVE: The view from the southern end of the Coney Island Boardwalk: the gated beach community of Sea Gate.

PLATE 4, BELOW: One of the many faces of Coney Island.

PLATE 5, ABOVE: Fourth of July, Coney Island..

PLATE 6, BELOW: Madam Marie's fortune-telling shop in Asbury Park, closed for years, being readied to reopen.

PLATE 7, RIGHT: Just past sunset on the Wildwood walk.

PLATE 8, BELOW: The perpetual carnival at Morey's Pier. There are more rides in Wildwood than in any other Boardwalk resort. Most are operated by the Morey Organization. (Photo courtesy of Morey's Piers.)

PLATE 9, ABOVE: Victorian homes, a block off the Cape May Promenade.

PLATE 10, RIGHT: The Ocean Gallery at Second Street, Ocean City: "It's Astounding!!!"

PLATE 11, RIGHT: Boardwalk carousel horses, Virginia Beach.

PLATE 12, BELOW: A row of Williams '57 Baseball games at Fun Plaza on the Boardwalk in Myrtle Beach.

PLATE 13, ABOVE: The Jantzen swimsuit figure, diving over the Daytona Beach Boardwalk.

PLATE 14, LEFT: Harry Perry in Venice Beach: "They've changed the definition of freedom."

PLATE 15, RIGHT: The Santa Cruz Boardwalk on a summer morning. (Courtesy Santa Cruz Seaside Company Archives.)

PLATE 16, BELOW: The Santa Cruz Boardwalk at night: a seductive, welcoming place. (Courtesy Santa Cruz Seaside Company Archives.)

and small but had a solid summer clientele. They also liked the idea of living at the beach. During the off-season, they struck a deal with Dentino to take over operation for the 1962 summer season. Settlement was scheduled for March 15, 1962.

But on March 6, the Ash Wednesday storm slammed the Atlantic coast. "We drove down afterward to have a look, not knowing what to expect. Coming into town, you couldn't see any evidence that there'd even been a storm. No sign. You didn't see trees blown over, you didn't see wires down or anything like that. Not until you got to within fifty, sixty, maybe seventy-five feet of the Boardwalk. Then you saw it: utter destruction. The Boardwalk completely gone. Buildings gone, toppled into the water. Businesses gone. Bumper cars were out on the sand. This building here had sunk seventeen or nineteen inches. We just couldn't believe it.

"Naturally, we had second thoughts about buying it after seeing that. Mr. Dentino, who'd been in Florida when the storm hit, came back up here. He said, 'If you decide you don't want to go through with the deal, I'll give you your deposit money back.' Which he didn't have to do. We said we'd talk about it on the way home. And then just as we were starting to drive away, Mr. Dentino came out waving his hands and he said he had just talked it over with his wife and they'd allow us fifty thousand dollars off the purchase price if we went through with it.

"We had no guarantee then that the city would put the Boardwalk back, of course. We didn't know what was going to happen to Rehoboth, although we were confident that if it was going to continue as a resort they would have to build another boardwalk. So we went ahead and bought it, and we were in business on Memorial Day. By next season, the whole Boardwalk was rebuilt. And we've been here ever since. It was the right decision."

At first, Fasnacht's parents ran the Rehoboth park while Allen, his brother Don, and their wives ran the Hershey picnic park. In 1968, they closed the Pennsylvania business, and the whole family began spending summers in Rehoboth.

The Fasnachts changed the name of the park to Funland. In the 1970s, they expanded, buying adjacent property where the bumper cars operate today. They added the Haunted House in 1980—which is still one of the most successful Boardwalk attractions—and several thrill rides.

"Overall we haven't changed much," says Fasnacht, walking among the kiddie rides. "Most of these rides are the same. The helicopter was here, the merry-go-round, the rocket ship was here, these boats were here, the fire engines were here. The fire engines are probably our oldest ride. They were made in Coney Island by the Pinto Brothers company in the early fifties. We're a small park, so we don't have room to add the real big rides. We change a little here and there in games and rides, although sometimes we'll go several years without changing anything. People like that. One of the things they say to us is 'Funland never changes.' We try to keep it a nice clean place that's family oriented and affordable. Our philosophy has always been to treat your customer well. That's the most important thing."

Fig. 45. Allen Fasnacht, co-owner of Funland, in his favorite part of the park.

Standing on the Boardwalk in front of Funland, Fasnacht says: "I'll tell you one thing that has changed here, though, if you want to hear a little story. This goes back to 1962, when we were cleaning up the debris out here after the storm. Dad, my brother Don, and I were clearing away timber right over there when a man appeared up on the sidewalk, and he said, 'Hi, are you the new owners?' We said yes, and he said, 'I'm Jack Strauss. I own property right across the street. Do you have any interest in buying it?' It was a hundred twenty-five feet by a hundred feet. I asked him how much he was asking for it. He said sixty-four thousand dollars. I said, 'I don't think so.' I found out later if I'd said fifty-five thousand, he'd have taken it. The same size property on the corner right over there just sold two or three years ago for three-point-two million. So I guess that's one way that things have changed."

"I'VE GOT TO TAKE out the trash. Can you come back in an hour?" It's Tuesday morning, and Allen Fasnacht is hauling trash out to the Dumpster before the park opens at ten o'clock.

"I have to say, my family's blessed with a lot of mechanics and I'm not one of them," he explains later. "So I have to do what I can, which includes emptying the trash and that kind of thing. With that in mind, you can see how running the rides at night is so much fun to me."

Fasnacht is at his kitchen table, in an old wooden building that serves as both the Fasnachts' summer home and the Funland offices. "We have two classifications of employees here: high school and college kids, and family. We just took a group family picture last week. There are now thirty-two family members who work here. We have fourth-generation family working in the park, and we're getting ready for a fifth generation."

On a bulletin board in the next room is a list of employees and former employees who met their spouses here at Funland—including his brother Don's three daughters. "Some join our organization," he says, "and some end up joining our family. One of the things that's gratifying is that this has stayed a family business for so long with only minimal friction. Everything you read about generational businesses, by the time you get to the third generation, usually you're in trouble. It's often a situation where mom and pop started it and worked round the clock, and the second generation picked up their habits, but by the third generation, they're interested in doing different things. That hasn't happened here, and I think that's in part because of the nature of the business but also the nature of this town."

The Fasnachts' home is actually in the park—so close to the Sea Dragon thrill ride that people sometimes ask if there has ever been a collision. "Obviously, we don't get to bed early," Fasnacht says.

Does he ever think about quitting? "No, this is too much fun. I think there's something very interesting about the Boardwalk. A lady the other day made the statement that the Boardwalk is the place where you can mix all types of people, all colors and creeds, and no one seems to notice. The banker rubs elbows with the migrant worker. People from all walks of life. People come here to watch the world go by. You never know what you'll see. I had a family in the park last night, they all had red shirts on, with a name on them and then another name underneath. I said to the older gentleman who was putting his grandkids on my helicopter ride, 'Tell me about your shirts.' He said, 'That's our family shirt. This is our family reunion. We're having it here at the beach.' "

The Price of Maintenance

After the March 1962 nor'easter, Rehoboth Beach sank a row of wooden pilings thirty feet into the ground, much as Cape May did, as a fortification against future storms and erosion. Unlike Cape May, though, Rehoboth chose to rebuild its wooden boardwalk rather than replace it with a concrete promenade. Three times since the 1962 storm—in 1985, 1992, and 1998—the Boardwalk has been seriously damaged by storms and, in part, rebuilt.

Even when Rehoboth Beach's Boardwalk isn't pummeled by storms, the city spends $25,000 annually replacing boards—11,600 planks of southern yellow pine wood make up the Boardwalk—and another $175,000 on general upkeep, according to Rehoboth Beach Public Works director Millburn Craig. "That's the price of maintenance," he says.

Fig. 46. Reversible seatbacks give people the option of watching the beach or the Boardwalk parade.

Maintenance comes in many forms. Millburn and a crew of three or four city workers venture out on the Boardwalk shortly after 6:00 A.M. three times a week during summer, hammers in hand, searching for loose nails. "When it's wet, the boards will stay swollen, but when we get a lot of dry weather, the nails will start popping up. So we go out there and hammer them back down."

Millburn also monitors the Boardwalk's 250 trash barrels. "I make sure you do not see any trash barrels overflowing on the Rehoboth Beach Boardwalk. Sometimes when you get a couple of large pizza boxes in one at lunchtime, it'll start to fill up. When I see that, I get a truck up there right away."

Trash is the top maintenance priority for the Public Works Department, according to Craig. In July and August, the city hauls between five hundred and six hundred tons of trash each month to an inland landfill. In June, the haul is about four hundred and fifty tons.

Craig arrives at work each day before six in the morning. He has a crew of about thirty-six in summer and about a dozen year-round. Workers empty trash cans at night, rake the beach sand for trash, and clean the Boardwalk with giant Billy Goat vacuums in the mornings. Several hours after he leaves work, Craig is back on the Boardwalk, monitoring its appearance. "Public Works cannot work regular hours. It's really a full day's job. Part of my job is to make sure the city fathers don't receive complaints. They've got enough to worry about. The public knows this as a clean, attractive beach and boardwalk. It takes a lot of work to keep it that way."

This Pizza Thing

Dominick Pulieri tosses a circle of kneaded pizza dough high in the air behind the counter at Grotto Pizza on the Rehoboth Beach Boardwalk. Grotto is a Delaware institution, with thirteen restaurants in the state, ten of them at the beach, and an army of loyal fans. Most of the tourists waiting for a table here, though, don't realize that this sixty-year-old cook tossing the dough is also the founder and owner of Grotto Pizza.

Pulieri started Grotto Pizza a few blocks from here back in May 1960. His first store was a take-out stand, which sold pizza and nothing else. There were no tables that summer, no soft drinks, no forks or knives, not even paper plates. Pizza slices, served up on napkins, sold for twenty cents each. A pie cost $1.60.

"It's a funny thing," says Pulieri, recalling that first summer, when he was seventeen. "I grew up in an Italian family in Pennsylvania, and I was always around pizza. My mother made it every Friday. I had worked in a pizza restaurant. We came to the beach in 1960 because there were no pizza businesses here. But what we found out, and this was a shocker, was that there was no market for it, either. Simply because people did not know what pizza was."

Pulieri, the son of Italian immigrants, grew up in Wilkes-Barre, where his father worked in a coal mine. His sister Maryjean, eight years his senior, married a man named Joe Paglianite who owned a pizza restaurant at Harvey's Lake, a Pennsylvania resort area. Pulieri began working at the restaurant when he was thirteen.

"It was a small place called Joe's Pizza. That's where I learned the business. At that age, most of what you do is wash dishes and mop the floors, that kind of thing, but when I had the opportunity, I'd also try to learn to make pizza. I became fascinated by it, by what makes a good pizza, so that by the time I was sixteen or seventeen, I had become very proficient at making pizza.

"One day this fellow happened to come in the restaurant who had a place down in Dewey Beach, Delaware. He said, 'You guys should come down to Delaware. There's no pizza down there at the beach.' I guess those were just the right words at the right time. I was graduating from high school, and I needed to get a real job where I could make some real money to go to college. And then Joe said, 'Why don't we drive down to the beach and have a look.' I'd never seen the ocean before, so it didn't take much to get me to go."

They explored the Delaware shore and wound up leasing a storefront space in Rehoboth Beach, right next to the Dairy Queen on Rehoboth Avenue. The rent for the summer was $1,300, which included a small room upstairs with a bed, where Pulieri would live. Paglianite covered the lease, provided a couple of used pizza ovens, and paid Pulieri a thousand dollars to run the business that summer.

"As I was getting ready to open, it dawned on me that I had to call it something. I wasn't going to call it Joe's, because Joe wasn't really there, and I couldn't call it Dominick's, because I didn't think it was appropriate. Up at Harvey's Lake, there was a bar called the Grotto Bar, and I just liked the sound of that word. It was short, it was Italian, and so I decided to call it Grotto Pizza.

Fig. 47. Grotto Pizza owner Dominick Pulieri: "To me, making pizza's like walking." (Photo courtesy of Dominick Pulieri.)

"It seemed like a summer thing to do, a way of making money to go to college. Of course, it became more than that, but at first it was just an opportunity to make a few bucks. Although I wasn't just doing it because of the money. I was in my element, making pizza. I loved doing that."

The only problem was, no one wanted pizza.

"My sister came down with me, and at first I had her on the sidewalk trying to give away samples, and people wouldn't take them. I'd go out on the beach for a while sometimes because there was no business, and my sister would call to me and say, 'Dom, you have to come back and make a pizza.' I think I ended up throwing away more dough that summer than I used for pizza."

Still, by the end of the season, Grotto's had a few regular customers as well as a clientele from the Washington area that knew and enjoyed pizza. "What we were doing was selling the idea of pizza to a lot of people, and by the time August came, I had started to gather customers. Each night, certain guys would stop by and get a couple slices."

Pulieri estimates that the business's gross income that first season was $30,000. "The next summer, I think we quadrupled that amount," he says. Today, Grotto Pizza is a $30 million business, with 1,800 employees in summer and close to a thousand year-round.

"It grew incrementally. The second year we had soda and put in a couple of tables. We kept knocking the partitions down and adding more tables. And then our third year we opened up a little stand on the Boardwalk."

Their success was a blend of foresight and fortune. Pizza was just starting to gain popularity around the United States when he launched his business. The first major pizza chain, Pizza Hut, had begun as a single restaurant in Wichita, Kansas, two years earlier. The first frozen pizza was introduced in grocery stores at about the same time.

Inevitably, other pizza businesses opened at the beach. "That never bothered me," says Pulieri. "The way I've always looked at it, customers have choices. Our obligation is to be the best choice. That's the philosophy that's kept us going. I've always said that if we do it better, they're going to come back to us. This country is about free enterprise, and I'm a great believer in that. Competition strengthens, it doesn't weaken. Our secret is attention to quality and growing to fill the marketplace."

The basic Grotto recipe—and what they advertise as "the Legendary Taste"—hasn't changed over the years, he says, although advances in cooking technology have changed how the pizza is made. "The pizza you ate in the 1960s was the same taste as the pizza you eat today. It's the same recipe."

Rehoboth Beach in the 1960s was strictly a seasonal resort, Pulieri recalls, which shut down after Labor Day. For five years, Pulieri left town at the end of the season and worked as a high school science and chemistry teacher in Smyrna, Delaware. "But what happened was, this pizza thing kept growing and growing. And I realized at a certain point that I couldn't do both and do both of them right. So I quit teaching in 1970. People would sometimes say to me, including my mother—she said, 'You're not *teaching* anymore, you're *making a pizza*?' I'm thinking, 'No, I'm running a business.' "

Pulieri still lives in Rehoboth during the summer and at a condo in Georgetown, Delaware, the rest of the year. He says he often receives offers to franchise the business but so far has resisted. "I have someone coming in tomorrow who's going to give me a spiel. I listen to them, but I think you lose something when you franchise. I think there's another way to go. I like the way we do things. I like the people we have working for us. We're not a public company. We have a control over quality that you don't always have when you franchise. I love the business.

"I never married, so I don't have children. But when I count my employees, I think I have about fifteen hundred of them. At some point, I'm going to have to figure out how I'm going to leave this. I'm not looking forward to that, but I'm going to have to do it. I want this to be a generational company. Hopefully, in some way, my employees will end up owning it."

Meanwhile, he still enjoys spending time in the restaurants. "There's really two reasons for that. One is controlling quality, working with my employees, but the other reason is the pizza. To me, making pizza's like walking. There's something very satisfying about seeing families sitting down and eating something you've created. There's a satisfaction in that I get every day.

"Every once in a while, I'll remember that when we came here there wasn't any pizza. And I'll remember how my sister used to give me heck for buying a dustpan and a broom. She said we couldn't afford it. Things like that. I take nothing for granted. I don't want to live in the past, but I don't want to forget the past, either. Because the past is what shaped me."

He speaks fondly of his sister Maryjean, who suffered from congenital heart disease and died in the late 1970s at age forty-two. "I called her my American mother. We were very close," he says.

"Now, of course," he adds, "pizza's up and down the beach. For a lot of people that's part of what the beach is all about. I can't tell you how many times a year people will ask me, 'Why does the pizza taste so much better in your restaurants at the beach?' Well, you know what, it's the same pizza. Trust me, we don't have a different formula here at the beach. I tell them, 'The difference isn't the pizza, the difference is you. You're at the beach, you're having fun, you're more relaxed, you're enjoying yourself more, you're in a different state of mind.' "

Night Falls

As daylight fades and the sky above the sea is veiled with streaks of muted sunset, the mood changes on Rehoboth's Boardwalk. Children in sweatshirts, shorts, and flip-flops walk several paces behind their parents, watching the storefronts, eating cotton candy that sticks to their faces. An artist seated at Wilmington Avenue sketches the sunset with colored pencils on a drawing pad. Three young people walk north, the boys carrying guitars, the girl a stand-up bass. They're passed by a pair of women holding hands. Two older couples watch, sitting on a bench near Playland, eating Grotto Pizza. Bob Marley blares from a sundries shop. Teenagers run wildly onto the sand, as if the horizons of their lives were as vast as the sea. At the Rehoboth Avenue bandstand, the First State Harmonizers are singing "Sunny Side of the Street."

Lurking behind the good-time, honky-tonk ambience of Boardwalk life here is a reassuring stubbornness, which becomes evident on this warm summer night. The Boardwalk becomes a kind of alternate reality, a thriving borderland of democracy, which has somehow remained impervious to corporate America. This boardwalk is more intimate than most. Its commercial core comprises only about five blocks in the middle of the twenty-block promenade. Here the Boardwalk has familiar though scaled-down attractions. To the north and south, the walk is darker and narrower—only about twelve feet wide—and resonates with the primal sounds of something wilder and much older. On this enchantingly modest boardwalk, nature serves as a foil to the man-made attractions, and vice versa.

There's a traffic jam coming into town tonight and not enough parking spaces to accommodate all the visitors. Later, there'll be traffic tie-ups leaving town. Up on Route 1, Delaware's main coastal drag, the congestion gets worse each summer, as new condo projects, outlet malls, and shopping centers are opened. But on the Boardwalk, with the sea breeze blowing and the pizza cooking, the mood is laid-back and lighthearted. The Rehoboth Beach Boardwalk has resisted the growth and change that has invaded much of coastal Delaware in recent years. Its endurance speaks for itself.

CHAPTER SEVEN

OCEAN CITY, MARYLAND

A Distant Glittering Shore

EVERY NIGHT after dinner, Granville Trimper takes his place on a bench by the south entrance to the Trimper's Rides amusement park. For the next several hours—until the park closes at midnight—Trimper sits amid the carnival lights and caramel-sweetened sea breeze, surveying the activity. He has done so for years, beginning his workday at nine thirty in the offices next door and ending it here in the park. Trimper's Rides, at the southern end of Ocean City's 2.7-mile Boardwalk, is one of the oldest seaside amusement parks in the country, with a merry-go-round that has been turning since 1902. Trimper's grandfather started the park in the 1890s.

"I never get tired of watching people enjoy themselves," says Trimper, who is seventy-five. "That's what this park is all about. That's what this town is all about. A lot of times people will come over and say, 'I used to bring my own kids here, now I bring my grandkids.' That's a good feeling."

Ocean City, Maryland (not to be confused, though it often is, with Ocean City, New Jersey), is a city of many personalities and many contradictions, with one of the country's best and most beguiling boardwalks. A small town at heart, with a year-round population of about seven thousand, Ocean City becomes Maryland's second-largest city in summer, when more than three hundred thousand vacationers crowd onto the narrow, ten-mile-long barrier

Fig. 48 (OPPOSITE) Ocean City's new Boardwalk arch, modeled after one depicted on an old postcard, is in keeping with the Victorian flavor of the renovated downtown. It's visible to guests as they arrive at the southern end of town. (Courtesy of Ocean City Visitor and Convention Bureau.)

island. The city has tirelessly promoted itself as a "family resort" but is known for its abundance of bars and nightclubs. Some call it "blue-collar," although new Boardwalk condos are selling for more than a million dollars. The city is packed with pizza parlors and crab shacks, but discerning diners can also find haute cuisine served in elegant settings. Visitors flock here to escape urban stress, yet on rainy summer afternoons the main highway resembles a ten-mile-long parking lot. A small but fervent antigrowth faction occasionally wins skirmishes against developers but perpetually seems to be losing the war. Much of the city is a mishmash of condos and strip shopping centers. There are also a few surprisingly attractive pockets of residential development and, in north Ocean City, an imposing line of condo skyscrapers known as High Rise Row.

Fig. 49. The Ocean City Boardwalk, circa 1900. (Courtesy of the Ocean City Life-Saving Station Museum.)

The jewel of Ocean City is its mostly low-rise southern end, where the Boardwalk meets the inlet, where the city was born. In recent years, the local government has enhanced this neighborhood, known as downtown, by putting power lines underground, installing old-fashioned streetlamps, and creating a Boardwalk tram lane. These improvements give south Ocean City a cleaner, more orderly and family-friendly feel than it used to have. Still, the essential draw of the city's south end is the exhilarating, at times overwhelming, sensory chaos of the Boardwalk.

"There have been a lot of changes in Ocean City," says Trimper, "but most have been north of here. The appeal of this area is the rides, the lights, the Thrasher's french fries, the Fisher's popcorn, that whole atmosphere. I think if we lost that, we'd lose what gives Ocean City a lot of its character."

Trimper's Rides and its neighbor Marty's Playland, also owned by the Trimper family, are a large part of that character, as is Charles "Buddy" Jenkins's amusement pier, with its water park, rides, and concessions, including the fabled Thrasher's. Ocean City's Boardwalk is old-fashioned in the best sense of the term, largely because the same families have controlled so much of it for generations—but increasingly, says Trimper, a new trend is threatening some of the old ways.

"MY GRANDFATHER CAME HERE from Baltimore," says Trimper, watching the swoop of his most popular ride, the Tidal Wave roller coaster. "He had a bar called the Silver Dollar Café on Hanover Street, and he wanted to come here and have a look. Back then, you had to take the train and also a boat to get here. So he came down, looked the place over and decided to move here. He sold his business in Baltimore, loaded his wife and seven children on the train, and brought them all down here. That was 1890."

Ocean City, incorporated fifteen years earlier, was still a small fishing village, but the railroad line had recently crossed Sinepuxent Bay, and the hospitality industry was beginning to grow. In 1892, the city's first Boardwalk, about twelve blocks long, was built by a land development corporation called the Sinepuxent Beach Company.

Daniel Trimper and his wife, Margaret, purchased property between South Division and South First streets, and for years they successfully operated two hotels there: the Sea Bright and the Eastern Shore. When a storm damaged the Sea Bright in 1900, the Trimpers decided to rebuild it in an exotic style based on Windsor Castle in England. The Trimper holdings—by this time two hotels, a theater, and a small amusement park—were named Windsor Resort, a name still used by the Trimper company.

In 1902, Trimper purchased a steam-driven carousel from the Herschell-Spillman Company of New York—which also produced one of Coney Island's early merry-go-rounds—and moved it to their resort site. The carousel had forty-five animals, three chariots, and a rocking chair. It cost a nickel to ride. Today the same ride, run by electricity, costs four tickets—$1.60.

"We've tried to keep the old-fashioned rides here, some of which never go out of style," says Trimper, who is dressed casually in shorts and a knit shirt. "But we always have to find something new, particularly for the teenage crowd and, increasingly, for kiddies who don't want to go around in circles anymore." Next year, Trimper's plans to replace its miniature golf course with a new thrill ride called Freak Out, he says.

As Trimper discusses the changing amusements business, two employees walk past, nodding hello. "That's my grandson," Trimper explains. The other is a summer worker from Belarus. Trimper has nine grandchildren; five of them work full-time in the park, as do three of his children. Each summer, dozens of foreign workers, many from Eastern Europe, join the ranks. "Most are

Fig. 50. Granville Trimper, on his bench at Trimper's Rides. Trimper's grandfather brought the amusements industry to Ocean City in the 1890s.

students," he says, "although we get all types. They tend to be very good workers. Very frugal. Some of them work two jobs. We've had some of them say, 'You don't know how bad things are in our country.' Two Czech boys working on the roller coaster one summer said they made more that summer than their parents made all year."

As night seeps in and the breeze cools, Trimper talks about the growth of Trimper's Rides over the years: the addition of outdoor amusements in the 1950s; the creation in 1983 of a fishing-village-themed shopping center, the Inlet Village; the purchase of the resort's largest arcade, Marty's Playland, after the death of owner Sam Gaffin, son-in-law of original owner Marty Mitnick. "We wanted to keep it the way their family always ran it, with the fortune-telling booths and Skee-Ball and all that. But, like he did, we also update it with the newest video games."

He talks, too, about the changes in Ocean City. When Trimper was born, the inlet—Ocean City's southern boundary—didn't exist. The city extended then to South Sixth Street. But in 1933, a hurricane tore a hole in the city, separating Ocean City from Assateague Island and forming a sea lane for the commercial fishing industry. Assateague Island is today a state park and national refuge, home to more than a hundred wild ponies.

The city's northern limit reached only to Fifteenth Street when Trimper was a child; today it extends more than eight miles farther north, to the Delaware line. "That's been the big growth in Ocean City," he says. "This area has tried to keep its flavor." He knows that may not continue, though: As Trimper follows the trends in the amusements business, he also follows trends in resort land use and property values. "The big issue here is becoming the value of land," says Trimper. "The most valuable use of this land right now would be condominiums and a hotel." Ocean City's condominium economy may be reaching a tipping point, some believe, and when that happens, the nature of downtown may change.

Fig. 51. Ocean City's Boardwalk in the 1940s. (Courtesy of the Ocean City Life-Saving Station Museum.)

"The reason we're taking out the miniature golf next year is that the land is too valuable," Trimper explains. "Instead, we're putting in the big ride. It's hard anymore in this business to make the bottom line come out right. Labor's so high, rides are expensive. They keep increasing taxes on everything. There aren't a lot of incentives.

"I'd like to keep this atmosphere . . . but because of the value of the land, I don't know how long that's going to be possible. Last year, we had a very poor season. We made very little money. We've had proposals to build town houses or a thirteen-story hotel. We're told that would be the best use of the land."

Trimper sits back and watches the families going past in the dusk. "I'm opposed to that," he says. "I'm opposed to it as long as I can afford to be opposed to it."

In the Family

To reach Ocean City from Washington or Baltimore—where many of its visitors live—you must drive for three hours, and the time it takes to get here adds to the resort's mystique, particularly for those who arrive after dark. The first shimmer of amusement lights on the inlet water, the scents of sea air and french fries cooking in peanut oil, the muted screams—all seem like a kind of treasure at the end of a rainbow.

Many of Ocean City's business owners were drawn here because of that mystique—and also, to paraphrase Willie Sutton, because Ocean City is where the people are. The resort is full of stories about fledgling merchants who came to town with a few hundred bucks and a love of Ocean City and, through hard work, established thriving businesses. The success stories say that even with its entrenched traditions, Ocean City makes room for outsiders.

On a hot late-summer morning, Rudolph "Bunky" Dolle sits in his small Boardwalk office at Dolle's Candyland and talks about some of the people who came here from elsewhere and built businesses: his grandfather, for instance, who arrived in Ocean City ninety-four years ago and bought a saltwater taffy store on the corner where Dolle's Candyland now operates. He also brought a Charles I. D. Looff carousel to town. Both businesses did well. In 1915, Dolle added caramel corn to the candy shop. After the carousel burned down in 1925, he began selling fudge and chocolates. More recently, Dolle's expanded its Boardwalk retail space from about 200 to 850 square feet and moved its kitchen to a building next door. Tours of the kitchen are now offered each Friday; they include demonstrations of the fifty-year-old taffy machine, which cuts and wraps the candy. In summer, Dolle's sells about 1,500 pounds of saltwater taffy a day, Dolle says. Its most popular item, though, is the warm, sweet Dolle's caramel corn—which to some is the very essence of the Ocean City Boardwalk.

"You'd be surprised how many people come here year after year wanting one product," Dolle says, "whether it's Dolle's caramel corn or Thrasher's fries or Alaska Stand hamburgers. That product defines their visit to Ocean City in some ways. People identify with a single product so much that it's actually hard to diversify."

Dolle began working in the family business when he was twelve, sweeping floors and packing candy. One of the secrets to making it in Ocean City, he says, is understanding the city's emphasis on family. "If there's a single reason why these businesses keep going, it's that phrase 'family resort.' Some people say that started as a gimmick, but I think it's true.

"Family has a double meaning in Ocean City," Dolle adds. "It's a place that is geared to families—I think Ocean City is about the closest you'll come to a resort that offers something for everyone—but it's also a place that in many ways is run by families. That's been a nice combination that seems to work." Dolle's is run by four people: Dolle, his wife, and their two children.

Many of the city's other success stories are family based. Brice and Shirley Phillips, for instance, arrived in Ocean City fifty years ago from an Eastern Shore hamlet called Hooper's Island and opened a carry-out crab stand at Twentieth Street. The Phillipses worked seventeen-hour days during the summers, and for twelve years added a dining room a year to their eatery. The family-run company now has six restaurants with seating for four thousand diners, along with a nationally distributed frozen food supermarket line. Last year, their most lucrative restaurant reported sales of nearly $14 million. Hale and John Harrison, from nearby Berlin, where their family ran a fruit business, bought resort hotels and restaurants in the 1970s and 1980s and came to dominate Ocean City's hospitality industry by the time they were in their thirties. Bill Gibbs worked as a beach umbrella boy in front of the Breakers hotel, then opened a pizza restaurant at age twenty-three. Today, Gibbs owns the Breakers, along with six Dough Roller restaurants. His three sons are general managers of the business and can sometimes be found, along with Gibbs, behind the counter, tossing pizza.

Fig. 52. In the family: Rudolph "Bunky" Dolle, right, and his son Andrew. Dolle's has been on the same Boardwalk corner since 1910.

Concrete into Wood

Until 1996, Ocean City's mayors were natives, men who spoke with distinctive Eastern Shore accents and told folksy stories about the Ocean City of old. The big-city media from Washington and Baltimore sometimes portrayed these mayors as backwoods sages, suffused with homespun wisdom about the weather, the tides, and the quirky nature of tourism. Last in a long line of native mayors was Roland "Fish" Powell, a plainspoken, business-savvy man who insists he does not know the origin of his nickname.

Powell's predecessor was the late Harry Kelly, a flamboyant promoter who enjoyed challenging the Baltimore/Washington media when their weekend weather forecasts called for rain at the beach. Before Kelly was Hugh Cropper, credited with charting the course for full-tilt development in Ocean City.

As more and more outsiders came to the resort—making the vision of Cropper and others a reality—it became inevitable that the tradition of the native mayor would eventually be lost. It finally happened in 1996, when Fish Powell stepped down and Jim Mathias, a Baltimore-born Boardwalk business owner, was elected.

Mathias, who previously served as a city councilman, talks with unabashed enthusiasm, and also some humility, about his job. "Knowing Ocean City and loving Ocean City, I feel honored, but also a sense of responsibility in having this position," he says, driving his city-owned SUV north in heavy summer traffic, past rooming houses, motels, sandwich shops, and sunburned tourists. He recalls the first time he visited Ocean City, as a child with his family. "I remember the smells, the creosote of the wood, the caramel popcorn, the cheeseburgers. I remember going into the arcades and the sound of the Skee-Ball machines. It was something that got inside of you.

"The toughest part about coming here on vacation as a kid was leaving," adds Mathias, a tall, intense man, dressed in khakis and a golf shirt with an Ocean City insignia. "I remember sitting in the back seat of the car. I was always turned around backward and had tears in my eyes because I wasn't ready to leave. I loved this place."

Harry Kelly, who died in office in 1985, was mayor when Mathias moved here in 1974. "Sometimes," he says, "I'll drive over to Evergreen Cemetery in Berlin and visit Harry Kelly's grave, you know, and just say, 'I'm doing the best I can.'"

Mathias's father, who worked in the arcade business in Baltimore, bought a property just off Ocean City's Boardwalk in September 1972 and opened an amusements arcade. Mathias worked his first job here that summer, at Ponzetti's Pizza on the Boardwalk, while earning a political science degree from the University of Maryland, Baltimore County. After his father died suddenly in March 1974, Mathias and his brother Jeffrey took over running the Ocean City business. Today he also has a Boardwalk T-shirt shop—in a space he leases from Bunky Dolle. His wife Kathy works for the city manager.

"One of the sustaining ideas, you could say, about Ocean City, is that this is still a place where the small businessman can come, and if he's got a quality operation, he can find success. A lot of places, like Atlantic City, have been overwhelmed by corporate entities. That's an important part of what sets us apart," says Mathias.

The mayor finds a parking space just off the Boardwalk. It's a hot afternoon. The sky is blue and nearly cloudless; the breeze smells of suntan oil and funnel cakes. Sunlight shimmers on the Atlantic Ocean. Vacationers in bathing suits and flip-flops are lined up at the Alaska Stand, which has sold hamburgers on the Boardwalk for seventy years.

As Mathias walks up the boards, several people call out to him. "Hey, Mayor!"

"How you doing?" he replies. "It's a beautiful day, isn't it?"

At an arcade, Mathias chats with the manager, then plays a game of Skee-Ball. Back on the Boardwalk, he stops to listen to two musicians from Delaware, Michael Truitt and Eugene Baryshnikov, who are sitting on a bench playing the blues. For a while, he claps along. Besides being an Ocean City businessman and the mayor, Mathias sometimes appears as guest vocalist with a Baltimore-based R&B band called Mary Lou & the Untouchables.

Fig. 53. Ocean City mayor Jim Mathias (left) joins an impromptu Boardwalk jam session.

"What this town doesn't need," he says, back in the thick summer traffic, "and the thing that would go against the grain of everything we stand for, is gambling." Gambling has occasionally been proposed for Ocean City, though never very seriously; recently, however, Maryland's governor has pushed for legalizing slot machines at the state's racetracks, a plan some in Ocean City see as a step toward bringing gambling to the beach. "There are people who would like to see gambling in Ocean City, but the fact is there's no reason to bring it here. We aren't Atlantic City; we don't have the problems Atlantic City had. To me, that would ruin the family atmosphere. If we let it in, we'd be killing what makes Ocean City great."

LATE IN THE AFTERNOON, the mayor is joined at Tommy's Sub Shop on Twenty-ninth Street by Bernadette DiPino, another Baltimore native, who shares his enthusiasm for Ocean City. DiPino is now Ocean City's chief of police.

"I'm a Boardwalk person, always will be," says DiPino, who previously worked for the Baltimore County Police Department. "My heart's always been with that Boardwalk. As a young child, my family brought me here, and the most exciting part was going to the Boardwalk, getting a bucket of Thrasher's french fries, sitting on a bench, and watching people—just observing how they acted, what they were wearing, how much fun they were having. I couldn't believe it years later that I was paid to do that same thing. I got to stand on the Boardwalk and watch people going back and forth. I felt it was an honor and a gift that I was being paid to do that. I would have done it for free. That's how passionate I felt about it."

DiPino was hired by the Ocean City Police Department in 1988 as an undercover Boardwalk officer. "The Boardwalk was different back then," she says. "I mean, there were people who would walk up and down smoking marijuana, people selling dope. That's changed, and it was really a community-wide effort that caused it, a commitment to clean it up. The city decided to make that Boardwalk a top priority. There's more lighting now, more of a police presence. If you live in an area where there's graffiti and there's trash, where it looks run-down, you're going to have crime. If it looks clean and the lighting is good and there's a police presence, you're not."

Her favorite part of Ocean City hasn't changed, she says. "I like to go down to the Boardwalk at least once or twice a week just to look at the people and have Thrasher's french fries. I still think there's nothing like it."

"THE TOWN'S NAME IS Ocean City, and the heart of the town is the ocean. But the soul of the town is the Boardwalk." The mayor is driving his city vehicle south now over the mostly deserted Boardwalk. It is well after midnight, and most of the businesses are closed, but a number of people are still out, walking in the cool breeze or sitting on benches. Some recognize the mayor and call out to him.

"How you doing?" he replies. "It's a beautiful night, isn't it?"

To a pair of police officers walking their beat: "How you doing? You guys are looking good."

He stops to point out the six-block section of the Boardwalk, from South First Street to North Division Street, that in the late 1990s was converted from concrete to wood. The same section was changed from wood to concrete back in the early 1950s, according to Ocean City historian Ken Jordan.

Mathias was a strong booster of the change. Others in government weren't. "The reason we did that," he says, "was, very simply, nostalgia. People used to come down to this southern end of the Boardwalk and say, 'What happened? Where's the Boardwalk?' We'd say, 'This is it,' and they'd say, 'No, this is concrete. It's not the same thing.' That was important to people. So that was one of the changes that was made to keep the Boardwalk nostalgic. It seems like a little thing, but it's made a big difference. It gives the south end of the Boardwalk a different feel," he says.

Driving north, the mayor talks about the massive seawall that now protects Ocean City's Boardwalk. Built in 1991, six years after Hurricane Gloria washed away most of the Boardwalk, the seawall rises about three feet above the wood, capping giant steel sheets that were driven thirty feet into the sand. It was part of a multiyear, $40 million federal-state-local beach protection plan that also included pumping more than five million cubic yards of sand from offshore bars to the beach and the creation of an eight-mile sand dune. The project, which will require periodic maintenance forever, protects the estimated $3.7 billion worth of property in Ocean City.

"If we get a bad storm, God forbid, you might not have a beach, but it'll never erode below the level of that seawall. The integrity of that seawall will not be breached. We didn't have that before," Mathias says.

Ocean City will no doubt have storms in its future, both literally and figuratively, but it is obviously a resort that is in good hands.

The mayor finishes his Boardwalk tour and drives back downtown, where he parks for a moment near the inlet. South Ocean City assumes a quieter beauty as waves crash over the rock jetty and beneath the darkened amusement pier. It's two thirty in the morning and the mayor finally seems talked out. "I love this place, man," he says.

Unlike Anything in the World

The most distinctive building on Ocean City's Boardwalk—on any board-walk, really—is the Ocean Gallery at Second Street. It's a patchwork of re-cycled building parts collected and assembled by owner Joe KroArt, along with a clutter of hanging paintings, posters, prints, and hand-written signs, which say such things as IT'S ASTOUNDING!!! and VOTED NO. 1 BEST IN THE USA! and HOME OF THE GREATEST FINE ART SALE ON EARTH! People often do a double-take when they pass the Ocean Gallery; KroArt says he wants them to do the same with fine art.

"My objective is for people to look at art in a way they've never looked at it before," he says, standing be-hind the register on a sunny weekday afternoon. "It starts with the building. People see this building and it's a surprise to them. It's unlike anything in the world. They may be coming up off the beach and they'll see it and they'll smile and laugh. It wins them over. And then they'll come inside and see what it is. A lot of peo-ple have never really been to a gallery before, and they walk out with a whole different feeling about art."

KroArt—who changed his name from Kroat to KroArt years ago—is both an entrepreneur and an art-ist who attended the Maryland Art Institute. "I hated it," he says. "It was everything that is wrong about art. I knew art was fun and that wasn't fun. That's what created the mindset that led to this gallery." An art gallery may seem an unlikely business for Ocean City's Boardwalk, among all the arcades and eateries,

Fig. 54. Ocean Gallery owner Joe KroArt making his case, on the Boardwalk in Ocean City.

but KroArt's wacky presentation makes it a good fit. "People thought it was crazy at first," he says. "Sell paintings? In Ocean City? On the Boardwalk? I knew it couldn't be a sterile gallery, with ten artworks on the wall for three thousand dollars apiece. That would never work."

Instead of offering ten artworks, the three-story Ocean Gallery contains about forty thousand items for sale, ranging from ninety-nine-cent posters to oil paintings priced at half a million dollars. On this summer afternoon, a steady stream of customers enters the gallery, and there is frequently a line at the register. KroArt says Ocean Gallery, which has been at the same Boardwalk location more than thirty years, "has more fine art per square foot than any other gallery in the world. . . . There's so much art you can't take everything in at first. You are overwhelmed by it all."

"The most rewarding thing for me is getting people hooked and then seeing their tastes mature," says KroArt, who taught school for seven years before opening the gallery. "Kids will come in and buy their first piece of art for their room—a poster for a couple of dollars. Then they'll come back the next summer and maybe buy a numbered print, and then maybe an original painting. Van Gogh said a good painting is one you like. Art is about what you want on your wall in your life."

As if the Ocean Gallery building weren't enough to draw people's attention, KroArt, who resembles an accountant with his short-sleeved white shirt and dark tie, blares John Philip Sousa marches for the Boardwalk passersby. Those browsing inside the gallery get a more subdued, jazzy soundtrack. It's an idea he says comes from P. T. Barnum.

"I'm not influenced by other galleries or by other people because I don't want the Ocean Gallery to look like anything you've seen before. But it's an interesting story about P. T. Barnum. Back around 1980, a Baltimore paper did a story on me, calling me 'the P. T. Barnum of Fine Art.' Some of the papers here picked it up. I went to Barnum's museum in Connecticut and studied him a little bit, and I was amazed by what I found. Barnum was six-two, two hundred and ten pounds; I'm six-two, two hundred and ten pounds. Barnum had an eighteen-acre farm; I have an eighteen-acre farm. We both had three children. The parallels were so incredible, I got goose bumps."

At his American Museum in New York, Barnum would program rousing music outside, to catch the attention of people passing by, and soothing music inside, to get them to stay. "What Barnum did was advertise in ways that people had never done before," says KroArt. "I do that with art. I try to generate curiosity so that people will come in and try to figure it out."

In television ads for the gallery, KroArt dons a blond wig and a tuxedo and is seen jumping from the roof of his building. A few weeks ago, he put up a sign outside the gallery urging people to scream "ART SALE BABY"!

"People were doing it all night," he says. "They were having fun with it, but at the same time I'm getting people to advertise for us."

Behind KroArt's wild-man image is an astute businessman—he owns several other less audacious galleries—and a serious artist. His offbeat humor doesn't encroach on his own art, which ranges from abstract painting to landscape photography. "I have a barn studio in Baltimore County where I go to paint when I need to," he says. "I never paint when I'm here. I can't mix this crazy energy with painting, so I don't try. It's really two different worlds. There it's quiet and introspective, and that's where the drive inside me says, 'It's time to paint.' I can't do that here."

Ocean Gallery has joined Ocean City's tradition of family-run businesses. KroArt's son Joey helps manage the store, and his wife Adele, says KroArt, is his barometer. "When she says one of my ideas is crazy, that's when I know I have something," he says. "If it's not wild enough, she'll say, 'It's good,' and I'll think, 'Oh, it's not good enough.' But if she says it's crazy, then I know I've got something." Among his current ideas: "I want to do an exhibition where the paintings are all hanging from the outside of the building. I want to be the first to display an exhibition on the exterior of a gallery." He also wants to drive the old car he calls his Batmobile off the Ocean City pier into the ocean. "I've proposed it to the city council. It would be an international story. That car cost twenty-eight dollars to build, but it would generate millions in publicity."

Philosophy and French Fries

Buddy Jenkins sits behind his ornate wooden desk, looking dapper in a pale green suit and matching tie, a handkerchief in his breast pocket. The view from his second-story office is of the water park portion of Jolly Roger, the thirty-six-acre amusement park he owns.

Jenkins is considered one of Ocean City's shrewdest businessmen. His holdings include hotels, the Jolly Roger, and the amusement pier franchise. A thoughtful, intellectually curious man—known to wax philosophical about politics, religion, world affairs, the state of the American vacation, and virtually any other topic—Jenkins is a refreshing departure in a town where most businesspeople show up to work in shorts and deck shoes and where intellectual curiosity can itself seem a curiosity.

The topic this day is Thrasher's, the Boardwalk french-fry phenomenon that first opened in 1929 and which Jenkins has owned since the 1970s. Thrasher's is a business that needs no advertising—other than the aroma of french fries cooking in peanut oil and the line of people waiting to buy them. Besides soda, Thrasher's offers just one product, available in three sizes, which sell for four, six, and eight dollars. The line sometimes stretches a hundred people long.

There has been speculation over the years as to why Thrasher's draws such ardent fans, but no one has quite been able to figure it out. Clearly Thrasher's fries taste different from others: Their texture is agreeably firm—neither crispy nor soggy—and their flavor addictive. Is it the peanut oil? The potatoes?

"Here is a precise, simple explanation," says Jenkins. "Our focus has been to produce one product with the highest possible quality standards. It has not been to develop new products, to expand, or to market it. Many people concentrate on making the transaction rather than on the repeat customer. Your repeat customer is the greatest single security blanket any business can have. Word of mouth is the single greatest source of advertising, and that can only come with a satisfied customer. People go into business and they don't realize that."

But what gives Thrasher's fries that taste?

"That's a secret," Jenkins says.

Although there are now three Thrasher's locations in Ocean City and two in nearby Rehoboth Beach, aficionados of french fries agree that none taste as good as those served at the original pier location.

"Lines are wonderful because lines attract people," says Jenkins. "People see a line and they figure this must be a quality product if people are willing to stand in line for it. But the quality has to be there or they would not stand in line a second time. Now, a line can also be too long, and when a line becomes too long, it's telling you a story. It's saying, 'Open up a different location.' There's a difference between quality and volume. If you maintain the quality, then you can increase the volume. But the first thing you do is maintain quality."

The same applies, in a way, to Ocean City.

"Here is the reason people continue coming here, whereas they stopped visiting some of those towns to the north of us," says Jenkins. "Because Ocean City has kept the trust for the working guy, the middle-class guy.

Ocean City has—and I give full credit to the business community, the local government, the state government—kept this a place that is affordable and offers quality attractions. It's not for the rich but for the working- and middle-class guy. And because we have kept that trust, we've had bridges built for us, we've had dual highways built for us, to get people here. We've had the beach replenished."

Keeping the trust doesn't mean that Ocean City shouldn't change, he says. "It has to change. Our responsibility is to pay attention and change with the times. There was a time when people came here and stayed for two or three weeks. Then all of a sudden, the hotels were very difficult to operate. Why? In 1952, [Governor] Preston Lane built the bridge across Chesapeake Bay, and that changed Ocean City forever. It was much easier to get here all of a sudden, so the vacation time shrank. And then a new word came along: the motel. And many of the old hotels became obsolete. Then, in the 1960s, condominiums became another new word."

Fig. 55. Buddy Jenkins in his office at the Jolly Roger Amusement Park.

Jenkins doesn't consider the city's current condominium trend a bad one. "In some cases, they're tearing down old, obsolete buildings that have fire code violations. Refurbishing is a good thing, as long as there is a plan.

"But we can't forget who our visitor is. The public will tell you what to do if you pay attention. They'll tell you exactly what to do. The reason people come to Ocean City is very simple. Let's not forget that. It's something that is ingrained in human nature. We as individuals need to periodically go off somewhere, to sit on a beach and reflect, to say, 'Where the hell am I, what am I doing with my life?' and get back to basics. People by nature want to be by the water. They always get as close as they can to the water because psychologically it makes them feel better. I call it 'the Tadpole Syndrome.' You are a tadpole and you're trying to get back into that ocean. Now, people will do that in whatever way they can afford. If they can pay a million dollars to be there, they'll do it. If a man can afford a hundred-thousand-dollar condominium, he will buy that. Or he may spend a few hundred dollars for a weekend here. In the back of his mind, he's tired of the hassle, tired of gridlock on the beltways. So people go to coastal counties. People are always going to want to come here if we do our job, and our job is to pay attention and keep the trust."

A LITTLE PAST DUSK, forty-seven people are lined up for Thrasher's french fries. Subtly, nighttime has arrived. The cooling winds add a brisk spice to the scents of caramel corn, cotton candy, and fries. Colored lights brighten in slow spinning patterns over Jenkins's amusement pier. The crowds become denser at the pier, where the walk is lined with temptations and diversions, a circus with many rings. When the human traffic reaches its peak, two hours before midnight, the crowds are so thick that you can't see the Boardwalk's timber. With a different perspective, you might sense, if only briefly, that what you are part of is not a sea of people so much as a wave—a collective, spontaneous motion.

From a Boardwalk bench or a balcony above it all, the human traffic is more interesting to watch than any organized parade, but if you walk out into the sand north of the pier, the Boardwalk seems to change like an optical illusion. Out on the wide empty beach there is a place where the music starts to fade, replaced by the steady crashes of breaking surf; where the scents of Boardwalk foods disappear and the air smells suddenly of wet sand and sea salt; this is a place where the eyes, no longer dazzled by amusement park lights, begin to adjust to darkness, to pick out specks of stars above the ocean. Walk to the edge of the beach and look back at the silent Boardwalk and it resembles a distant, glittering shore, a vibrant city celebrating the notions of American leisure and free enterprise. From a distance, there is a beauty and symmetry to this carnival skyline, reflecting the city's dichotomy: For all its craziness and its seeming embrace of anarchy, Ocean City is a fairly conservative place, anchored by family traditions and an old-fashioned American spirit.

Board Walk, Virginia Beach, Va.

CHAPTER EIGHT

VIRGINIA BEACH, VIRGINIA

Recreational Walk

W HEN LANDSCAPE architect Barry Frankenfield interviewed for a planning position with the city of Virginia Beach back in the mid-1980s, he was particularly intrigued with one aspect of the job description: helping to redesign the resort's two-and-a-quarter-mile Boardwalk.

"I've always liked the idea of the Boardwalk," says Frankenfield, who grew up in the suburbs of Philadelphia. "The basic idea was to reconstruct what we had, to make it better. But also to create a different atmosphere. . . . For a while, nothing was happening on the Boardwalk. We wanted to make it happen. Our mission was to reprogram the Boardwalk experience."

Since the 1980s, Virginia Beach has not only successfully reprogrammed the Boardwalk experience, it has also reprogrammed the resort experience. In 1989, a racially charged riot on Labor Day weekend put Virginia Beach in the national spotlight—and forced civic and business leaders to take a hard look at long-festering problems. In the ensuing years, Virginia Beach has built a new image, as well as a new Boardwalk. The timing was mostly coincidental— plans were under way to redo the Boardwalk when the riot occurred—but the two campaigns dovetailed nicely. The physical appearance of the oceanfront and the image the resort conveys to vacationers are now largely in synch: it's clean, fun, modern, and safe, a place to take your family. Along Atlantic

Fig. 56. (OPPOSITE) *The Boardwalk in 1913. People dressed in their Sunday finest to walk the boards. (Courtesy of Virginia Beach Public Library.)*

Avenue, the commercial strip where the riot occurred, the resort presents free family-oriented entertainment every night during summer—puppeteers, jazz trios, magicians, vocal ensembles. The result is a happy chaos rather than the more unpredictable, sometimes edgy mood of fifteen years ago. Signs posted around the area gently stress the point, asking visitors to refrain from "wearing revealing attire, . . . engaging in any behavior which is likely to intimidate, harass or disrupt the peaceful enjoyment of others," and "using obscene or vulgar language or gestures."

One block east of Atlantic Avenue, the recently widened Boardwalk provides a parallel environment, both literally and figuratively. It's a twenty-eight-foot-wide concrete sanctuary with virtually no commercial enterprise other than hotels and a few cafés and restaurants. Beside it to the west, separated by a belt of grass, is a ten-foot-wide concrete bicycle path, which runs the length of the walkway. Other boardwalk towns have wrestled for decades with the problem of what to do about bicyclists on a pedestrian thoroughfare. Virginia Beach has solved the problem. Most boardwalk resorts, because of space constraints, safety concerns, or property rights issues, have been unable to construct a separate bike path and are forced to restrict bicycling to early morning hours. In Virginia Beach, you may bicycle any time you want.

Although boardwalk towns are by nature resistant to corporate franchising, the franchising of ideas is a different matter. From saltwater taffy to amusement piers to rolling chairs to—more recently—decorative pavers, old-fashioned benches, and street lamps, boardwalk towns have always taken ideas from other boardwalks and made them work at home. Virginia Beach, too, has borrowed—but in a different way. It has created something unique: a recreational boardwalk—a place to run, walk, bike, and Rollerblade—that is linked to the commercial strip of Atlantic Avenue by handsome connector parks and concert pads. To this it has added a layer of free entertainment—and lots of benches.

"Going back to the 1980s, we envisioned the Boardwalk being kind of the pedestrian Main Street of the town," says Frankenfield, who worked on the early stages of Boardwalk planning and is now design and development administrator for the city's Department of Parks and Recreation. "One of the ideas with that was to have a lot of benches, so that people would be encouraged to sit, to linger and enjoy the Boardwalk. Some of the hotel owners were opposed to that. They thought it would attract bums. That hasn't happened, because it's not that kind of atmosphere." Frankenfield recalls when his relatives came down to visit from Pennsylvania. "They said, 'What is this? It's nice, but it's not a boardwalk.' That's because it's clean and it's attractive. It's not the idea people have in mind when they think boardwalk."

Aesthetics versus Engineering

The first Virginia Beach Boardwalk, built in 1888, was an eight-foot-wide wooden walkway constructed on top of pilings and bulkheads. It extended four blocks, from the Princess Anne Hotel at Sixteenth Street past the Arlington Hotel to Twelfth Street. Perpendicular wooden walkways connected the Boardwalk with the hotels.

As new hotels were built, the Boardwalk was lengthened, eventually stretching from Rudee Inlet to Thirty-ninth Street. After a storm in 1927 destroyed the timber walk, town officials decided to create a more permanent structure and rebuilt it in concrete. The new walk was dedicated with a parade in June 1928. The walk has been concrete ever since, although everyone calls it "the Boardwalk."

Rough seas have several times washed away the shoreline of Virginia Beach and battered the concrete Boardwalk. The 1933 hurricane caused a nine-foot tidal surge and more than $105 million worth of damage in today's dollars. Longtime residents recall that the March 1962 storm, which cost more than $64 million in damage, took much of the beach and opened up troughs around the Boardwalk; one hotel owner trucked in crushed-up cars from the city dump for use as reinforcement fill. Afterward, the Army Corps of Engineers recommended a long-term sand renourishment program and a hurricane protection project for Virginia Beach.

There was also talk, for years, of a new Boardwalk. By the late 1980s, city maintenance crews were periodically removing sections of the damaged and cracked concrete and repouring them. It was clear that a large-scale project was needed to rebuild the Boardwalk and solve other problems, including the lack of adequate storm-water drainage along the oceanfront, but it took years of discussion and debate among the city, the Army Corps of Engineers, and the citizens before it happened.

"The planning for the project really goes back to the 1962 storm," says Rob Hudome, project development manager for the city's economic development department. "That's when they started talking about it. It just took thirty-five years for everyone to agree how to do it."

Hudome worked with Frankenfield and others in the 1980s on plans for Boardwalk improvements. He later helped coordinate the Boardwalk rebuilding and hurricane protection project, a joint effort between the city and the Army Corps of Engineers. At times, says Hudome, it was a case of aesthetics versus engineering. "We had different objectives. The Army Corps of Engineers was charged with building a seawall with steel sheet-piles

Fig. 57. The Boardwalk and beach in 1955. (Courtesy of Virginia Beach Public Library.)

driven into the sand. You could just build a seawall that wasn't very attractive, but that would go against what Virginia Beach wanted to be. Our idea was build all these improvements into the project, aesthetic elements like lighting and the wider bike path. For us, it was important that it be an inviting place, a clean, safe setting. Being engineers, and being tasked with building the hurricane protection, the Corps didn't think those things should be a part of it. They just wanted to build the wall.

"We had several designs brought to us that made sense from an engineering standpoint, but from a tourism, pedestrian, and aesthetic standpoint, they just weren't acceptable. One of the designs was a wall that went the length of the Boardwalk. The elevation of the beach rises as you go south, so by the time you got to the south end, to get the maximum protection you'd be walking next to a four- to six-foot wall and you literally couldn't see the ocean, which was totally unacceptable. So there were years of going back and forth before we got them to agree that all of this should be built together."

There was also the issue of funding. The project wound up costing more than $121 million, of which the city paid 35 percent, or $44.8 million. The city debated for years where the funding would come from, finally deciding to tap into the Resort Revitalization Program, a source created in the mid-1980s that generated millions of dollars a year from hotel, restaurant, and amusement taxes. This fund had been used to pay for improvements to Atlantic Avenue.

"Once we realized this fund had the ability to support the debt of the project, things came together," says Hudome. "Plus, by this time the old Boardwalk was getting to the point that something had to be done. It wasn't in good shape. It looked bad, there were safety issues. If the Corps didn't do something, we were going to have to come in and do some major maintenance on it. But things just came together at the right time."

The Boardwalk and seawall project, which was dedicated in June 2000, sank a sheet-pile seawall into the sand topped by a new walk that was up to ten feet wider than the old one. It also built the new bike path, lamps, foot showers, and other amenities. Storm water, which up until then had been pumped directly onto the beach, along with trash and other debris, was relayed through a pipe to stations at Sixteenth and Fortieth streets, where it was pumped to sea. The following year, more than three million cubic yards of sand was dredged from offshore hoppers, widening the resort beach to three hundred feet from Rudee Inlet to Eighty-ninth Street. It was the final phase of the five-year project—although maintenance will continue indefinitely.

Phil Roehrs, the city's coastal engineer, notes that Virginia Beach closely studied beach replenishment projects elsewhere before deciding on its own. "We visited other cities. We saw what Ocean City had done, for instance, which is a good project, but they built their seawall three feet above the Boardwalk, and we decided we didn't want to do that. We wanted to preserve the view of the ocean. That was important. And as insurance, we also widened the beach."

Although the ocean view was preserved, it turned out to be a view obstructed by railings. According to Hudome, "The only thing that ever bothers me about the Boardwalk is the railing. I was an advocate of not having a railing. To me, when you have a railing you're fencing off the thing that people came here to see. It just seemed so much more inviting without one. Now, if you're sitting on a bench, you're looking through a railing. The Army Corps of Engineers kept saying, 'If you don't have a railing, people are going to fall off it.' I said, 'If you have this three-hundred-foot beach you can grade it so that there's only a foot or two drop-off.' But everybody kept using that term 'falling off' the Boardwalk. We went around and around about it. There was one group that was for the railing, one group against. And as you can see, the railing group won."

Fig. 58. The new, widened concrete walk: "It took thirty-five years for everyone to agree how to do it."

IN THE MORNING, A crisp breeze blows along the oceanfront. In Boardwalk cafés, hotel guests are dawdling over coffee and breakfast platters, watching the sea brighten and the walkers, joggers, and bicyclists parading past.

At Fifteenth Street, near the Virginia Beach Amusement Park, a Rollerblader pulls to a graceful stop, then turns to wait for her three charges. The children have gold-brown hair like hers and appear to be about two years apart, the youngest perhaps seven years old. The woman's name is Susan Maguire. She is visiting from the suburbs of Richmond.

"We started coming here as a family eight or nine years ago, but then we stopped," she says, her blue-gray eyes glinting in the clear morning light. "I used to visit as a kid. I thought my girls might like it, but there really wasn't a lot for them to do. We took them to Cape May a couple of times, where their aunt lives, but they didn't like it there much, either. We'd have to drive them up to Wildwood, where they liked the Boardwalk rides and the water parks okay. But Wildwood was a little rough.

"We came back here two years ago, and they had this new Boardwalk and I couldn't believe it. I found out they allowed Rollerblading all day long. I was amazed. Rollerblading is my passion. I told these girls, 'Next year, we're going to come back and we're all going to Rollerblade together.' And they were into it. So they all learned to Rollerblade together last spring. And here we are."

Is Virginia Beach, then, her favorite boardwalk?

"Are you kidding? I mean, we've got all these other things, too. Like we go to the Jewish Mother for lunch, you know, and eat out at least once at Captain George's. We go on the rides one night and always get Forbes saltwater taffy to take home. But the main thing is Rollerblading. I mean, this is awesome."

Moments later, the four of them are skating south, the youngest a little unsteadily, as the sun rises higher in the sky.

Fig. 59. Virginia Beach's Boardwalk (right) and parallel bike path.

Telling the Story

Fielding Tyler is something of a maverick historian, a retired military man who has been director of the Old Coast Guard Station Museum since 1991. "I'm a native of Virginia Beach," he says. "I knew nothing about maritime when I came here. If they'd asked for a normal museum director's resumé, I'd never have been hired. I didn't know bow and stern, port and starboard, nothing. But I said, 'I know Virginia Beach, I know where the money is, and I can run this museum like a business,' and they said, 'Okay, you're hired.' So over the past thirteen years, I've learned all of this stuff."

Tyler is in his office at the museum, on the Boardwalk at Twenty-fourth Street. "What we do," Tyler says, "is tell the story of the oceanfront." Through exhibits, artifacts, and photographs, the museum preserves the history of the Coast Guard and its forerunner, the Life-Saving Service.

Several years ago, the museum expanded its scope to also tell the history of the Virginia Beach resort.

The most impressive artifact here is the building itself, a Life-Saving Station dating to 1903. It was one of five stations built on the Virginia coast between 1874 and 1915, a period when there were more than 185 shipwrecks in these waters. Tyler's office is upstairs, where the surf men used to sleep. The history of the Coast Guard, one learns, goes back to 1790 when the first United States Congress authorized the construction of ten ships to enforce tariff and trade laws and protect federal revenue collecting. It was known then as the Revenue Cutter Service. The service's responsibilities grew as the country did, to include rescuing sailors in distress and enforcing slavery, piracy, and smuggling laws. The organization was named the Coast Guard in 1915 when the Revenue Cutter Service merged with the Life-Saving Service.

The museum is one of the treasures of the Virginia Beach oceanfront, although attendance is modest, Tyler concedes. Sometimes vacationers come in to use the rest rooms. "This is a resort area. History is not really appreciated here, as you can imagine. The historic society here consists of six dedicated people. We're a struggling nonprofit. We have to do anything we can to make a buck. We are whores. But we serve a function, and we've got good people. My main mission is to save this

Fig.60. Fielding Tyler, director of the Old Coast Guard Station Museum, at the Boardwalk's northern end.

building. There are some who would like to convert it into bathrooms, a restaurant, or something that would make money for the city. I'm not going to let that happen."

Tyler's direct, matter-of-fact manner is balanced by a quirky, sometimes self-deprecating humor. He criticizes developers who are building luxury hotels "that the city doesn't need." He talks of a city councilman "that some say is an evil man" who would like to build a fast-food restaurant on the site where the museum now stands. At one point, he describes himself as a "revisionist historian."

"You know what a revisionist historian is? It's someone who, if he doesn't know the answer, he'll make one up. So you have to be very careful about what you use from this guy. But the problem is, he's the only real source, so you have no other place to go. You're sort of doomed." He waits a beat and smiles.

When asked about the history of the Boardwalk, Tyler says, "Let's go for a walk."

OUTSIDE, THE AIR IS warm and breezy with a faint mist of sea spray. Tyler stops to let a family of five on bicycles of varying sizes ride by.

"The city's history is really about hotels," he says. "Hotels and cottages. This up in here is what used to be known as the Cottage Line. They called them cottages, but many of them were like small hotels. The Boardwalk was built so hotel guests could walk along the ocean. It's a great mover of people. But there were never a lot of commercial businesses on this boardwalk like you see in other towns. People walked here to look at the ocean."

A bikinied Rollerblader slices past, weaving backward, followed by two shirtless male joggers, their conversation punctuated by grunts.

Tyler stops at the Norwegian Lady, a nine-foot-tall bronze statue at Twenty-fifth Street, which commemorates the sinking of a Norwegian ship called the *Dictator*. It's a story some visitors miss: On March 27, 1891, the *Dictator* was sailing with a load of lumber from Pensacola, Florida, to West Bartlepool, England, when it ran into a vicious storm south of here. The ship's captain, Jorgen Jorgensen, steered the ship north along the coast, hoping to make it to Norfolk for repairs, but the ship began to break apart and sank along the Virginia Beach coast. Jorgensen's wife and son drowned in the wreck, and the captain came ashore unconscious. Eight of the seventeen crew members died.

The ship's wooden figurehead, known as "the Norwegian Lady," washed up on the beach in front of the Princess Anne Hotel, where it was found by Emily Gregory, a hotel guest who later married the first mayor of Virginia Beach. The Norwegian Lady was a fixture at that site for decades, until she was damaged in a storm and removed in 1953. Nine years later, the city of Moss, Norway, commissioned a nine-foot bronze replica of the original wooden figurehead and gave it to the city of Virginia Beach, where it has stood ever since, facing the sea. The plaque on it reads: I AM THE NORWEGIAN LADY. I STAND HERE AS MY SISTER BEFORE ME TO WISH ALL MEN OF THE SEA SAFE RETURN HOME.

Thirty-seven hundred miles away, in Moss, the *Dictator*'s port of origin, an identical statue stands, looking toward Virginia Beach.

ENGLISH COLONISTS DROPPED ANCHOR at the southern tip of Virginia Beach almost exactly four hundred years ago, Tyler points out. They were traveling up the Chesapeake Bay, on a mission that would eventually establish the settlement of Jamestown. Led by John Smith, the colonists stayed here for three days and named the point Cape Henry. One member of the first landing party described the region's "fair meadows and goodly tall trees, with such fresh waters running through the woods as I was almost ravished at the first sight thereof."

Soon the Cape Henry waters were crowded with merchant ships. Before the first lighthouse was constructed in 1792, bonfires were used to guide ships into Chesapeake Bay. The advent of a railroad line from Norfolk to the coast in 1883 ushered in the cottage and hotel era and turned Virginia Beach into a resort. The Princess Anne, which opened five years later, was considered the resort's first luxury hotel. A newspaper at the time described it as "magnificent . . . with electric lights, bath houses with a veranda and a good ballroom." The even grander Cavalier hotel, which opened in 1927, is still in business, on a rise northwest of the Boardwalk's northern end.

Virginia Beach was incorporated as a town in 1906 and as a city in 1952. In 1963, it merged with Princess Anne County. As Tyler points out, the resort known as Virginia Beach is actually one small edge of a huge municipality, the largest in the state. The city of Virginia Beach comprises 248 square miles and has a population of about 450,000. The beachfront area is a six-mile strip of land with about 8,500 hotel rooms. It draws about three million vacationers annually.

In the late 1970s and early 1980s, the oceanfront changed from a cottage and mom-and-pop hotel resort to a midrise, franchise hotel resort. By most accounts, it is changing again, into a more upscale, high-rise convention resort, whose centerpiece will be the new $200 million convention center, which will open in 2007. Thirty-first Street, once home to a sprawling amusement park, is now the site of a twenty-two-story Hilton convention hotel. "People want to change things. They think Virginia Beach is going to attract the rich and famous down here. I don't think so," says Tyler. "Are people going to stay at a luxury hotel and then walk across the street and buy a T-shirt at Sunsations? What do you think?"

Sunsations, the T-shirt and sundries department store chain, was started in Ocean City, Maryland, in 1983 by developer Avi Siboni. There are now seven Sunsations stores in Virginia Beach and forty-five elsewhere, mostly in resort towns.

"The riot was up there," Tyler says, pointing toward Atlantic Avenue. "It was a full-blown riot that some think we're still recovering from. Over the past fifteen years, the city has put a lot of care and money into the development of Atlantic Avenue. It's gone from the tacky sixties and seventies feel to a much more friendly, polite place. And in doing that, they've changed it so that the locals don't come down here anymore. They've put an emphasis on making the tourist feel welcome, so it's less of a hangout for locals. But the locals all use the Boardwalk."

No Cursing

The Labor Day riot of 1989—during which black college students fought with beach police and smashed store windows along Atlantic Avenue—is still an open wound for many resort business and political leaders. Some are unwilling to talk about it on the record, and those who do pick their words carefully. What became known as "the Greekfest riot" lasted for several hours, but it branded the resort with an ugly national image that stuck for years.

The students, fraternity members who came from Norfolk State University and elsewhere for an end-of-summer celebration, had made similar pilgrimages to the beach on past Labor Day weekends. The previous year, some business owners say, a mood of racial tension had hung over Greekfest, with students claiming that the city deliberately made them feel unwelcome. Some Virginia Beach merchants feared the 1989 event might explode into violence. It did. The riot happened early Sunday morning, when thousands of students were walking up and down Atlantic Avenue. As one eyewitness later described it, "There were police everywhere, some in riot gear; the only thing missing was a riot." The sight of police clubbing students and students looting stores reminded onlookers of race riots from the 1960s.

"It was a terrible event, and you sort of could see it coming," says one business owner. "The city decided to look the other way and hope it wouldn't happen. Maybe that was a mistake. Obviously, that was not a high point for Virginia Beach."

The Greekfest riot was indeed a low point, but it also served as a pivot, the event that would transform Virginia Beach, in just a few years, into one of the most attractive boardwalk towns in the country.

Jimmy Capps, owner of the Breakers Resort Inn, an oceanfront hotel located at Sixteenth Street—where the Princess Anne once stood—was on the resort committee that studied the riot. "In my lifetime, I've never been around anything like that. I came to work the next morning and it was like a war zone. There were National Guard on the streets. Everything was shut down. It was a situation I had never seen and hope to never see again. It had been brewing, yes, but I don't think anyone anticipated it would reach that level. There was a lot of broken glass, windows boarded up. There was a tremendous amount of physical damage and a lot of hurt feelings. A lot of hurt pride."

Capps says the riot revealed some of the resort's weak spots. "There was plenty of talk about what caused the riot, but basically it was this: There were a lot of people on the streets with nothing to do. We knew they were coming and we didn't give them anything to do."

Greekfest returned in 1990, but it was a scaled-down version, without the turbulence. City leaders and business owners, meanwhile, scrambled to create a new identity for Labor Day weekend, with such attractions as powerboat races and monster truck pulls. In 1994, the city decided to go for broke, inaugurating the four-day American Music Festival. Billed as the largest music event in the history of Virginia Beach, the festival rolled out about forty bands and solo artists on five outdoor stages, among them the Beach Boys, the Four Tops, the Temptations, and Billy Ray Cyrus. The music festival is now a Labor Day staple.

In 2001, another event was added to the weekend: the Rock 'n' Roll Half Marathon, an offshoot of San Diego's Rock 'n' Roll Marathon, which features bands playing live along the race route. The event brings more than fifteen thousand runners to Virginia Beach.

Along with the nightly free concerts during summer, these events have given a theme of music and entertainment to the new Virginia Beach. What the resort didn't have, it is now known for. "What we've done is create an atmosphere that simply doesn't lend itself to a crowd waiting around to throw bottles at people," says Capps.

Some visitors have carped quietly that campaigns such as the NO CURSING signs that now dot the oceanfront go too far—that the city leaders have become "morality police." Capps points out that the signs aren't a mandate. "I don't know how anyone can be opposed to being nice. That's all we said. It doesn't force you to do anything. It simply asks you to be nice."

Fig. 61. *Sign of the times in Virginia Beach: No cursing.*

Gordon Parker, a financial planner and Virginia Beach native, says: "Some people visit Virginia Beach who haven't been here in a while and they don't recognize it. . . . The business community has become more aware of the responsibility we have to keep track of our image."

Capps recalls talking recently with a group of college students about their impressions of Virginia Beach. "They told us that if they go to McArthur mall in Norfolk, which is one of the big shopping malls, they act better than they do when they come to Virginia Beach. We asked them why. They said because they're supposed to. That was their answer. But when they come down here, the perception is, they can let their hair down. That was the perception. We've had to work to change that perception."

The new Boardwalk, he adds, has helped do that. "To me, the signature of Virginia Beach is now the Boardwalk. It wasn't free—it cost us well over a hundred million dollars—but it's the catalyst for the whole resort. I'm not a big world traveler, but I've been a few places and I've never seen one like this."

IT'S SEVERAL MINUTES PAST two o'clock, and clubgoers are spilling out of the Cave, Peabody's, Club Lagoon, Hammerhead's, and the other bars along Atlantic Avenue, where most have been drinking and dancing for several hours. Voices are raised, their pitch uninhibited; several women shout raucously. Then, subtly, they adjust to the unexpected: The street is unusually bright, and smooth jazz plays from loudspeakers. The incongruity of where they have been—the blaring music, black lights, and anything-goes atmosphere inside Peabody's, for example—and the well-lit, mellow ambience outside seems disorienting to some. It's as if they have entered a different country and can't go back.

This is, it turns out, another of the city's strategies to control its environment. If a street is brightly lit when the bars let out, and there's mellow, jazzy music playing, people are less inclined to be rowdy, goes the thinking. On this night, at least, it seems to work.

Virginia Beach continues to try harder than most other resorts to moderate the behavior of its visitors, overcompensating, perhaps, for a time when it didn't try hard enough. Because of its demographics—which include several military bases within the city limits—and the nature of beach resorts, the oceanfront will always face challenges to maintaining the peace, but for now it seems to be succeeding. The resort has engineered a happy chaos along its oceanfront, a temporary corrective to the ruthlessness of the world—particularly down on the Boardwalk, where the noise of Atlantic Avenue can't even be heard tonight. There's a clear, cool sky above the beach. The lights of freighter ships blink out at sea. A couple walks by slowly, holding hands. They stop and look to the water, letting a good feeling flow through them.

Being Seen

Ask longtime residents what's changed about the Boardwalk over the years and the most frequent answer will be dress. It used to be, people dressed up to walk the boards; now, it seems, they dress down. Early twentieth-century photographs show men in three-piece suits and women in fancy dresses—and virtually everyone wearing a hat. Beginning in the 1950s, Boardwalk attire became much more casual. By the 1960s, no one dressed up. This shift seems to reflect a mysterious change in the culture, and is echoed in every boardwalk town in the country, from Santa Cruz to Wildwood to Coney Island.

Julie Pouliot, a Virginia Beach native who collects old photographs and postcards, thinks too much is made about it. "If you look at the pictures from those days," she says, displaying several old black-and-white postcards of tourists on the Virginia Beach Boardwalk, "you see the ladies put on their dresses, and the men put on their suits. That's true. But what they're doing is, they're showing off. People come here on vacation, and they act a little different. They walk a little different. They show off. The Boardwalk is their stage. That hasn't changed. The kids go up there now and they're all strutting their stuff, they're showing off their clothes, their hair, their body jewelry, their piercings. They're acting differently than they would elsewhere.

"The first function of the Boardwalk is protection. The second thing is it's a showoff walkway. You sit out there and you can see everything. I did it when I was a teenager, and they still do it now. The best way to get yourself seen is to walk up and down that Boardwalk. It's a very basic thing."

CHAPTER NINE

MYRTLE BEACH, SOUTH CAROLINA

Crossroads at the Seashore

MARCUS SMITH remembers riding his bicycle down the Boardwalk to the Myrtle Beach Pavilion back in the 1930s. "It was the place everyone went. It was wonderful. As you'd get there you'd smell the hot dogs and popcorn. You'd go inside and on the second floor there were these big arches, so you always felt the breeze from the ocean. They had rocking chairs all around the room, and the parents sat in the rocking chairs while we played. Monday was children's night."

When Smith was born in 1926, the population of Myrtle Beach was about two hundred. Today it's more than twenty-five thousand, with a surrounding area nearly ten times as populous. Myrtle Beach lies in a sixty-mile stretch of South Carolina coast known as the Grand Strand, which attracts close to fourteen million visitors a year. Tourism is South Carolina's largest industry, and Myrtle Beach is its main engine. Over the past fifteen years, Myrtle Beach has numbered among the country's fastest-growing tourist destinations, with a cornucopia of attractions including country-western theaters, water parks, and 120 golf courses. In 1995, a $250 million outdoor entertainment mall called Broadway at the Beach opened a mile and a half from the ocean. The 350-acre complex includes a Hard Rock Café, Planet Hollywood, and Jimmy Buffet's Margaritaville.

Fig. 62. (OPPOSITE) Myrtle Beach's original boardwalk and pier, circa 1920. (Courtesy the Horry County Museum.)

At the heart of Myrtle Beach's oceanfront is a lot of history: a three-block concrete Boardwalk with businesses that date to the 1930s and the eleven-acre, fifty-six-year-old Pavilion Amusement Park. The Pavilion is owned by Burroughs & Chapin, the same company that built Broadway at the Beach. The park's thirty-five rides include the Hurricane—a twenty-four-passenger wood and steel roller coaster—go-cart tracks, and a 1912 Hershell-Spellman carousel with twenty-seven hand-carved animals, which was moved here in 1950.

Most of the beachfront that Marcus Smith remembers was destroyed by Hurricane Hazel in 1954. "The sea tore it up and took it away," says Smith, who was for years Myrtle Beach's only optometrist. The three-block concrete Boardwalk that now stands, between Eighth and Eleventh streets, segues nicely into the amusement park. Recently, power lines have been moved underground and decorative pavers installed, lending a contemporary, generic veneer to these old-fashioned attractions.

More dramatic changes are ahead. The city wants to lengthen the Boardwalk to about a mile during the next few years—from the Second Avenue pier to the Fourteenth Avenue pier. Planners are also exploring redevelopment of the entire Pavilion property—replacing all or some of the amusements with high-rise condos and boutique-style shops. In the late 1990s, Burroughs & Chapin proposed moving the Pavilion Amusement Park inland to property it owns at the Route 17 Bypass, near Broadway at the Beach. The city responded in 1999 by forming the Myrtle Beach Downtown Redevelopment Corporation (DRC), which is spearheading oceanfront redevelopment plans.

The trouble with the Pavilion, some city officials say, is that it's only open half the year. "What we really need, what the city really needs and what the oceanfront really needs, is something there that is open twelve months a year," says Kelly Mezzapelle, project manager for the DRC. "Because when the Pavilion shuts down, everything around it has to shut down, too. We would like to keep an amusement atmosphere there, but we'd like to introduce other attractions, too, making it an area that would appeal to families and maybe also to a more upscale visitor. [Burroughs & Chapin] has been very open to working with us on this. They realize it's not 1940 anymore."

The question is, what sort of attractions would work best on the Myrtle Beach oceanfront—and be a good match with the expanded Boardwalk?

On an afternoon in May 2004, Barry Landreth, a California developer, stood before a gathering of residents and businesspeople at the Myrtle Beach Convention Center and unveiled plans for a sweeping overhaul of the oceanfront. These included a rotating amphitheater, two ten-story condominium towers, a Saks Fifth Avenue store, and a roller coaster. Both the city and Burroughs & Chapin were impressed, and Landreth—whose proposal was one of fifty submitted to the city—won the job of planning the new Myrtle Beach oceanfront.

For months, Landreth worked with the city and Burroughs & Chapin, fine-tuning his concepts into a workable plan. Along the way, his role in the project seemed to shift from planner to developer. In October, Landreth told Burroughs & Chapin that he had raised more than $40 million to fund the project. Later, the amount reportedly doubled to $80 million. Landreth also entered into a separate project during this time with John Reyelt, vice chairman of the DRC, to build a time-share resort five blocks from the Pavilion. The deal, which eventually collapsed for lack of funding, was not revealed to other corporation members.

Questions about Landreth's background were finally raised by both the DRC and Burroughs & Chapin, which was concerned that he had missed meetings and failed to produce monthly progress reports. A brief investigation by the DRC yielded what an earlier check had missed: apparent discrepancies in letters of reference and earnings statements. The city also learned that Landreth faced charges in California of writing a bad check for $64,500. In January 2005, the DRC demanded that he produce financial statements and tax returns. Instead, Landreth resigned from the project. Reyelt stepped down from the DRC the following day.

The final act in the Landreth episode seemed to confirm the fears of many Myrtle Beach residents and business owners: that the city was proceeding recklessly with a plan that would forever change the oceanfront. It also raised questions about whether a city built around working-class vacationers can, by force of will, attract a more upscale clientele.

Photographer and historian Jack Thompson doesn't think so. "I've been here fifty-four years," he says. "Some people want to get rid of the nickel-

and-dime aspect of Myrtle Beach and bring in dollars, big dollars. They don't realize that the nickels and dimes add up to big dollars. The first visitors to Myrtle Beach were the mill workers, and through the years their children and grandchildren have come here. They're still coming. What I ask is 'Why kill the goose when it's still laying the golden eggs?' "

Futurists

Two years before the Pavilion Amusement Park opened, Eloise and Justin Plyler started a smaller, 140-foot by 180-foot amusement park and gift shop, on property just north of the current Pavilion site. They called their business the Gay Dolphin.

Fig.63. The Seaside Inn, Myrtle Beach's first oceanfront hotel, circa 1901. (Courtesy the Horry County Museum.)

"What happened was, they saw dolphins playing out in the ocean one day, and that seemed to Dad just the right symbol," says their son Buz Plyler, who runs the business today. "Myrtle Beach is one of the calmest stretches of ocean you'll find anywhere. It's actually a bay. It has a gentle slope. There aren't many waves. Dad was looking for a name that would have a happy sound. He realized that dolphins were among the nicest, happiest, and most intelligent creatures, and he wanted the business to reflect that."

The amusement park shut down in the late 1960s, but the Plylers' gift shop grew. The three-story Gay Dolphin is now a landmark of the Myrtle Beach Boardwalk, with a glass lookout tower and aisles of mostly inexpensive souvenirs that include shark's tooth jewelry, sea shells, rubber fish, coconut pirate heads, and apparel emblazoned with MYRTLE BEACH. "Gay," of course, has taken on new meaning since 1946, but Plyler says that hasn't hurt business. "It's actually been a positive. People see us as old-fashioned, a business that has been here for generations. They feel comfortable with that."

This feeling reflects a larger truth about Myrtle Beach, Plyler maintains. "The oceanfront here is the historical center of the resort. If you replace it with condominium towers, you'd be changing the organism. We would be real-estate oriented then as opposed to amusements oriented. That's the decision we have to make. Either provide a view for people who want to retire or give visitors a place to be entertained. We need to decide that. I think if we decide we want to give them a view, it's important that we be futurists about it.

"It's difficult to be a futurist, to be able to accurately foresee change and to build within your means. This city used to have some good futurists. We have some people on the council now who are making decisions who maybe don't have the experience necessary to be making those decisions. That's dangerous. It's hard to be a futurist if you don't have the experience."

He cites not only the Landreth case but also expansion of the city's convention center. Myrtle Beach has wagered millions of dollars in recent years on becoming a major convention destination, but it's still waiting for a winning hand. When expansion of the Myrtle Beach Convention Center did not result in an expected business boom, city leaders decided they needed a convention hotel to provide on-site lodging. In 2001, the city issued $65 million in bonds to cover the hotel's construction, becoming one of the first cities to use public backing to finance a hotel operated by a private company. The Radisson opened in January 2003 with a projected 65 percent occupancy rate during its first year of operation. The actual occupancy was 46.6 percent. It lost $1.7 million that year, twice the projection. In 2004, the city defaulted on its bonds and had to refinance $47.7 million in bonds to cover losses.

"The city has rushed forward with a few things and maybe made some poor judgments," says Plyler. "Now they're talking about bringing in upscale businesses. I'm not sure that's what people want when they come to Myrtle Beach.

"Right now we're seeing a collapse of the industrial infrastructure in America, and tourism patterns are going to change. People aren't looking at that closely enough. This may not be the best economic use of the land in the long run. I don't think it's wrong to change, but I think it would be wrong to change too much, without proper consideration.

"I can see it from both sides. We really only have a hundred days of good weather here. But I think with some of these plans, they're forgetting the families. If you talk with children, you might be surprised. I ask children all the time, 'Do you have more fun in Myrtle Beach or in Orlando at the theme parks?' And every single time they say they have more fun here. They love the beach and the ocean and the Boardwalk and the rides. They don't want to wait in long lines for fancy rides. You should ask children what they think."

Burroughs & Chapin

The history of Burroughs & Chapin is, in a sense, Myrtle Beach's history as well. The company's roots date to the mid-1800s when Franklin Burroughs opened a turpentine distillery and mercantile store in nearby Conway, South Carolina. What is today Myrtle Beach was then a remote, forested coastland, cut off by rivers and inlets from the plantation societies of coastal South Carolina. Burroughs, a Confederate soldier, returned to Horry County after the Civil War and expanded his business to include timber and riverboats. Unlike some companies that bought timber rights, Burroughs and his partner Benjamin Collins bought the land itself—more than a hundred thousand acres, eventually—establishing the foundation for what would become one of the largest beach resorts on the East Coast.

After Burroughs died in 1897, his sons took over the business and oversaw the establishment in 1900 of a rail line from Georgetown to the beach. The next year, they opened the first oceanfront hotel, where the Pavilion Amusement Park now stands. Rooms at the three-story Seaside Inn were priced at two dollars a night, which included dinner. A wooden walkway ran about a thousand feet from the hotel porch to the beach. The company also sold nearby beachfront lots for twenty-five dollars apiece.

The first Pavilion, built in 1908, was a wooden octagonal building on the beach, which served as a dance hall and a gathering spot. By this time, bathhouses and small hotels dotted the shore, catering to mill workers, many of whom arrived by boat from Charleston.

The potential of the resort area, then known as New Town, was soon seized upon by Simeon Chapin, a wealthy New York stockbroker. Chapin partnered with the Burroughs brothers in 1912 to launch a development company called Myrtle Beach Farms, Inc. It was Burroughs's widow who named the proposed resort town Myrtle Beach, after the native wax myrtle trees along the coast. Chapin's business acumen and financial resources proved to be a good fit with the Burroughs company's extensive land holdings.

As Myrtle Beach evolved, the Burroughs & Chapin company controlled its growth and sometimes acted as its conscience, donating land for churches and backing a number of charitable causes. Later, the company would convince city leaders to clamp down on loitering, cruising, and the sale of drug paraphernalia at the oceanfront. When a Gay and Lesbian Pride March came to Myrtle Beach in the 1990s, the company urged its tenants not to participate, running a newspaper ad stating: "Burroughs & Chapin Company, Inc., past and future, rests on traditional family values. The South Carolina Grand Strand, like our nation, was founded on family values. Our company was also founded on these values. Myrtle Beach has always been a family beach. Our goal is to do our best to celebrate and reinforce that priceless legacy."

The growth of Myrtle Beach was guided by population and travel patterns as well as by nature. After Hurricane Hazel wiped out homes and forest land in 1954, the city rebuilt the oceanfront with a row of motels. In the 1960s, Myrtle Beach became known as a golf resort. The 1970s saw a boom in high-rise condominium development.

A quiet turning point for the city came in 1990, when the Myrtle Beach Farms company reorganized, forming Burroughs & Chapin. Three years later, stockholders hired the first non-family-member to captain the firm, a local businessman named Doug Wendel. Under Wendel, the company became markedly more aggressive, targeting high-end vacationers. One of Wendel's first announcements was Broadway at the Beach. The company also developed expensive housing projects, such as the 2,200-acre Grande Dunes, where condominiums are priced at $1 million and houses go for up to $4 million.

Many tourism officials applaud the work of Burroughs & Chapin, saying the company is helping steer the Grand Strand away from its reputation as a "Redneck Riviera." The average visitor to South Carolina spends only $262, tourism officials recently pointed out, considerably less than the national average of $464.

On the Myrtle Beach oceanfront, meanwhile, redevelopment remains something of a balancing act for the city's Downtown Redevelopment Corporation. Plans for the Boardwalk extension have been modified to quell the protests of some oceanfront hotel owners who worried that the walk would attract loiterers. A new plan, which places the walk on the ocean side of the dune, still needs Office of Ocean and Coastal Resource Management approval. Under that plan, no commercial businesses will exist along the Boardwalk, but officials want to see some eventually. "We're hoping that over the years, the hotels would appreciate the value of having something on the Boardwalk, cafés or little restaurants, kind of like the hotels in Virginia Beach have," says DRC director Mezzapelle.

As for the Pavilion, the city has abandoned Landreth's plans and is starting over again. "I think we're dealing with a lot of misconceptions," says Mezzapelle. "It's unfortunate that when Barry Landreth first came to town, one of his slides showed a Saks store. There was not going to have been a Saks in his final plans. We weren't, and aren't, trying to turn the oceanfront into an upscale shopping mall or a shopping mall at all. What we're looking at is a variety of things that the current clientele would enjoy, but also things that a different clientele might enjoy. We don't want to do anything crazy or drastic, but we want it to be developed. We want to make it a twelve-month-a-year attraction."

'57 Baseball

Along the south wall of Red Waldorf's Fun City arcade is something you won't find at any other boardwalk in the country: Dozens of '57 Williams Deluxe baseball machines, a classic pinball-style game that was manufactured only one year. For aficionados of arcade games, discovering this bank of baseball machines is sort of like finding three dozen '64 Mustangs lined up side by side in a parking lot.

"People are always telling me they used to play these as a kid," says Waldorf. "It's a great game. Many people say they had forgotten about them and they sit down in here and become fascinated with them again. It brings back memories. People associate them with childhood. Many people bring their children in and show them the game they used to play when they were kids."

To play the wooden, glass-topped game, you press a button, dropping a metal ball from the pitcher's mound. With your other hand, you pull a lever and bat the ball toward the outfield. Results are frequently gratifying: It's easy to rack up runs, and congratulatory bells clang each time you hit a home run.

Early on a summer evening, as cool sea breezes blow in through the open-front arcade, all of the baseball games are in use. Players range from children to old-timers. Blinking red neon arrows point toward the machines, framing the words BASE BALL on green-and-white hanging electric signs. Outside, the sky darkens above the ocean. Interiors become more focused. In this fast-changing resort, the long row of Williams Deluxe '57 machines seems like a mechanical monument. The well-worn metal of the levers, the clacking sounds of balls on wood, the softer click of the rigid base runners spinning around the diamond, the painted baseball field through a looking glass: In Myrtle Beach, participants can still enjoy the simplicity and mystery of a perfect game.

Waldorf, who owns Fun City, has been collecting these machines since they first came on the market. Most arcades phased them out decades ago, replacing them with electronic games, although many larger arcades still have one or two. The machines, which cost $185 brand-new, now sell for about $3,000. He compares the game to automobiles. "Some years a classic design comes along and it's never duplicated. This was the 1957 model. In 1958, they came out with a variation. I think it was named Four Bagger. Similar, but it wasn't the same. They do that to get people to buy new games, just like with cars. They make little changes, and pretty soon it's not the same game.

"I remember once back in the late 1960s, I went to Williams Manufacturing in Chicago and I sat down with the head man—and by then I'd bought up all of these games that I could find—and I said to him, 'You

Fig. 64. Red Waldorf (left) and his father, E. T. Waldorf Sr., on the Boardwalk in 1966. (Courtesy of Red Waldorf.)

really ought to manufacture another game like that '57. People really liked that game.' He said to me, 'There is no way.' He said, 'I'll be very honest with you. We don't want a game that'll last over two or three years. That game was too good.' "

Waldorf has been on the Myrtle Beach Boardwalk almost as long as the Williams '57 game has existed. His first day at the arcade was Fourth of July

1958. Born and raised in Mobile, Alabama, he transferred to the Myrtle Beach area after serving with the air force in Africa.

"I worked in electronics, radar maintenance. When I started here at the arcade, my first job was making change, but then they realized I knew electronics, so I went to work on the equipment. I got married in 1961. I married a girl from Pennsylvania, and we didn't have any family here, either one of us. But the owners of the arcade kind of took me in like a son and treated us well. One man owned the property, and another man owned the business. Both of them were like a daddy to me. They taught me a lot. They told me when I did wrong, they told me when I did right. The man who owns the property, A. E. Jackson, is still here. He will be ninety-one in October. I took him to buy a new car in March. He's still sharp. In all of these years, I've never heard him say anything bad about anybody, nor have I seen him do anybody wrong. And there's very few people I can say that about."

Fig. 65. Fun Plaza in 1965. (Courtesy of Red Waldorf.)

Waldorf, who bought the Boardwalk business about fifteen years ago, is in the arcade every day; his two sons work with him. "I don't need to do this," he says. "I don't need the money. But I enjoy it. All these people that have been coming here for years, it's like a community. I enjoy seeing them come back, seeing that life's good for them. I keep addresses, and I send out Christmas cards. If somebody doesn't show up one year, I try to find out what's wrong. Is there something I can do? Did somebody make them mad here? If they don't come here this summer, I get on the phone and find out where they are, what happened."

Waldorf supports the plan to build a longer Boardwalk but says changing the commercial atmosphere of the oceanfront would alienate the resort's bread-and-butter visitors. "The Boardwalk, to me, is an extension of the beach. I take the attitude that people don't come to Myrtle Beach to visit the Fun Plaza or the Pavilion, they come because of that ocean. A longer Boardwalk would give people a chance to get out of their hotels and motels and walk up and down the beach. That's something everyone enjoys.

"Now they're talking about putting in these upscale restaurants and shops down here. Listen, when a Burger King, a McDonald's, can't make it here, that tells you something. People have got all of that at home. They're not looking for a Gap. They're here on vacation, and they're looking for something different. If you were going to buy a fourteen-carat gold necklace, would you buy it in New York City, Chicago, or would you buy it on the Boardwalk in Myrtle Beach? That's not why people come to the Boardwalk."

Fig. 66. Skee-Ball still costs a quarter for nine balls.

Waldorf would prefer the city concentrate on making tourists feel welcome. "I would like to see better cleaning, better public facilities. I've said for the last fifteen years, the chamber of commerce has done its job so much better than the city. The chamber has gotten people here, but the city has not been able to take care of them. They spent millions of dollars putting in these brick pavers. It looks good, but have you tried cleaning those things? Not easy. Not easy getting cigarette butts out. Chewing gum won't come up at all. They spent all this money putting in parking meters, and it just put an extra burden on the visitors and on the merchants, with people asking them to make change. I'd like to see some way that if you and your family came down to the beach just for the day you could find a place to put on a bathing suit without breaking the law. I'd like to see some police visibility.

"We have a serious problem here with the management of the city. The authorities are working banking hours, Monday through Friday, nine to five. But the beachfront here doesn't work those hours.

"My arcade is the only place in this area that has public rest rooms and an ice water fountain. Other places, you walk in and get an ice water, you're going to pay the same thing you would for a Coca-Cola. Ninety percent of the places in Myrtle Beach, it seems, have a sign on the door, saying NO PUBLIC REST ROOM. I have a problem with that.

"One of the things you'll find about Myrtle Beach historically is that everyone's always been welcome here. I get a real mixed bag—we get some very high-income people, some blue-collar people, mill workers, tobacco farmers. But you know what? I don't care what color you are or what your background is. As a businessman, my only concern is that your money's green and that you behave and you have a good time."

The Right to Be Here

Veins of lightning illuminate the ocean. The surf is gentle, barely noticeable. On the beach, two young men are strumming guitars, singing a Green Day song, while several friends sing along. The air is salty, sulfurous.

Up on the Boardwalk, a little brunette-haired girl walks dizzily beside her parents, in her own world, singing "I'm a *soul* man" over and over.

Two older couples finish ice creams and walk into Fun Plaza. They watch the Williams '57 players and wait for a game to open up.

A group of young people in the next block is huddled together. When a stranger approaches, one of them steps toward him and says, "Hi!"

"Hi," says the stranger.

"Don't you recognize me?"

"I don't think so."

"It's me! Jesus Christ!"

"Oh."

The young man asks the stranger if he has been saved. The stranger walks past.

A half block north, a man with matted hair and soiled skin asks, "Do you have a quarter you could spare so I could get a cup of coffee?"

There is a bottle in a paper bag between his legs.

People walk by without acknowledging him.

"Do you have a quarter you could spare so I could get a cup of coffee?"

A woman looks at him closely for a moment and shakes her head. She is holding hands with a much older man.

"Do you have a dime?" the man says. "For a cup of coffee?"

Later, a heavyset man in khakis and a blazer stops, elaborately reaches deep into his pockets, and spills a handful of change in the man's opened palms. It must be close to three dollars.

The man with matted hair does not thank him. He counts the money, puts it in his pockets and waits for someone else.

A car goes past, blaring the Allman Brothers Band, drowning out the thumping sounds of the amusement park. Down at Peaches Corner, people sit on swivel stools at a long Formica counter, eating hot dogs and hamburgers and drinking beer. A huge group of teenagers walks toward the beach, most of them eating ice cream. The nocturnal streets of the oceanfront are mobbed, charged with a healthy anarchy. The wind smells of rain.

JACK THOMPSON WAS THIRTEEN when he ran away from his home in Greenville, South Carolina, and hitchhiked with two friends to Myrtle Beach. "It took us two days to get here," he recalls. "Back then, we'd get a ride for fifteen or twenty miles and then we'd have to find another ride. Mostly it was in the backs of trucks, often with chickens or hogs or some other animals."

Thompson, a Myrtle Beach photographer, claims that when he arrived at the beach on that day in 1951 he knew he was here for good.

"When we got here, my little friends ran into the ocean, but I stopped at the Pavilion because I saw this photo stand there. My father was editor of the *Greenville News,* and I used to hang out in the photography department. I had photography in my blood even then. I saw that photo booth, and I asked if they needed any help. This fellow said, 'Can you pick up that prop?' They had props for the Myrtle Beach Jail and a skinny man and a fat woman, those things where you put your head in them and they'd take your photo. I picked it up and went in, and I smelled the chemicals that I associated with photography and the newspaper. It was in my blood. The man asked me if I wanted to work there. I did.

"My parents sent my brother down to get me, but he met a pretty girl and he stayed, too. Pretty soon I met a girl and then another girl, and I didn't want to go home. The man who hired me became my guardian. His name was Dwight Lambe. I worked in his other studio during the winter and at the Pavilion during the summer.

"I always liked Myrtle Beach. I liked the girls and the beach music. I like everything about it. I believe in fate," he adds. "And I believe it was my fate to come here. If I hadn't done that, I wouldn't have taken all the photos I did and had the archives of photos showing Myrtle Beach in the fifties, sixties, seventies, and eighties. Some people came down and they got homesick. I never did."

FOR MOST PEOPLE, THE oceanfront represents freedom—but freedom comes in many varieties. To some people, it's simply a view; to others, it's riding roller coasters and walking barefoot in the sand. Freedom can mean permissiveness, the taste of sea breeze, the chance to meet like-minded people. Or it may be something more intangible.

For two weeks each spring, Myrtle Beach is a meeting place for motorcyclists from across the country. First, during the third week of the month, tens of thousands of cyclists visit the beach for the Carolina Harley-Davidson Dealers Association Myrtle Beach Rally, a sixty-three-year-old event that is the third-largest biker rally in the country. It's followed by the five-day Black Bike Week, which calls itself "the largest black beach week event in the world." Black Bike Week drew nearly twice as many participants last year as did Harley-Davidson Week.

In 2003, the National Association for the Advancement of Colored People and eighteen individual plaintiffs filed a federal discrimination lawsuit against the city of Myrtle Beach, claiming that it uses excessive police force during Black Bike Week, that it unfairly restricts the traffic flow along Ocean Boulevard to one-way during the event, and that businesses close deliberately to avoid serving black bikers. The suit also cites a disparity in the city's handling of the mostly white Harley-Davidson Week and its handling of Black Bike Week. City officials counter that the greater police presence is commensurate with the greater number of people in town. Participants in Black Bike Week, city officials have said, tend to be younger and rowdier than those who come for Harley Week.

Some merchants and hoteliers complain that motorcyclists have ruined the family market for the month of May and, more generally, damaged Myrtle Beach's image. One oceanfront shop owner says his Memorial Day receipts have dropped from $100,000 to $8,000 as Black Bike Week has grown. There is worry in some quarters that tensions associated with Black Bike Week will erupt into violence, as tensions over the Virginia Beach Greekfest led to the 1989 riot.

But can any resort that sells the universal allure of "freedom" tell one group that it isn't welcome? It's a question that Myrtle Beach will struggle with as it charts its future. Increasingly, the American coastline is a place of conflicting visions, as more and more people journey there—not just to play but to live. What Ocean City's Buddy Jenkins calls "the Tadpole Syndrome" is a national trend: About 54 percent of Americans now live in coastal counties, even though these counties make up only about a fifth of the country's land area, according to Census Bureau figures.

The larger question for Myrtle Beach will be what it ultimately wants to do with its valuable share of the coast. Can the resort consciously change its tourism and resident base by changing its environment, as South Miami Beach has done and Virginia Beach seems to be doing? By offering more upscale attractions, will it necessarily be able to attract more upscale visitors? Or is there some more elemental appeal about this beachfront that will resist change?

Each boardwalk resort has its own complicated character, shaped by history, memory, demographics, real estate, and travel trends. The answers are different and difficult for each one. What Myrtle Beach needs as it contemplates these questions is what every beach town needs: some good futurists.

CHAPTER TEN

DAYTONA BEACH, FLORIDA

Sea Change

Visitors to the Halifax Historical Museum in Daytona Beach will discover an enchanting four-foot by fourteen-foot model depicting the Daytona Beach Boardwalk and beachfront as it looked in 1938. The diorama was built that year by Lawson Diggett, a Daytona Beach lumber mill worker and well-known local model maker.

Mary Luellen, a volunteer at the museum, gazes through the glass case at a little wooden house just west of the Boardwalk. "See that teeny place? That's where I lived. We moved there when I was five years old. It was only a short walk from there to the Boardwalk, and we went there all the time. Every night. That's all we had. These were the days before air-conditioning. They had benches, you could walk around and have an ice cream cone. It was nice back then. Now they've gone and ruined it."

Some of what the Boardwalk model shows still exists—the signature 1937 coquina bandshell at the north end, the Main Street overpass, the granite clock tower, the Pier. Some is gone—Pepp's swimming pool, the miniature golf course. But the most striking difference between 1938 and the present is the towering hotel/condo/restaurant complex that now stands on the north end of the tiny two-block Boardwalk. Much more is in the works. If the model were rebuilt in a few years, it might include two twenty-

Fig. 67. (OPPOSITE) WACs parading on the Daytona Beach Boardwalk. Pictured at top left is the coquina bandshell. (Courtesy the Halifax Historical Museum, Daytona Beach, Florida.)

story condominium towers on the south end, along with a widened pier full of amusement rides.

The Boardwalk model is one of the Halifax Historical Museum's most popular displays, according to director Suzanne Heddy. Sometimes, she says, people tell her they wish the Boardwalk still looked the way it did in 1938. Of course, she points out, a lot happened between those seemingly idyllic days "before air conditioning" and the present. "To look at this model from 1938 and say that was a better time for the Boardwalk may be true. But it doesn't take into account those years when the Boardwalk became very seedy and run-down. I remember going there in the seventies and eighties and people were sleeping in the underpasses and using drugs. It had really deteriorated. So what I'm saying is, it may not be better than it was in 1938, but it's much better now than it was twenty years ago."

Heddy, a Daytona Beach native, says she hopes the Boardwalk will continue to get better. The developer of the proposed hotel/condominium project, Bill Geary, president of California-based Carlsberg Management Company, has visited the museum and seems to care about Daytona's history, she says. She also speaks highly of the longtime Boardwalk merchants, some of whose businesses will be torn down to make way for the new project.

Fig. 68. The Boardwalk looking south. Decorative pavers and palm trees were added to make it more attractive.

"You have to find a balance. I hope they don't get rid of all the classic old things that people have been coming here to see for years and years," she says. "When people go on vacation, they want to see things that are familiar and things that are landmarks. I hope they're able to keep those things here."

THE GLORY DAYS FOR Daytona Beach, it is often said, were the 1920s and 1930s. That was when the fastest cars in the world were shipped here to chase after land-speed records on the hard-packed beach sand. The first man to drive a car faster than 200 mph did so in Daytona. "Right down there," says Heddy, pointing toward the beach.

It's lunchtime now, and Heddy and Luellen are eating sandwiches outside at the Daytona Beach Pier Restaurant. The Pier is one of the best lunch spots in Daytona Beach—not that it's fancy, or the food extraordinary, but just because it's out over the water, with a view of the Boardwalk and the coastline looking north.

Until the spring of 2000, cars were allowed to drive along the twenty-three miles of beach here, a tradition left over from the speed-racing days. Then, at the urging of developers and some business owners, traffic was banned along a one-mile stretch in front of the Boardwalk. Boardwalk merchants say the ban has taken away more than half of their daytime business.

"It's perfectly stupid," says Luellen. "Driving on the beach was part of what made Daytona Beach special. It used to be solid cars along here."

Over lunch, Heddy and Luellen share stories about Daytona Beach, as a pleasant breeze blows in from the sea. They talk of the "rogue wave" that crashed ashore here on July 3, 1992, with a wall of water supposedly eighteen feet high. They explain that the Saint Johns River is one of only a few rivers in the country that flow north; that Volusia County was originally inhabited by Timucuan Indians; that the Boardwalk was first known as "the broadwalk"; and that Daytona Beach is, surprisingly, the summer home of the London Philharmonic Orchestra. Luellen recalls that in the days before air-conditioning, the resort advertised itself with the slogan "It's cooler in Daytona Beach." Back then, bathing suits were called "beach pajamas," she adds, and the Pier casino was "the best dance floor in Florida." Heddy talks of growing up in the Ponce de Leon Lighthouse, where her father was the keeper. Standing at Daytona's southern end, it was built in 1887 and is the tallest lighthouse on the East Coast still in its original location. Heddy was the last person to be raised there; it's now a museum.

They tell the story of Mary McLeod Bethune, the daughter of freed slaves, who moved to Daytona in 1904 and started a one-room school, which eventually became Bethune-Cookman College. They talk, too, of Daytona Beach's origins: Named for Matthias Day, an Ohio newspaper publisher, Daytona was incorporated in 1876. Six years earlier, Day had bought up

2,144 acres of land on the Halifax River and built the resort's first hotel, Palmetto House. In 1890, railroad tycoon Henry Flagler laid tracks to the beach, and a building boom followed. Daytona and two settlements across the Halifax River incorporated as Daytona Beach in 1926. The city built the first section of its two-block concrete Boardwalk, between Main Street and Auditorium Boulevard, three years later.

And they tell how, and why, by the 1930s, Daytona Beach had become known as "the World's Most Famous Beach."

Birthplace of Speed

Almost as soon as the automobile was invented, the race was on to make it go faster. Initially, the competition was centered in France, where Gaston de Chasseloup-Laubat set a land-speed record of 39.24 mph in 1898. (Within six years, another Frenchman, Louis Rigolly, broke the 100 mph barrier.) Soon it shifted to the United States and, for a while, to Daytona Beach.

In 1903, with the auto industry in its infancy—two years after Ransom Olds introduced the Curved Dash Olds, the first car produced in quantity— Ormond Beach, Daytona's neighbor to the north, hosted its first time trial on the sand. The event, known as Sandfest, was the idea of two local businessmen, William Morgan and J. F. Hathaway, who envisioned the unusual hard-packed, miles-long beach surface as a perfect track for timed speed runs. Hathaway wrote an article that year in *Motor Age* magazine predicting that Daytona's and Ormond's beaches would become "a place where world records will be made in the future." He was right.

At the first meet, on March 26, 1903, Horace Thomas drove a car owned by auto-maker Olds to a speed of 54.38 mph, setting an American record for cars under a thousand pounds. Alexander Winton, another early automotive pioneer, also set an American record that day, driving 68 mph in a heavier car.

The success of the 1903 time trials launched a tradition, which drew car manufacturers and enthusiasts from around the world to Florida's coast. The sand-and-coquina-shell beaches at Daytona and Ormond became a proving ground for the latest experimental steam- and gas-powered engines, and a showcase for the world's fastest cars. The speed runs also drew hundreds of spectators, who lined the beaches from Ponce Inlet to Silver Beach for a chance to witness a world record run. The futuristic-looking custom racers—some of which suggested spaceships—needed about three miles to reach top speed, then ran a measured-mile time trial, followed by another three miles before they coasted to a stop. Official times were counted as the average of two runs, one in each direction, within a one-hour period.

The time trials grew in renown during their first two decades, as engines became bigger, speeds increased, and records fell. By the late 1920s, speed racing had earned Daytona Beach an international reputation. The twenties was in many ways an American decade, a time of heroes and record breakers, of innovation and optimism—from the invention of talking motion pictures to Lindbergh's solo flight across the Atlantic to Babe Ruth's home-run record to the advent of commercial radio. The nation's mania for record breaking lured many of the top drivers and automakers to Daytona Beach during this time. But the two men who came to personify the quest for speed were not Americans. They were British drivers Malcolm Campbell and Henry Segrave, whose brief rivalry caught the world's imagination and made them heroes.

Fig. 69. Sir Malcolm Campbell and his car Bluebird at Daytona Beach in 1928, after setting a new land-speed record on the hard coquina shell beach. (Courtesy Halifax Historical Museum, Daytona Beach, Florida.)

Campbell, a successful appraiser at Lloyd's of London, began racing as a hobby while studying the diamond trade Fiercely competitive, he broke the world land-speed record nine times between 1924 and 1935, five of them on the sand in Daytona Beach. Campbell named each of his record-breaking cars Bluebird, after the play The Blue Bird by Belgian writer Maurice Maeterlinck—an allegorical fairy tale about two children's elusive search for the "blue bird of happiness."

Segrave, a handsome former fighter pilot and war hero, was a champion grand prix racer. In 1927, he told skeptical colleagues that he was going to Daytona Beach to break the 200 mph speed barrier. Over the previous two years, Campbell, Segrave, and another British driver, John Parry-Thomas, had pushed the speed record over 170 mph, but 200 mph still seemed an elusive, some thought unattainable, mark.

Several days after Parry-Thomas was killed in Pendine Sands, Wales, trying to break Campbell's record of 174.88 mph, Segrave arrived in Daytona Beach. With him was an entourage of mechanics and reporters, along with his new car, the *Mystery S*, a six-thousand-pound machine powered by twin aircraft engines. On March 29, Segrave defied the skeptics and shattered the 200 mph barrier, setting a new record of 203.79 mph.

The following February, Campbell came to Daytona Beach for the first time and reclaimed the record, posting a time of 206.95 mph. Others arrived that spring, also seeking the record. In April, Ray Keech drove a car called *Triplex*—powered by three aircraft engines—to a time of 207.55 mph. Frank Lockhart, a twenty-six-year-old Indianapolis 500 winner, was seeking to top 220 mph when his car blew a tire and flipped, killing him instantly.

Segrave returned to England and built a new, streamlined, aluminum-bodied car with a nine-hundred-horsepower engine. He called it the *Golden Arrow*. At Daytona on March 11, 1929, the *Golden Arrow* pushed the record to 231.36 mph.

The speed game helped to build Daytona's economy in the 1920s, while imbuing the resort with a distinct, free-spirited character, which survives today. The pre-Depression years were an optimistic era in this country, when mavericks challenged the limits of what was considered possible. Segrave and Campbell, though British, imbibed this exuberant American spirit. Two days after breaking the 200 mph barrier at Daytona, Segrave recounted to a colleague words that newspaper publisher Alfred Harmsworth had shared with an editor off to America for the first time: "You are going to the greatest country in the world, the land of big ideas, big men, big business, big talk, big buildings, big everything. . . . As long as you are among Americans, they and their country are the biggest things that ever happened."

Segrave's and Campbell's accomplishments won them not only worldwide fame, but also knighthoods. Their rivalry ended suddenly and tragically, though, in June of 1930 at Lake Windemere in England. Segrave had gone there with his seven-thousand-pound torpedo-shaped boat *Miss England II*. He was hoping to break the world water-speed record, becoming "the fastest man on land or sea," but his boat struck a floating log during his record attempt, ejecting Segrave at a speed of nearly 100 mph. He died shortly afterward, at age thirty-five.

Campbell went on to break the land-speed record at Daytona Beach four more times and also to set several water-speed records. His last run at Daytona was on March 7, 1935, when he drove the twenty-nine-foot-long, twelve-thousand-pound *Bluebird V* to a record speed of 276.82 mph. The car is now on display at the Daytona USA museum here.

Several months later, Campbell shattered the 300 mph barrier. By this time, though, the center of speed racing had shifted to the wide-open Utah desert. Daytona time trials were discontinued after 1935, replaced the next year with a beach-and-road stock car race, the precursor to the Daytona 500. In 1937, Daytona hosted its first Bike Week, coinciding with the Daytona 200 motorcycle race, an event organized by Bill France.

France, a former banker who also raced cars, was a key promoter of racing in Daytona Beach and the rest of the country during the 1940s, 1950s, and 1960s. In December 1947, France invited members of the racing industry to his Daytona Beach bar, on the roof of the Streamline Hotel, to discuss forming a national racing association. Out of that meeting, the National Association for Stock Car Auto Racing, or NASCAR, was born. Beach racing continued in Daytona Beach until 1959, when France opened the Daytona International Speedway.

Land-speed records, NASCAR racing, and motorcycle rallies gave Daytona Beach worldwide renown. It was a free-spirited place with an outlaw sensibility, which seemed to celebrate American individuality.

But by the 1970s, its rebellious nature clearly had an underbelly.

Dreamers, Drifters, and Condos

With its long strip of oceanfront hotels and its prized, driveable beach, Daytona continued to cater to families during the 1970s and 1980s. Increasingly, however, it also saw an influx of less desirable visitors, drawn by some vague appetite for a better, more vital life. The promise that Daytona's outlaw spirit held for these people was often quickly broken or forgotten, but many found something else that tethered them: a loose, gritty subculture of drifters who hung out in seedy bars and dealt drugs in run-down rooming houses. One of those who landed in Daytona during the early 1980s was serial killer Aileen Wournos, who lived here off and on throughout the decade. Wournos met her girlfriend Tyria Moore at a Daytona Beach gay bar in 1986 and killed the first of her seven male victims in the woods north of here in 1989. She was arrested for the last time in 1991 at a biker bar just south of Daytona Beach called the Last Resort.

Daytona's fringe culture haunted the Boardwalk, as well. While its rides and arcades always attracted families, the Boardwalk for a while also drew drug dealers, panhandlers, and what one Boardwalk business owner called "leftover hippies." In the 1980s, pedophiles frequented a park just north of the Boardwalk, preying on runaways.

Mark Wesley, who waited tables in Daytona Beach during the late 1970s and now lives in the Orlando area, says, "The Boardwalk was like an anthropological study. There were a lot of freaky people there. Also a lot of people who were just strung out. The way I described it was, it seemed to have a perpetual hangover."

Bob Szerokman, who still works on the Boardwalk, remembers it more fondly. "This used to be a poor man's beach, the place where the working man could come. In the seventies, this time of year, everyone came here and had a good time. It was always crowded. There were a lot of characters back then. We don't have so many characters anymore. The characters were better in the seventies."

As Orlando shifted into high gear, with the expansion of Walt Disney World and the addition of Universal Studios and other theme parks, Daytona became stuck, failing to capitalize on the fact that it was only fifty miles away. Its underbelly, meanwhile, grew. The oceanfront became known for its biker bars and tattoo parlors.

In the 1980s, city officials finally took steps to reinvent the Boardwalk, declaring the area "blighted" and creating a redevelopment district that gave rise to what is now sometimes called "the New Daytona Beach." The result so far is a $200 million complex known as Ocean Walk Village and Shoppes on the north end of the Boardwalk, which includes two condominium/hotel towers, restaurants such as Bubba Gump's and Johnny Rocket's, a Starbucks, and a ten-screen movie theater. It was built with the help of $22 million in city bonds. Carlsberg Management Company, a partner in the

Ocean Walk complex, now plans to add two 250-room condo/hotel buildings on the south end of the Boardwalk, along with fifty thousand square feet of retail and restaurant space.

The most controversial aspect of Carlsberg's new $20 million project is the displacement of longtime Boardwalk businesses, including the Joyland arcade, Midway Fun Center, Lisa's Gifts, Captain Darrell's Oyster Bar and Restaurant, Fun Fair go-cart track, and Pizza King. These Boardwalk establishments are all slated to be torn down and replaced with condo/hotel rooms and chain restaurants. The Daytona Beach City Commission has given its blessing to the plan, and filed circuit court suits to force several Boardwalk property owners to sell through the process of eminent domain.

The Carlsberg project will in effect replace the existing Boardwalk with a new one, which will be integrated into the adjacent high-rise condo/hotel/retail projects. The walk will also be extended about a half mile south, as part of a planned $1.3-million park project; there will be no businesses along the extension.

Not surprisingly, several Boardwalk business owners are upset about the new Daytona Beach that is being foisted upon them. Some say that what's planned shouldn't even be called a boardwalk; it's more a residential/retail complex with a sidewalk. Proponents say this is what a twenty-first-century boardwalk should be: slick rather than honky-tonk, with an upscale blend of commercial and residential development. The controversy here mirrors debates in other boardwalk towns, where escalating land values are "changing the organism," as Myrtle Beach's Buz Plyler says—where the tried-and-true traditions of midway games and carnival rides are literally losing ground to developers who want to build condominiums.

In Daytona Beach, it turns out, there may be room for both.

A New Postcard

Bill Geary became interested in Daytona Beach in the late 1980s, he says, when the city was looking to turn a corner and redevelop its Boardwalk area. "The more we studied Daytona Beach," Geary says, "the more we realized the tremendous potential that existed there. And the more we saw how its resources weren't being utilized."

Geary, who is sixty-one, is president of Carlsberg Management Company, the Los Angeles–based real estate firm that is redeveloping the Boardwalk. Carlsberg, which owns and manages forty-seven properties in eight states, bought land near the Boardwalk fifteen years ago, with plans to build a Sheraton hotel, but, as Geary describes it now, "The real estate market went into a depression, and it was never built." That property, along with several Boardwalk parcels purchased since then, will be used for the new development.

Although the bulk of the Carlsberg project will be two condominium towers, Geary maintains that amusements will play an important role in the new Boardwalk. Carlsberg's plans include a widened pier, with a ninety-foot Ferris wheel, a roller coaster, an old-fashioned carousel, and other rides— something akin to the Santa Monica Pier in California, says Geary.

"It's not just to preserve the historic nature of the Boardwalk," he says. "There's also the fact that Daytona Beach has a tremendous number of tourists each year—about eight or nine million—and there's very little for them to do, other than the beach. It's kind of amazing, when you compare it to places like Myrtle Beach and the other beach communities. I think we're all convinced an amusement facility on the pier would be a great success.

"What's happened over the years in Daytona Beach is that for some reason this community sat back and watched as Orlando became such an explosive city with thirty or forty million visitors. But the one thing Orlando doesn't have is the beach. And if we can bring the Orlando tourist here, we're going to multiply the business and income in the community. But in order to do that, you've got to have the facilities that these people want, which is theme restaurants and a nice hotel and modern attractions. I see the pier amusements as being part of that."

Although Geary's plans won the approval of the Daytona Beach City Commission, he still had to contend with the strong and vocal opposition of a few Boardwalk property owners, one of whom has been likened to a modern-day David, battling the Goliath of big-money development.

DINO PASPALAKIS'S FAMILY HAS owned Boardwalk property here since the early 1960s, when his father, Augustine Paspalakis, bought the Joyland amusements arcade for $300,000. Today Dino owns Joyland, and his sister owns the adjoining Lisa's Gifts. Paspalakis also holds a ninety-nine-year lease on the Midway Fun Center.

"I grew up working here on the Boardwalk," says Paspalakis. "My sister and I have been running the business since my father passed away in 1987. My father didn't build this business and give me this property on the Boardwalk to have it stolen by some greedy developer and some greedy city staff."

It is an early autumn afternoon in Daytona Beach, several weeks before a scheduled court hearing on the eminent domain case.

"The city staff thinks penny arcades attract a low class of people. The fact of the matter is, boardwalks attract families. Whether you're wealthy or not, every child loves to play video games. Every child loves to play Skee-Ball. Many of the people running the city don't even come down to the Boardwalk and see the type of families that we get on a daily basis. Sometimes we are jam-packed. They don't see that. They don't know what they're doing. The only difference between our boardwalk and Wildwood or some of the others is that we're a lot more compact. But if you look at the industry average and see what the top video games are, this boardwalk has every one of them. It has the same basic attractions as other boardwalks. It's a place you go to walk and watch people. It's got the hot dogs, candied apples, pizza, rides, games.

Fig. 70. Dino Paspalakis, with his grandfather on the Daytona Beach Boardwalk in 1971. (Courtesy of Dino Paspalakis)

"What the developer, Bill Geary, wants to do is take half the Boardwalk away, put in restaurants and a swimming pool that caters to his private hotel, and then get rid of most of the amusements. That goes against the idea of what a boardwalk is. Once you make the hotel control such a large portion of it, it's not the same place. It's not a boardwalk. So I'm going to fight this."

Traditionally, Paspalakis explains, eminent domain has been used to facilitate new roads or bridges, but in the past two decades, it has often been a tool helping developers to seize property from small businesses or homeowners so they can construct large-scale shopping centers and hotel complexes. "It's not American," he adds. "It goes against the American Dream of working hard to build a business."

"You have to understand, they're taking my property for what they say is the 'elimination of blight,' but the definition of blight is so broad that it can mean anything. Whenever the city says it wants a piece of property and asks a consultant if it's blighted, they come back and say it's blighted. If they were truly looking for blight, they would go to property that has devalued, but what they do is blight the most profitable areas, then give it to developers that they favor."

In 2003 and 2004, the eminent domain battle over Paspalakis's arcade property received national attention. Paspalakis says he felt he was fighting over more than just the Daytona Beach Boardwalk. "What I feel is that I'm fighting everybody's fight. Property rights should be sacred in America. If my property can be taken, anyone else's can, and that's not right. If you can build a bigger house than your neighbor, should that entitle you to take your neighbor's property away? The answer is no."

To Bill Geary, on the other hand, eminent domain is a necessary process. "One part of redevelopment that some people don't accept is that there has to be some pain for there to be some benefit, and there has to be a way to prevent one business owner from standing in the way of progress. . . . I've known Dino for years, and I'm sympathetic, but, you know, it's the market that's demanding the change, not us. The land is too valuable. It just doesn't make sense to use it for a bunch of arcades. The fact is, it's going to happen whether you like it or not. That's how the market works. If it wasn't me, it would be someone else."

Fig. 71. The saltwater taffy pull, in a window on Main Street.

IN LATE OCTOBER 2004, just weeks before the court hearing over the eminent domain case, Paspalakis and Carlsberg reached a settlement after a fifteen-hour mediation. It was a compromise of sorts for both sides. Carlsberg purchased the Paspalakis properties, Joyland and Lisa's Gifts, for a reported $2.6 million, while Paspalakis was guaranteed that he could operate an arcade on the Boardwalk "in perpetuity," as part of the Carlsberg project. Geary says the agreement will leave the three stores on the south end of the Boardwalk intact, "which actually worked out, because if we put in the amusements pier, it will all flow together with the arcades." Three other property owners were still awaiting eminent domain proceedings.

More recently, Carlsberg raised some eyebrows when Geary's partner Jerry Fincke said at a public meeting that the plan to put amusements on the pier had been shifted to the back burner. Geary calls it a misunderstanding. "Amusements are an important part of what we want to do," he says. Geary predicts the amusements will be operating by 2007 or 2008. "I think when we put that Ferris wheel back on the pier, it's going to become the new postcard for Daytona Beach."

Waiting for the Storm

Sheets of plywood are stacked against a wall at the Pizza King restaurant on the Boardwalk as Hurricane Jeanne spirals on a collision course with Daytona Beach. It's a Friday afternoon, normally a busy time here, but today much

Fig. 72. The Mardi Gras arcade, one of the businesses that was at the center of the eminent domain controversy.

of the oceanfront is deserted. Several Boardwalk arcades and food stands are already boarded up. Behind the counter, a television is tuned to the Weather Channel, where a reporter is relaying the latest news. He's standing on the beach only a few blocks south of Pizza King, using the Daytona Beach Pier as a backdrop.

"We just took down the plywood from the last storm, and now we're putting it up again," says Pizza King owner Steve Petras. He opens the oven to check on a slice of pizza. Jeanne is the fourth hurricane in the past six weeks to threaten Daytona Beach. Two of the previous storms, Charley and Frances, left behind considerable damage. "I've never seen anything like this in all the years I've been here."

Petras is the man who introduced pizza to Daytona, back in 1958. As he tells it, speaking with a strong Greek accent, "I came down to visit a friend. I am from one of the islands in Greece. At that time, I was living in St. Louis, Missouri. I came down here and I liked it very much. I had lived by the water in Greece, so when I saw the opportunity to come here and be by the water again, I did."

Thirty-seven years before Petras arrived, Jim Forest, a Greek immigrant who had recently Americanized his name from Demetrios Fooriotis, stepped off a train in Daytona Beach and went to work in the restaurant business. Later, he opened the Forest Amusement Park on the Boardwalk and, through a partnership with other Greek business owners, bought up a large parcel of Boardwalk property. Today most of the Boardwalk businesses in Daytona Beach are owned or operated by Greek families. That will change with the new Boardwalk.

Fig. 73. Steve Petras, in front of Pizza King: "They're making a mistake."

"There are going to be a lot of changes in Daytona Beach," says Petras. "That's too bad." When Petras opened his restaurant, he says, "our visitors used to come from Tennessee, Georgia, Alabama. The northern people didn't come here yet. They went to Miami, Fort Lauderdale, places like that. That changed in the 1960s. That's when the college students started coming here. That was one big change.

"Now the big change is that all the old motels are being turned into condos. That's the future of Daytona Beach. They're making a mistake trying to take away the Boardwalk, though. The Boardwalk was always the place where everyone could come and feel comfortable. It's the place where if you're a doctor, lawyer, executive, priest, it doesn't matter. Anyone comes here and no one knows who you are. You don't have that anywhere else. You don't have it in a shopping center. A lot of my customers, they've been coming here for years and years, and they sit in here and they tell me they're very upset they closed the beach [to automobiles]. They say they don't like the changes they see on the Boardwalk. All these plans, I don't think it's going to work. I think it's going to fail."

Outside, palm trees are whipping wildly up and down the Boardwalk. There's a spray of rain in the wind. Petras pulls out the pizza slice and serves it to his only customer, then checks CNN for a storm update. Ironically, the devastating 2004 Florida hurricane season seems to be hastening what has been happening in Daytona Beach for years. Many motels along Atlantic Avenue are still boarded up because of damage from Charley and Frances. Some will never reopen. Daytona Beach's long-standing reputation as an "affordable" resort has for many years kept its land values below those elsewhere on the Florida coast, but that's all changing now. More than two dozen mom-and-pop motels have been bought up by developers who plan to tear them down and build upscale condominium projects.

As evening approaches, the Boardwalk is all shuttered closed. Torn palm fronds litter the streets. On the beach, a few people are standing in the wind, watching the roiling sea. There are always those who linger as a hurricane approaches, who pause to contemplate the savage power and unpredictability of what is coming. The approaching storm compresses time, heightens awareness. It lets us marvel for a few moments at the immensity of all that is beyond our ability to forecast or prevent.

Suddenly, it begins to rain.

CHAPTER ELEVEN

VENICE BEACH, CALIFORNIA

Land unto Itself

I T STARTED with a coin toss and a choice. Abbot Kinney won the toss and made the choice: He would take the uninhabited parcel of marshland to the south, leaving the developed, seemingly more valuable half of Ocean Park to his former partners, who had bought their way into Kinney's land development company two years earlier. The choice surprised them. They did not know what the brilliant and eccentric speculator planned to do with the property.

Kinney was a distinguished, bearded, red-haired man with eclectic interests and large appetites—an author, businessman, botanist, and world traveler who spoke seven languages. Among his numerous endeavors, Kinney had started and built a lucrative tobacco business, translated a history text for Ulysses S. Grant, and toured West Coast Indian territory with author Helen Hunt Jackson, a trip that became the basis for her best-selling novel *Ramona.*

An asthmatic, Kinney came to Southern California in 1880 to stay at a health spa east of Los Angeles. Finding the climate agreeable, he wound up building a hilltop house nearby, selling his shares in the tobacco company, and becoming a Los Angeles land speculator. In time, Kinney formed a partnership with businessman Francis Ryan, and together they purchased the

Fig. 74. (OPPOSITE) Abbot Kinney, the founder of Venice-of-America, circa 1912. (Courtesy of the Kinney family.)

Ocean Park Casino in Santa Monica, along with several hundred acres of beachfront property. Kinney married in 1884 and soon after built a beach cottage in Santa Monica. He was, by most accounts, content with his land development business and his life in Southern California, but that changed after Ryan died suddenly in the fall of 1898. Six months later, Ryan's widow married Thomas Dudley, a Santa Monica businessman who was often at odds with Kinney. The strong-willed Kinney also did not get along with the three businessmen who purchased Matilda Ryan's 50 percent interest in 1902. In 1904, the four men agreed to dissolve the partnership, dividing their land with a coin flip.

Fig. 75. The crowds on Windward Avenue in 1905, the opening season for Venice-of-America. (Courtesy of the Los Angeles Public Library.)

Kinney's grandiose plan was to turn his marshy portion into an Old World–themed seaside village, based loosely on Venice, Italy. Venice-of-America, as he called it, would feature colonnaded Venetian-style architecture, an auditorium for dance and theater performances, art galleries, European gardens, strings of lights, and miles of canals with gondolas and gondoliers. The planned community would also include a pier with a ship-style restaurant, amusements, and a two-and-a-half-mile miniature railway. Kinney hoped the development would spark a cultural renaissance in the United States.

People thought his idea a little kooky at first, some calling it "Kinney's Folly." As the exotic-looking community took shape, however, skepticism turned to excitement, and building lots were snapped up along the canals. Kinney set July 4, 1905, as the grand opening date. When a storm battered the coast on March 13, destroying the new pier and auditorium, Kinney hired 600 men to work around the clock to ensure that Venice-of-America opened on time. It did. Some forty thousand people showed up for opening day, most arriving by trolley, to stroll amid the Byzantine- and Renaissance-styled architecture, to ride gondolas through the sixteen miles of canals, to enjoy the arcades and eateries, and to swim in the saltwater plunge. About $400,000 worth of property was sold that day.

Venice-of-America was an unqualified success—although Kinney had misjudged one thing: People were less interested in the community's cultural attractions than they were in being entertained. It was the rides and games they lined up for, not the art and music. The next year, Kinney added more amusements and built the Midway Plaisance, based on the midway model created for the 1893 Chicago World's Columbian Exposition. Attractions included a funhouse, games of chance, a wild animal arena, belly dancers, and such sideshow attractions as Filipino headhunters and the eight-foot man and thirty-inch woman. Venice soon became known as a thriving seaside amusement park with such rides as Race Thru the Clouds, which was the first roller coaster on the West Coast, the Scenic Railroad, the Tunnel of Love, the Giant Dipper, the Captive Airplane, and the Dragon Slide.

Unfortunately, though, the city of Venice, which incorporated in 1911, was frequently mired in political and financial difficulties. By the 1920s, the novelty and usefulness of Kinney's canal system had disappeared. Many of the canals were filled with silt, and the city often reeked of dead fish. Kinney had underestimated the effect the automobile would have on American culture and travel patterns.

With the city's financial difficulties mounting, residents bitterly debated Venice's future, some favoring annexation to the city of Santa Monica, others wanting to join Los Angeles. Several bond initiatives and annexation proposals were voted down before finally, in late 1925, Venice became a part of Los Angeles.

The city filled in most of Kinney's canals and turned them into roads. Venice's attractiveness as a resort was further diminished after the Ohio Oil Company discovered oil in south Venice in 1929. Suddenly, Venice's skyline consisted of dozens of oil derricks. With only limited environmental laws on the books, oil often soiled beaches, closing them to swimmers. For several decades, until its resurgence in the 1970s, Venice was seedy and run-down.

Today Venice Beach is neither a sophisticated cultural center nor an amusement park. It is a place so compellingly odd that it defies simple description. The concrete Oceanfront Walk—commonly called "the Boardwalk"—is the focal point of Venice Beach, crowded every weekend with street performers, Rollerbladers, bodybuilders, panhandlers, psychics, movie stars, drug addicts, street preachers, merchants, and plenty of people just there to watch. Venice still seems run-down in places, but property values are among the highest in the country. It's a fiercely tolerant, though often politically contentious, resort, which seems to have its own unwritten rules of behavior and logic. Freedom here is defined differently than it is elsewhere.

Fig. 76. Skateboarders on a late afternoon in Venice Beach.

The Venice Beach of today, while not what Abbot Kinney envisioned when he opened Venice-of-America in 1905, can, in a sense, be traced to him—to his sense of individuality and to his idea of building a land unto itself. Historian and author Elayne Alexander, who is writing a biography of Abbot Kinney, points out: "History isn't places, it's people. That's especially true in Venice Beach. There has always been a welcoming attitude here. People are accepted whoever they are—and even valued for their unusual thought processes, more so than anywhere else I've ever been. That all goes back to Abbot Kinney, who was a very egalitarian man."

One Step at a Time

On a gray, drizzly winter morning, Elayne Alexander drives through the streets of Venice Beach, telling stories about some of the people who lived here and passed through: George Freeth, who introduced surfing and lifeguarding to Southern California; Orson Welles, who shot scenes for *Touch of Evil* at Windward Avenue; Charlie Chaplin, whose first Little Tramp appearance was filmed on the Boardwalk; Arnold Schwarzenegger, who pumped iron for years in Venice; and Jim Morrison of the Doors, whose towering image is painted on a building a block off the Boardwalk.

Mural art decorates the sides of buildings all over Venice, she says. It's a tradition that goes back to the beatniks who used to hang out at the Gas House and the Venice West Café.

On Pacific Avenue, she stops at the original Gold's Gym, opened in 1965 by a self-described "beach bum" named Joe Gold with equipment he built from old cars. During the late 1960s, Gold's Gym was the mecca of American bodybuilding.

Driving north, she indicates where the old Kinney canals once flowed and points out the homes of actors Dennis Hopper, Julia Roberts, and Orson Bean.

Fig. 77. Rip Cronk's giant mural of singer Jim Morrison, a onetime Venice resident. Cronk painted it in 1991.

"This building used to be the King George Hotel. That was where Aimee Semple McPherson—Sister Aimee—was last seen before her disappearance," she says. McPherson, founder of the Church of the Foursquare Gospel, came here to Venice Beach one morning in May 1926 to go swimming. "In those days, you checked into a hotel, changed clothes, and then came out onto the beach. She came here with her secretary, and she walked out onto the beach and promptly disappeared." Divers searched for days without finding her. The story of Aimee McPherson's disappearance became national news, with "sightings" reported all over the country. Then, five weeks after she vanished, Sister Aimee showed up in the Arizona desert, claiming to have been kidnapped. "But the story didn't ring true, and another story began to circulate: that she was in Carmel with her radio operator boyfriend and they had staged this whole thing to get away for a while. In those days, you didn't do things like that. Especially someone who was an evangelist." The city of Los Angeles brought charges against Sister Aimee, although they were mysteriously dropped the next year. "Back then, you could pay people off very easily in the city," says Alexander. "I suppose you probably still can."

She stops at an old green wooden house and gazes at it for a moment before speaking. "That was Kinney's place," she says. "He moved here in 1905."

The Kinney house doesn't look a hundred years old—which, she says, has been one of the problems with efforts to have it declared a historic site. "The second floor was made into an apartment in the forties, and for that reason we can't historically landmark it. We've had a terrible time trying to save this house. We've tried to landmark a number of buildings, and the city of Los Angeles does everything they can to prevent it."

Although Kinney moved here with his wife and sons, he also had a mistress, Winifred Harwell, who lived in nearby Santa Monica with their two illegitimate children. After his wife died in 1911, Kinney married Winifred and adopted the two children. Kinney died in 1920, of lung cancer, at age seventy.

Driving back toward the Boardwalk, Alexander talks about her own migration to Southern California in 1968. "I was living in the Washington, D.C., area. I made the decision quickly," she recalls. "I just got in my car and decided to drive to California. I'd been working as a model, and I thought I could continue my modeling career out here. Boy, was I surprised. All these actresses were trying to get into movies. So that was the end of my modeling career. I was twenty-six years old.

"I was a photographer and a writer. I came down here to roller-skate, but I also became very interested in the history of Venice Beach and in taking pictures of the old canals that were still left.

"I see my role here as trying to save as much as I can and to educate people. This city has a fascinating past, but there aren't many people interested in saving it. The city is trying to change the character of Venice, one step at a time. They want to turn this into Miami Beach. It's gradual, so many people don't see it happening."

She talks again about Kinney and his failed dream of a cultural renaissance by the sea. "What Kinney wanted to do was very daring for a number of reasons. At the time he created Venice, Ocean Park was an already established resort. Here he was putting another one right next to it. They were very powerful men who owned the other part, and they fought him every step of the way. You may have noticed that a lot of fighting goes on in Venice. That, too, can be traced to Kinney."

Free Speech Zone

Before the sun rises over the waterfront, dozens of people are camped out along the east side of the Oceanfront Walk, waiting for nine o'clock, when they can cross to the west side. The damp air is scented occasionally with marijuana and breakfast meats. Some of the people are sleeping. Others are talking, smoking, playing cards, listening to music. For vendors, there are literally two sides to the Venice Beach Boardwalk. Those who sell merchandise along the east side are either property owners or renters. For many of them, rents have jumped in recent years with the rise in property values. On the west side, vendors open up card tables and sell their goods to the same passing promenaders, without paying rent, taxes, or overhead. In some cases, they sell the same products that store owners across the walk are selling.

How things got to this point says a lot about the nature of Venice Beach. Back in the 1970s, the west side of the Boardwalk was mostly the domain of street entertainers—jugglers, magicians, musicians, comics. They were part of the carnival atmosphere that, along with roller-skating, had bestowed a new cachet upon Venice Beach. Gradually, though, that changed. Although vending was prohibited by city law on the west side, artists would paint there and sell their works for "donations." Incense sellers claimed they were exempt from the no-vending law by their right to religious freedom.

The west side is nicknamed "the Free Speech Zone," but the definition of free speech can be very nebulous in Venice. When police allowed the vending to continue, more and more people took advantage. By last summer, the whole west side was lined with merchandise sellers. There wasn't even room to cross over to the beach in places. Now, with people arriving before dawn to fight over spaces, the city is finally taking action, creating a lottery that it hopes will control the problem.

Venice Beach has always been a welcoming place that encourages what Alexander calls "unusual thought processes." Solving problems here is seldom simple. As businesswoman Carol Tautau says, "Venice is the only city in the world where if you get three people together in a room to discuss an issue, you'll end up with four different points of view."

THE BUILDING THAT HOUSES Small World Books, with its distinctive red-and-white awning, was a boarded-up warehouse when owner Mary Good-fader moved here from Marina del Rey. Someone had spray-painted GET OUT OF CAMBODIA on the front, she recalls.

"Venice was a more troubled place then," says Goodfader. "My husband saw this building and thought things might get better. They did. With the roller-skating boom in the late 1970s, it changed. I think Venice is a really unique community because of the artists and the writers, and the Holly-wood element now. The thing I like best about Venice is its diversity. There are many smart people who live here. They're good readers. There are also some things that I don't like."

Goodfader has supported the lottery plan. Because of that, a sign re-cently went up across the Boardwalk urging strollers to BOYCOTT SIDEWALK CAFÉ. The adjoining Sidewalk Café, owned by her son Jay Goodfader, is a Boardwalk tradition and a prime place for people-watching.

"It's just a good idea," she says of the lottery. "It's gotten out of hand to the point that people start camping out at five a.m. now for a spot, and they can't go over there until nine. So the people who live around here just have to be woken up by these horrible goings-on. They're fighting now because there aren't enough spaces for everyone. And they all think they're entitled to have a rent-free spot."

FOR THE PAST FIFTEEN years, Noel Kehrlein has watched the Venice Beach parade from a beach chair on the west side, where she works as a psy-chic five days a week. "My readings are psychologically based, not fortune-tellings," she explains. "The real purpose of a reading, or the way people should use them, is as a tool for self-knowledge."

Kehrlein, who grew up in San Francisco, says she was "one of those pi-oneering unwed mothers back in the sixties." She went on to earn two de-grees in psychology.

"What I like about working here is that it's outdoors and people from all over the world come here. I've read for princes and princesses and for movie stars. I read for someone who had just gotten off death row and for another man who just had a sex change to a woman and said he was afraid he'd made a mistake. One of my most unusual readings was Roseanne Barr, because when I put her cards down, I said, 'Wow, I see babies everywhere.' She wasn't even married at the time. I had no idea she was trying to get pregnant. And she said on Jay Leno a few days later: 'A psychic told me she saw babies everywhere.' "

Although it's rare that people leave San Francisco for Los Angeles, she says, Kehrlein prefers the mood here. "Venice Beach promotes free expression. Everyone here is creative. San Francisco seems more yuppiefied. The thing I like least about Venice is the crazies. Not the homeless—the homeless are fine. They sometimes even help us set up. But the crazies are scary, especially when they get on drugs.

"The most remarkable thing about the Venice Boardwalk is that we've really formed a community. We have people from all different countries, all different socioeconomic classes. We have no boss, but we have managed to become a community and to police ourselves, with rules that seem to work. There are street rules and there are cop rules, and we've been able to form this community with our own rules.

"The way we do that is, we decided we would each pick a space and stay there, and then we would help each other keep it. We wouldn't bounce all around. Everyone on this block looks out for one another. So if you have to go to the bathroom, you feel no one will take your stuff. And each block sort of does the same thing, some better than others. Of course, this was easier when there weren't as many people. Now, you've got times where two people are fighting for the same spot. We decided that if a new person comes in on this block and tries to take someone's spot, we'll all group together and talk that person out of it. So we sort of formed a system, respecting each other and helping each other."

She says she isn't worried about the new lottery, although it will probably reduce her working hours. "In some ways, it'll be easier. I've been through the lottery system in Berkeley. Others haven't been through it, so they're freaking out. They don't know what a lottery is. I've been on this

Fig. 78. Noel Kehrlein has worked as a psychic on the Boardwalk for fifteen years.

same block for fifteen years and now I'll have to move around. It will cost me my spot some days, but if they do it right, it should be okay. It's out of control right now."

THE IDEA OF IMPOSING a lottery to regulate a boardwalk that operates almost like its own country has riled up some of the longtime Boardwalk habitués. Probably the best-known Boardwalk performer is Harry Perry, who plays Jimi Hendrix–style electric guitar riffs while Rollerblading back and forth along the walk, dressed in a white robe and turban.

Perry came to Los Angeles from Detroit in the 1970s, he says, "to break into the music business. I started doing this in Hollywood. It was the same thing there except there's more smog. It's more breathable here. I'm a professional street performer. I call myself a guerrilla artist. Being a street musician, there's a lot of freedom in that. But freedom is not automatic. The idea of freedom is different everywhere you go. I came here because Venice Beach has always been a Free Speech Zone."

Perry says he defines freedom as the right to pursue his livelihood. "They've changed the definition of freedom now in Venice by saying you have to buy a license and enter the lottery. That's not what Venice is about.

"This is the Free Speech Zone, and it will stay that way. The people will determine that, not the city. The city can do anything. They can build casinos here if they want, and as long as we keep our freedom, it's okay. You can't change that. The people here will not allow it. The reason this is happening now is because an appointed councilperson pushed for it. We didn't vote her in. She snuck in when they rearranged how the districts were set up. This is our world. It'll stay a free zone."

Perry, who says he is a Sikh, calls his music "an extension" of his religious beliefs. "I practice that there is but one God. Truth is his name. Great and indescribable is his wisdom."

"No Place Else in the Country"

"After being here for a number of years, I find everywhere else boring," says Larry Gutin, co-owner of the Boardwalk shop Ocean Blue. "It's really a bizarre little place. There is always something crazy going on. There are characters everywhere. You can see hobo bums sitting out there, or you might see Robert Graham and Angelica Huston taking a beach walk with their dog—they live right around the corner. But the thing that's cool is that everybody down-dresses. So the really rich and the really poor are all in shorts and T-shirts. I didn't even know Faye Dunaway was in my shop until my wife came up and said, 'By the way, that's Faye Dunaway.' She was on Rollerblades. Arnold used to come here every weekend with his wife and kids. David Bowie was in the shop once."

Guiton, who owns Ocean Blue with his older brother Jeff, is eating a casserole lunch out of a Styrofoam box on a picnic table behind the store he rents on the Boardwalk. He grew up in Rockland County, New York, and has worked in Venice for more than twenty years. Ocean Blue sells jewelry, aromatherapy products, salts, oils, incense, imported candles, metal crafts, and other items. The Guitons import most of what they sell.

"The funny thing I've found about Venice," he says, "is that people always come back here. Whether it's a trip, a vacation, or they live here and they leave, something always brings them back. And I laugh because basically it's the last stop. You can't go any farther. It's the end of the road."

He eats in earnest for a while, then looks up. It's a warm, sunny afternoon in Venice Beach. "But here's the other side of it. The playing field here isn't level. And what's insane is that there's nothing you can do about it. Nothing at all. Across the Boardwalk there's a sign that says NO COMMERCIAL VENDING. If I were to ask you what that is over there, you would look at it and say it's all commercial vending. But if you ask any of them, they'll tell you it's their right to free expression. They'll say they're allowed to sell incense under freedom of religion because frankincense was sold by the Christians two thousand years ago. And the police don't do anything about it. If you read the law, it's very clear. Nothing's allowed on that side.

"This side of the Boardwalk is governed by variances, conditional-use permits. You can't set up poles. Your signs can only be so big. Over there, they don't even need to have a sales tax license. The city comes out here and they check each of our licenses, but they don't even talk to those people, and some of those people are taking in as much money as those on the private side.

"I used to be really involved in this," he adds. "I spearheaded a merchants' association, and we had almost every merchant involved. We put money together and we lobbied, but it never went anywhere. It's worse today than it was before. People do have a right to exercise their freedoms. Do they have a right to run businesses without the proper permits? I don't think so.

"What happens is, as soon as you get a good item, they'll set up on the public side and start selling it for less. I'll give you an example. I was one of the big incense stores on the beach. I sold a lot of incense, imported stuff, handmade, hand dipped. All that stuff used to do well for me. Then, for some reason, they allowed people on my side to move to the other side and set up and sell incense. Police said, 'You can't be there,' but they all said, 'Yes we can, we have a religious right.' They all banded together and the police laid off it. In 1998, 1999, 2000, I did about eighty thousand dollars a year in incense sales. I'm lucky if I do fifteen thousand now. It's all commercial boxed incense they're selling, the same product I'm selling. But I can't do anything about it.

"There is no place else in the country where this sort of thing happens. That's what sort of blows me away. Why don't people set up in downtown L.A.? Nobody sets up in downtown L.A. because the police don't allow it. And I wonder why the police allow it here. It's the same law, it's the same city."

Guiton isn't so frustrated that he intends to leave, however. "I'm a working guy. I have children. And I like it here." He's pleased that the Boardwalk was recently rebuilt with new recreation areas and bathrooms. "It could have been real vanilla and it isn't. I like the fact that it's the playground for a major urban city and it's free."

He's heard the stories about developers turning Venice Beach into South Beach West but doesn't buy it. "There are too many different factions here," he says. "There are also some real zoning issues. They can try to get variances, but this community is hardcore. I mean, they'll come out in droves. I don't think it's mature enough for that yet."

Out on the Boardwalk, a man is juggling chainsaws. A Rollerblader goes by in a clown suit, followed by two sinewy girls in bikinis. In the next block, two men with dreadlocks are selling shirts and smoking marijuana. A gray-haired woman in a long flower-print dress shouts incoherently at the bicyclists and skaters. An old man whose belongings are in a shopping cart bangs his hand against an electric bass guitar and laughs, pretending to be a street performer. A pair of buffed men jog past, shirtless, talking baseball. At the Boardwalk Café, a couple is sipping white wine, watching it all. The man's wearing a beret. On a warm weekend afternoon, it's easy to become a little intoxicated by the hypnotic rhythms and strange logic of this place— even knowing the bitter conflicts beneath the surface—and to understand why people always come back to Venice Beach.

CHAPTER TWELVE

SANTA CRUZ, CALIFORNIA

Perfect Composition

C HARLES CANFIELD is sitting in his office above the Santa Cruz Boardwalk, watching Monterey Bay and the Municipal Wharf, considering a
question: Why does this boardwalk continue to prosper when so many
other West Coast amusement parks have been forced to close down?

"I think some of it goes back to our philosophy," he says, "which is,
we try to maintain our history but also incorporate the new. We've stayed
pretty authentic, which is not always easy to do. We keep a lot of the old
things even though they don't make much money, and we reinvest in them.
We do things that sometimes don't make economic sense, but they make
sense in other ways."

The Santa Cruz Beach Boardwalk is a quintessential American boardwalk. Conceived a hundred years ago as the Coney Island/Atlantic City of
the West, it retains the look and feel of a model seaside amusement park,
with its Cyclone-like Giant Dipper roller coaster, its beautifully restored
1911 Looff carousel, and dozens of other rides, games, and food concessions.
While the real Coney Island is today a place of faded glory, this western version has managed to stay shiny and colorful.

The best explanation is this: Santa Cruz is the only major American
boardwalk that is privately owned. Charles Canfield's family has operated

*Fig. 79. (OPPOSITE) The Santa
Cruz Beach Boardwalk, as seen
from the Municipal Wharf with
the Santa Cruz Mountains in the
background.*

189

the Santa Cruz walk since 1952, guiding it through some choppy waters while keeping it clean and attractive, classic yet current. Private ownership brings opportunities that municipally run boardwalks don't have. The Boardwalk here is patrolled by private security, for example, not by police, and it has been able to establish some unusual rules, by the standards of other beach resorts. This is the only boardwalk where smoking is banned (although strollers are allowed to carry open beer cans as long as they purchased them on the Boardwalk). Private ownership is not in itself an advantage, but Canfield's company has made it one.

Canfield, who is sixty-three and slightly gruff in an agreeable way, gives much of the credit to his father, Laurence Canfield, who became president of the Santa Cruz Seaside Company in 1952. "My father anticipated the future," he says. "He started consolidating the property across the street to get the parking that would drive our business. He kind of got his arms around that early on. I don't know if we'd be in business now if we didn't have the parking. Then, in the sixties, he brought in the private security to give us more control."

Canfield was eleven when his father took over the company, and he has good memories of traveling around the country with him, visiting other parks and boardwalks. "My father studied the industry. He paid attention. Of course, everyone was watching Disney when they came online in 1955. Their whole program was the enclosed environment. In a sense, we have that here. We just don't have an admission gate."

When his father died in 1984, Canfield took the reins of the Seaside Company, and he has managed to keep the balance that distinguishes this park, bringing in new rides, while refurbishing older attractions. Senior staff members (at least one of whom does a pretty good, entirely respectful impersonation of the boss) credit his vision and instincts with keeping the Boardwalk progressive in an increasingly competitive and complicated amusements industry.

In the halls of the Seaside Company offices are a number of penny-a-play mechanical arcade machines that Canfield has collected, some going back a hundred years. The older ones are mostly test-your-strength games or machines that give the player a slight electric shock. Recently, the Seaside Company paid fifty thousand dollars for a 1930s funhouse animatronic figure known as Laughing Sal. The bloated, clownlike Sal fascinated and scared generations of amusement park patrons with its toothy smile and crazed laugh. This one comes from Playland, the giant waterfront amusement park in San Francisco that closed in 1972. Laughing Sal will be displayed on the Boardwalk at the entrance to the Neptune's Kingdom arcade, along with a Boardwalk history exhibition. At the same time, the Seaside Company is about to unveil its new 125-foot "drop" ride, the Double Shot. "So we're doing both," says Canfield. "We're bringing in something new, bringing in something old."

IT'S A WINTER MORNING, and the sun is sparkling on Monterey Bay as Canfield walks the Santa Cruz Boardwalk, talking about changes over the years and plans for the future. Four-tenths of a mile long, the Boardwalk is a compact mix of thirty-five rides, twenty-seven games, thirty-six food vendors, and fifteen shops. He begins his tour at Cocoanut Grove, once a famous dance hall that hosted most of the great big bands— Artie Shaw, the Dorseys, Benny Goodman. It was converted into a convention and banquet facility in the 1980s. Next to Cocoanut Grove are the Grand Arcades: Casino and Neptune's Kingdom, which contain about three hundred games, ranging from a 1910 fortune-telling machine to a laser tag arena to a pirate-themed miniature golf course to pinball games and simulators.

As his father did, Canfield studies the industry, traveling to trade shows and to other resorts. "The flip side of staying authentic," he says, "is that the industry is always changing." Canfield stops at the site of the new Double Shot ride. "This tower will give us a new dimension. We needed to introduce this sort of thing because young people are watching extreme sports now and some of the old rides are just a little too tame for them."

The proliferation of corporate theme parks over the past three decades has forced many old-fashioned amusement parks out of business. Canfield says the Seaside Company has learned to adjust. When Paramount's Great America opened across the mountains in Santa Clara in the mid-1970s, "we were a little worried about it. We were flat the year they opened. Then we kind of analyzed

Fig. 80. Charles Canfield, president of the Santa Cruz Seaside Company, riding the 1911 Looff carousel.

what they had and what we didn't have. What they had were two flume rides. So we thought, 'Let's put a flume ride in.' That equalized things a bit.

"In a funny way, the corporate parks have helped us to be more of a family park," he adds. "Before they came along, I think we had more of a teenage market here. Then the bigger parks put in the thrill rides, and those attracted more of the teenagers. We can't compete with them in that kind of arena, so we sort of went the other way. We added more kiddie rides, and it became more attractive to families."

The clanky 1924 Big Dipper roller coaster is still the most popular ride in Santa Cruz, he says, with more than a million riders a year.

"You have to keep in mind, the Boardwalk appeals to a very basic need: the need to recreate. It's our instinct to go out and have fun. A lot of people struggle through the week at work, and if they can go out and just have a good time, it rejuvenates them. It's like going to a movie, something to distract them from the humdrum of everyday life. So I think we fill a definite need along with these other entertainment attractions. We have to give them something that does that and is also different from what they get elsewhere. That's our challenge."

His explanation puts the endurance and vitality of this boardwalk in perspective, although a more immediate explanation can be found on virtually any summer evening. The task of a boardwalk is to seduce, and Santa Cruz's does it better than most. The warm smells of caramel corn, fried Twinkies, and roller-coaster-track grease, the sounds of band organ music and screams, the cool sea wind, the colorful, whimsical façades, the glow of moonlight on the water through arcade arches, the muted cries of gulls and sea lions—everything fits together here the way things do in a perfect piece of music. Some boardwalk towns painstakingly plan their futures, while others are stalled in debates over what they want to become. Canfield and the Seaside Company don't have those problems. "Sometimes," he says, "I think we're kind of a steward for Americana here. That's not such a bad thing to be."

Swanta Cruz

The man responsible for developing the Santa Cruz beachfront as a major tourist destination was a local businessman named Fred Swanton. Born in

Brooklyn, New York, Swanton grew up in Santa Cruz and graduated from business school in San Francisco. He was a persuasive and driven man who launched several successful businesses in the Santa Cruz area before developing the Boardwalk—among them an electric railway, a billboard company, a fish hatchery, and, with several partners, the Santa Cruz Electric Light and Power Company.

The earliest tourists to Santa Cruz came, beginning in the 1860s, for the hot saltwater baths and for the supposed "medicinal" value of sea air and saltwater. The lure was similar to that of East Coast beach resorts. It wasn't until 1881, however, that train service reached the coast and Santa Cruz began to flourish as a resort. By this time, hot-water bathing had become popular throughout the country, not only on the coasts but also at "hot spring" resorts inland. With train service, grand hotels and other commercial establishments were built to serve the guests.

By 1903, close to a hundred thousand people were taking the train to Santa Cruz each year, and Swanton anticipated, correctly, that the beachfront was ripe for new, more diverse attractions. In October of that year, he formed the Santa Cruz Beach, Cottage and Tent City Corporation, known familiarly as the Santa Cruz Beach Company. Swanton was able to sell his vision of a recreational casino to the community—along with shares of stock in his company. The next year, the Santa Cruz Beach Company built the giant, Alhambra-style, onion-domed Neptune Casino. The Neptune featured a giant, heated saltwater swimming pool called a "plunge," a café, a ballroom, roof gardens, five hundred dressing rooms, and a theater. For guests unable to afford the expensive grand hotels and rooming houses in Santa Cruz, Swanton created a "Tent City" by the beach with 220 red-and-white-striped tent cottages where visitors could stay for as little as $3.50 a week. In effect, Swanton made the Santa Cruz seaside a resort for working- and middle-class visitors, setting a tone for the Boardwalk that continues today.

The first two seasons of the Casino were hugely successful. Swanton expanded the enterprise for 1905 by adding a skating rink, an ice cream parlor, and hot-air balloon rides. Early in the third season, though, a fire started in an upstairs kitchen and quickly spread, burning down the entire Casino. In this era of wood-frame buildings, fires were not uncommon in boardwalk towns. Some of the great amusement parks and beachfront hotels on the East Coast were lost to them. But unlike Coney Island's Dreamland, which burned down in 1911 and never reopened, Swanton's Casino was back in business the next season. Almost immediately after the fire, Swanton convinced investors to rebuild on a grander scale—most importantly financier John Martin, who ended up contributing nearly a million dollars.

Fig. 81. Fred Swanton's first Casino building was destroyed in this 1906 fire. (Courtesy Santa Cruz Seaside Company Archives.)

The new, larger Casino and adjacent Boardwalk opened on June 15, 1907. Mixing Moorish architecture with California Mission style, the Casino included a dance pavilion, dining rooms, a theater, and a roof garden. John Philip Sousa provided entertainment at the inaugural ball. President Theodore Roosevelt, who had visited Santa Cruz several years earlier, sent a congratulatory note. "The New Santa Cruz" was a spectacular sight, with thousands of lightbulbs illuminating its windows, railings, and arches.

Swanton's company also invested in other projects. In 1910, it built the Casa del Rey Hotel across the street from the Casino, to replace the Tent City cottages. By 1912, though, the company was in trouble. Train traffic to the resort dropped significantly as the automobile grew more popular. This, combined with an economic downturn, forced the financially overextended Boardwalk company to consider bankruptcy. In 1916, the Boardwalk and its related businesses were purchased by a group of local investors called the Santa Cruz Seaside Company. The company still owns it today.

Fred Swanton, the great promoter of Santa Cruz, went on to serve three terms as the city's mayor, beginning in 1927. So strongly was he associated with the concept, birth, and early success of the Santa Cruz beachfront that some people called the resort "Swanta Cruz." Although he managed to convince investors to funnel more than $7 million into developing Santa Cruz's oceanfront, Swanton died nearly broke in 1940, at age seventy-eight.

Looff

Entering the Looff carousel building from the bustle of the Santa Cruz Boardwalk is a sort of time travel. The 1911 carousel is a functioning ride, but it's also a window on a lost American art form. A century ago, carousels were often the centerpieces of American boardwalks and amusement parks, with their bejeweled, intricately carved horses galloping in slow-motion circles.

A German-made 342-pipe band organ, built in 1894, provides waltzing calliope sounds. The lights, music, mirrors, and richly painted wooden horses—all frozen in midstride—convey the hypnotic spell that the carousel once cast on its riders. Everything is old, but nothing seems like it. Each of the seventy-three restored horses is different— some appear playful, others sinister. Seventy-one are jumpers, which move up and down; the other two are stationary.

This carousel was created by Charles I. D. Looff, the furniture maker from Denmark who built the first Coney Island carousel in 1876. Looff built about forty carousels in all. The Santa Cruz carousel, valued at several hundred thousand dollars, is one of eight or nine still operating. It's also one of the few carousels with a dispenser for rings, which riders grab and try to toss into the mouth of a giant clown's face. Most of these horses are the same ones that galloped here in 1911. Some were purchased later from parks in Myrtle Beach

Fig.82. The second Casino building, photographed in 1911. (Courtesy Santa Cruz Seaside Company Archives.)

and San Diego. The horses are periodically restored, at a cost of about two thousand dollars per horse.

As rides go, carousels are pretty tame. Still, they have a gentle allure that epitomizes the aura of early American amusement parks. The carousel is not a thrilling ride, it's an enchanting one.

The heyday of the carousel stretched roughly from the 1870s to the mid-1920s, when roller coasters and other thrill rides were in vogue. For a while, then, the carousel seemed an anachronism. Many were torn down. But as the old always seems to become new again in this country, interest revived in the 1970s. Early carousel horses became recognized as an American decorative art form, and prices for them soared to several thousand dollars per horse.

Fig.83. The Boardwalk carousel in 1912. Rocking chairs were provided so mothers could sit and relax to the music of the 1894 Ruth and Sohn band organ. (Courtesy Santa Cruz Seaside Company Archives.)

Charles Looff's son Arthur built the other classic old ride here: the half-mile Giant Dipper roller coaster, which opened in 1924. In 1987, the National Park Service named the Looff carousel and the Giant Dipper roller coaster National Historic Landmarks. The Boardwalk was declared a California Historic Landmark in 1989.

Controlling Destiny

"Back in the 1960s, the city police department maintained the Boardwalk beat," recalls Seaside Company vice president Ted Whiting III. "Then, for budget reasons, they pulled back and there wasn't much of a police presence at all. In the 1960s, there were a few problems. There used to be a bunch of honky-tonks across the street, five or six bars. Those properties have since been bought by the Seaside Company and turned into other things. Then sometimes we had motorcycle gangs that would show up. So we realized we needed to have a tougher presence. In the late sixties and early seventies, the decision was made to take control of our own destiny."

As vice president of general services, Whiting oversees the security department for the Santa Cruz Boardwalk. Whiting's family has run food concessions on the walk for generations. "When I was seven years old, in 1953, I used to sit at the knee of my great-grandfather and he'd show me how to make popcorn," he says. Sitting in a conference room now, in the Seaside offices, Whiting discusses the Boardwalk's security detail, which employs seven full-time officers and more than thirty officers during the summer season.

"We can enforce policies. We don't allow loitering; we don't allow panhandling. If gang members come here, we ask them to not fly their colors. If they don't agree, we ask them to leave. We can issue them a trespass warrant. That tells them they're not welcome here for a year. It works pretty well.

"One of the things we believe is that if the presence of authority makes people uncomfortable, then those are probably the people we want to be uncomfortable. Those are not the people we want on the Boardwalk."

The result of the private security force is a clean and safe-feeling Boardwalk. Santa Cruz has homeless people, but you don't see them on the Boardwalk. It has college students, but they don't get drunk and rowdy on the Boardwalk. "We encourage people to have fun and enjoy themselves. That's what we're here for. But if you come to the Santa Cruz Beach Boardwalk for spring break and think you're going to find Fort Lauderdale, you'll be sadly disappointed."

UNDER THE BOARDWALK IS a world that most visitors to Santa Cruz don't see. It's where a lot of the Boardwalk's magic is created—by the carpenters, painters, mechanics, and engineers who repair and renovate the rides and games.

"One thing we work hard to do is keep the park looking new, even though a lot of it is old," says Marq Lipton, vice president of sales and marketing, standing outside a room where a lighthouse model from one of the rides is getting a fresh coat of paint. "This is where all the work goes on to make sure everything looks new. What we deal with here is memories and nostalgia. But we have a saying: We need to keep our nostalgia current."

It's early in December, the only month that the Boardwalk is closed. Outside, workers are replacing boards on the Giant Dipper. "I'll give you an example of how that can be tricky," says Lipton. "We have this popular product on the Boardwalk called Dip 'n' Dot ice cream. As popular as it is, we thought we should bring in a new stand for it, just to give it a fresh look. It's the same ice cream. So we brought in the new stand, and what happened? Dip 'n' Dot sales dropped by 50 percent. So we brought back the old stand and it went back up.

Fig. 84. Buddy King's Big Band in the Cocoanut Grove ballroom, 1947. (Courtesy Santa Cruz Seaside Company Archives.)

"Sometimes, we change things and people say they don't want us to change, they want it like it was," says Lipton, who has been with the Seaside Company for twenty-six years. "We have a ride on this end called the Cave Train, which is a dark ride. It takes you through a lost, prehistoric world. It's Flintstone-ish. We were going to take that out. But then this group got together and called themselves Save the Cave Train. People didn't want us to get rid of the Cave Train. So we threw away all the other concepts, put this back in, and modernized it.

"There's a sense of ownership here, and there's a sense of continuity. People show their children the experience they had as a child, and it becomes a shared experience through the generations."

Lipton stops to chat with Sam King, a technician who repairs arcade games. King displays a Pong game from the 1970s. Other games lying around range from Pac-Man to pinball to old mechanical strength machines. "Things change so fast," King says. "Now they're putting PCs in the games.

What you get in the home now is better than what was in the arcades just a few years ago. So we have to keep up and have things that are bigger and different. There's one horse-race game now where you can actually breed a horse. You don't just race it but you also breed it and name it."

THE NEW DOUBLE SHOT ride was originally planned to be 185 feet tall, but some Santa Cruz residents complained that it would be an eyesore. Santa Cruz is very conservative about growth and about change. A small faction here doesn't much like the Boardwalk, thinks it brings in too much traffic and riff-raff. Charles Canfield and the Seaside Company understand this. They have been able to control their destiny in the context of what Santa Cruz is and what its residents want. In the case of the Double Shot, they scaled the ride down to 125 feet, and the city gave its approval.

Santa Cruz's population has hovered at around fifty thousand for many years. The city saw some pro-growth activity in the 1960s, when the University of California at Santa Cruz opened, but it was replaced in the 1970s with a movement to preserve Santa Cruz's small-town character. In 1979, a growth management initiative was passed limiting growth. There are only about 1,500 hotel and motel rooms in Santa Cruz and will probably never be oceanfront high-rises.

Maggie Ivy, CEO of the Santa Cruz County Conference and Visitors Council, grew up in Southern California and says she is still struck by the natural beauty of the Santa Cruz coast. "When I walk on the beach here, I see dolphins and whales and otters. You don't see that much in Southern California. It's better preserved up here. What's great about the Boardwalk is that it's set against such a beautiful backdrop. When you go on the Giant Dipper or one of the other rides and you get to the top, you have this incredible view. I don't know that you'll find that anywhere else."

Marini's

Most of the concessions on the Santa Cruz Boardwalk have been family owned for generations. Marshall Miller, who operates Sun Shops Gifts, a Boardwalk retail store, says he and his wife, who met while working as

Boardwalk ride operators, are "sort of the newcomers. We've only been here thirty-three years."

The oldest concession is Marini's, which started on the Boardwalk ninety years ago as a popcorn and peanut wagon. Best known for its saltwater taffy, Marini's has four stores in Santa Cruz, including two on the Boardwalk and one on the Wharf.

"We stay the same and the park stays the same. I consider that a positive," says Joseph Marini Jr. "Some of the names and methods have changed, but not much else. Sno-Cones are now shaved ice. Milk shakes come out of a machine. Popcorn is still around, but it's air popped. We sell a few more apples than we sold then, but other than that, it's the same."

It was Marini's grandfather Victor who first brought saltwater taffy to the West Coast. Among taffy aficionados, Marini's is considered one of the best in the country.

"It's still pulled saltwater taffy here, which gives it a little different consistency. We do the pull right here in the window. You can stand right there and watch the whole thing. It takes about twenty minutes to see the whole process. We do it all day long."

Fig.85. Joseph Marini Jr. (left) and his son Joseph III dipping candied apples. The Marinis' Boardwalk business started ninety years ago as a popcorn and peanut wagon.

Joseph's son Joseph III, who runs the business today, puts on his cooking smock and dips a candied apple for his guest. Marini's uses ninety-five thousand apples a year and twenty tons of sugar.

"Taffy is the most popular item," he says. "They used to offer five flavors of taffy. Now there are seventeen, but the most popular flavors are still the same: chocolate, vanilla, peanut butter, molasses, cinnamon, peppermint."

Joseph Jr. offers a sample of peanut brittle, one of his favorite candies. "One of the reasons this boardwalk is successful is you can bring your children here and show them what you did when you were a kid and have them enjoy the same things. That's pretty unusual these days."

Kris Reyes, a fourth-generation resident of Santa Cruz who worked in Marini's for ten years, says, "The kitchen is exactly the same as when I worked there. Down to where the paddles are. Nothing's changed. I'll still come here sometimes and kind of push one of them out of the way and dip apples for a while." Reyes, who is now director of community relations for the Seaside Company, says his grandmother, mother, brother, and sister all worked on the Boardwalk. "I have a nine-year-old adopted brother and I suspect he will, too....

The histories of Santa Cruz families have been written for generations by their experiences at the Santa Cruz Beach Boardwalk, whether that means working here, owning family concessions, or just spending time here. The overriding theme of the Boardwalk is the families. It's deeply ingrained."

The Edge

It's a perfect summer evening in Santa Cruz, the dusky colors changing over Monterey Bay, a smoky cotton-candy glow darkening into the mountains. You buy a warm candied apple and feel the excitement of the crowd as you move south, pausing to watch the Riptide and the Speedway and the Giant Dipper. Later you stroll into the quiet shadows of the Casino arches, and wind up on the Wharf, where fresh seafood is cooking, blues music is playing, and the sea lions are barking. Leaning on a rail, you look east as the stars come out, feeling the wind, and imagine all of the land between here and the other coast, where the first boardwalks were built by immigrants back in the 1870s. Bay water splashes the pilings and the shoreline, reflecting the Boardwalk rides like a funhouse mirror. As night closes in, everything else disappears.

Fig. 86. Casino arches mark the north end of the Santa Cruz Boardwalk.

Although every boardwalk town is unique, the most successful embody a similar paradox: They have been able to preserve American traditions while at the same time feeding a hunger for the new.

The boardwalk seduces us with its rides, carnival lights, music, and sweet confections, but also because, like the country, it is a welcoming place. It beckons us to take a vacation from our habits and our routines, to re-imagine ourselves, if only for a few hours. Seduced for different reasons, from different places, those who have joined the parade tonight are unwitting collaborators, creating a fluid American folk art out here on the edge of the land on a breezy honky-tonk summer night.

Acknowledgments

I AM GRATEFUL TO all of the people who spent time sharing their thoughts and memories about boardwalks, many of which are included in this book.

I'm indebted to the talented staff at Rutgers University Press who worked on the book, including Marilyn Campbell, Kendra Boileau, Alicia Nadkarni, and Melanie Halkias.

A special thank you to Bert Krages, my agent, for finding a home for *America's Boardwalks*, and to India Cooper, for her exceptional editing.

I owe a debt of gratitude to Myra Janco Daniels for giving me the time and encouragement to pursue this project. Thanks also goes to a number of friends and co-workers, among them Janet Johnson and Tibbie and China, for their support and advice; George Hierro for the photography lessons, and his assistance on the cover design; and Linda Gordon and Lilybelle, for their uncommon friendship.

Selected Bibliography

CHAPTER ONE. *ATLANTIC CITY, NEW JERSEY: AMERICA'S PLAYGROUND*

Bary, Andrew. "Rolling the Dice: Will Borgata Rejuvenate Atlantic City?" *Barron's*, July 21, 2003.

Cunningham, John T., and Kenneth D. Cole. *Atlantic City.* Charleston, S.C.: Arcadia Publishing, 2000.

Curran, John. "Under Atlantic City Boardwalk, Luckless, Homeless Cling to Life." Associated Press, October 25, 2003.

Johnson, Nelson. *Boardwalk Empire: The Birth, High Times, and Corruption of Atlantic City.* Medford, N.J.: Plexus Publishing, 2002.

Kent, Bill, with Robert E. Ruffolo Jr. and Lauralee Dobbins. *Atlantic City, America's Playground.* Encinitas, Calif.: Heritage Media Corporation, 1998.

Levi, Vicki Gold, Lee Eisenberg, Rod Kennedy, and Susan Subtle. *Atlantic City: 125 Years of Ocean Madness.* Berkley, Calif.: Ten Speed Press, 1994.

Simon, Bryant. *Boardwalk of Dreams: Atlantic City and the Fate of Urban America.* New York: Oxford University Press, 2004.

Sokolic, William H. "Reborn Atlantic City Marks 25 Years of Casinos." *Camden Courier-Post*, May 23, 2003.

Van Meter, Jonathan. *The Last Good Time: Skinny D'Amato, the Notorious 500 Club, and the Rise and Fall of Atlantic City.* New York: Crown, 2003.

CHAPTER TWO. *CONEY ISLAND, NEW YORK: SHADOWS OF A SPECTACLE*

Burns, Ric. *Coney Island.* Video documentary, PBS American Experience, 1991.

Burns, Ric, and James Sanders. *New York: An Illustrated History.* New York: Alfred A. Knopf, 1999.

Caro, Robert A. *The Power Broker: Robert Moses and the Fall of New York.* New York: Alfred A. Knopf, 1974.

Carryl, Guy Wetmore. "Marvelous Coney Island." *Munsey's Magazine*, September 1901.

"Coney Island: To Heaven by Subway." *Fortune*, August 1938.

Denson, Charles. *Coney Island Lost and Found.* Berkeley, Calif.: Ten Speed Press, 2002.

"End of the Season at Coney Island." *Harper's Weekly*, September 13, 1903.

Gorky, Maxim. "Boredom." *The Independent*, August 8, 1907.

"Human Need of Coney Island." *Cosmopolitan*, July 1905.

Immerso, Michael. *Coney Island: The People's Playground.* New Brunswick, N.J.: Rutgers University Press, 2002.

Register, Woody. *The Kid of Coney Island: Fred Thompson and the Rise of American Amusements.* New York: Oxford University Press, 2001.

Thompson, Frederick. "The Summer Show." *The Independent*, June 20, 1907.

CHAPTER THREE. *ASBURY PARK, NEW JERSEY: THE CURRENCY OF MEMORY*

Ayres, Shirley. *Asbury Park: Postcard History.* Charleston, S.C.: Arcadia Publishing, 2005.

Capuzzo, Jill P. "Asbury Park's Long Recovery." *New York Times*, December 7, 2003.

Dorfman, David. Asburyboardwalk.com.

Mansnerus, Laura. "15 Years Later, Rebuilding Asbury Park." *New York Times*, December 5, 1999.

Martin, Antoinette. "At Last, Asbury Park Starts to Reawaken." *New York Times*, October 10, 2004.

Pike, Helen-Chantal, *Asbury Park.* Charleston, S.C.: Arcadia Publishing, 1997.

———. *Asbury Park's Glory Days: The Story of an American Resort.* New Brunswick, N.J.: Rutgers University Press, 2005.

Shields, Nancy. "Governor Touts Asbury Park Beach." *Asbury Park Press*, April 9, 2004.

Ward, John T. "Why Is This Man Smiling?" *New Jersey Monthly*, January 2004.

CHAPTER FOUR. *WILDWOOD, NEW JERSEY:*
EVERY NIGHT IS SATURDAY NIGHT

Francis, David W., Diane DeMali Francis, and Robert J. Scully Sr. *Wildwood by the Sea.* Fairview Park, Ohio: Amusement Park Books, 1998.

Kent, Bill. "How to Save Wildwood? Make It Even Wilder." *New York Times,* July 11, 1999.

Rozhon, Tracie. "Be-Bop-a-Lula, Wildwood's My Baby." *New York Times,* August 31, 2000.

Scully, Robert J. Sr. "A Brief History of the Wildwoods." Wildwood Historical Society George F. Boyer Historical Museum.

Stewart, Doug. "Doo Wop by the Sea." *Smithsonian,* June 2003.

Strauss, Robert. "In Wildwood, It's a Family Affair." *New York Times,* August 10, 2003.

Vanderbilt, Tom. "Doo-Wop Modern: Rediscovering the 1950s in Wildwood, N.J." *Washington Post,* May 7, 2000.

CHAPTER FIVE. *CAPE MAY, NEW JERSEY:*
THE ECHOES OF HISTORY

Dorwart, Jeffrey M. *Cape May County, New Jersey: The Making of an American Resort Community.* New Brunswick, N.J.: Rutgers University Press, 1992.

Jordan, Joe J. *Cape May Point: The Illustrated History, 1875 to the Present.* Lancaster, Pa.: Schiffer Publishing, Ltd., n.d.

Kent, Bill. "Dr. Frankenstein of Cape May." *New York Times,* May 25, 1997.

Lawlor, Julia. "Cape May Point, N.J." *New York Times,* September 3, 2004.

Mansnerus, Laura. "In Cape May County, a Time of Growing Pains." *New York Times,* September 5, 1999.

Minnix, Bruce M., Mary T. McCarthy, and Harriet Wise. *Cape May for All Seasons.* Cape May, N.J.: Preservation Media, 1998.

Salvini, Emil R. *The Summer City by the Sea: Cape May, New Jersey, an Illustrated History.* New Brunswick, N.J.: Rutgers University Press, 1995.

CHAPTER SIX. *REHOBOTH BEACH, DELAWARE:*
RESISTANCE AND CHARM

Church, Steven. "Rehoboth's Heart and Soul Is Made of Yellow Pine." *Wilmington News Journal,* July 4, 2004.

Devincent-Hayes, Nan, and Bowen Bennett. *Rehoboth Beach in Vintage Postcards.* Charleston, S.C.: Arcadia Publishing, n.d.

Goodman, Peter S. "Shoring Up So People Show Up." *Washington Post,* May 21, 1998.

Morgan, Michael. *Pirates and Patriots: Tales of the Delaware Coast.* New York: Algora Publishing, 2004.

Munroe, John A. *History of Delaware.* Newark: University of Delaware Press, 2001.

Strum, Charles. "Where History and Beaches Meet." *New York Times,* July 3, 1998.

CHAPTER SEVEN. *OCEAN CITY, MARYLAND:*
A DISTANT GLITTERING SHORE

Arney, June. "O.C. Vital Artery Is Wood." *Baltimore Sun,* June 9, 2004.

Corddry, Mary. *City on the Sand: Ocean City, Maryland, and the People Who Built It.* Centreville, Md.: Tidewater Publishers, 1991.

Devincent-Hayes, Nan, and John Jacob. *Ocean City, Maryland.* Charleston, S.C.: Arcadia Publishing, 1999.

Hurley, George M. *A Pictorial History of Ocean City.* Virginia Beach: Donning Company Publishers, 1979.

Mirabella, Lorraine. "Condo Fever Alters Face of Ocean City." *Baltimore Sun,* May 3, 2005.

Sullivan, C. John. *Old Ocean City: The Journal and Photography of Robert Craighead Walker, 1904–1916.* Baltimore: Johns Hopkins University Press, 2001.

CHAPTER EIGHT. *VIRGINIA BEACH, VIRGINIA:*
RECREATIONAL WALK

Chewning, Alpheus J. *Virginia Beach in Vintage Postcards.* Charleston, S.C.: Arcadia Publishing, 2004.

Dunn, Joseph, and Barbara Lyle. *Virginia Beach "Wish You Were Here."* Norfolk, Va.: Donning Company Publishers, 1983.

Gowen, Annie. "Good Clean Fun in Virginia Beach." *Washington Post,* May 25, 2003.

Holden, Tom. "Beach Has High Hopes for Labor Day Event." *Virginian-Pilot,* August 10, 1994.

Liu, Kimberly. "Morality Police in Virginia Beach." *Cavalier Daily,* June 12, 2003.

"Norway's Queen Will Attend Ceremony." *Virginian-Pilot*, October 13, 1995.

Tibbs, Marc. "Oceanfront Taking Steps to Shed Ghost of Greekfest." *Virginian-Pilot*, September 1, 1994.

Yarsinke, Amy Waters. *Virginia Beach, Jewel Resort of the Atlantic*. Charleston, S.C.: Arcadia Publishing, 1998.

CHAPTER NINE. *MYRTLE BEACH, SOUTH CAROLINA: CROSSROADS AT THE SEASHORE*

Bryant, Dawn. "The Twists, Turns of the Pavilion Plan." *Myrtle Beach Sun News*, January 23, 2005.

Bryant, Dawn. "Myrtle Beach, S.C., Council Agrees to Bail Out the City-Financed Radisson Plaza Hotel by Issuing $47.7 Million in Bonds." *Myrtle Beach Sun News*, April 2, 1004.

Floyd, Blanche W. *Tales along the Grand Strand of South Carolina*. Winston-Salem, N.C.: Bandit Books, 1996.

Gragg, Rod. *Planters, Pirates, and Patriots: Historical Tales from the South Carolina Grand Strand*. Nashville, Tenn.: Rutledge Hill Press, 1994.

McMillan, Susan Hoffer. *Myrtle Beach and the Grand Strand*. Charleston, S.C.: Arcadia Publishing, 2004.

Moredock, Will. *Banana Republic: A Year in the Heart of Myrtle Beach*. Charleston, S.C.: Frontline Press, 2003.

Mysak, Joe. "Study of Convention Hotels Has Lesson for Los Angeles." *Los Angeles Business Journal*, June 28, 2004.

Riddle, Lyn. "What Kind of Growth Is in Store for Myrtle Beach?" *New York Times*, December 6, 1998.

Schmid, Randolph. "Coastal Zone Growth Places Millions in Hazard Areas." Associated Press, March 2, 2005.

CHAPTER TEN. *DAYTONA BEACH, FLORIDA: SEA CHANGE*

Bozzo, John. "Deal Ends Boardwalk Impasse." *Daytona Beach News-Journal*, October 30, 2004.

Cardwell, Harold, Sr. *Daytona Beach: 100 Years of Racing*. Charleston, S.C.: Arcadia Publishing, 2002.

Cardwell, Harold Sr., and Patricia D. Caldwell. *Daytona Beach*. Charleston, S.C.: Arcadia Publishing, 2004.

Frederick, Henry. "Property Takeover May Change Boardwalk." *Daytona Beach News-Journal*, April 19, 2003.

Hinton, Ed. *Daytona: From the Birth of Speed to the Death of the Man in Black*. New York: Warner Books, 2002.

Hurtibise, Ron. "Enthusiasm for Change Not Shared by Everyone: Some Worry Daytona Beach Is Selling Its Soul." *Daytona Beach News-Journal*, July 20, 2003.

———. "A Glittering New Coastline Will Bring Prosperity but Won't Solve All Our Problems." *Daytona Beach News-Journal*, January 25, 2005.

CHAPTER ELEVEN. *VENICE BEACH, CALIFORNIA: LAND UNTO ITSELF*

Alexander, Carolyn Elayne. *Venice*. Charleston, S.C.: Arcadia Publishing, 1999.

Garza, Mariel. "Are Rules Taking the Funkiness out of Quirky Venice?" *Los Angeles Daily News*, April 6, 2005.

Groves, Martha. "Sore Spots on a Split Venice Boardwalk." *Los Angeles Times*, October 26, 2004.

Jablon, Robert. "L.A. Cracking Down on Freewheeling Venice Beach Vendors." Associated Press, October 31, 2004.

Stanton, Jeffrey. *Venice, California: Coney Island of the Pacific*. Los Angeles: Donahue Publishing, 1987.

CHAPTER TWELVE. *SANTA CRUZ, CALIFORNIA: PERFECT COMPOSITION*

Beal, Chandra Moira, and Richard A. Beal. *Santa Cruz Beach Boardwalk: The Early Years—Never a Dull Moment*. Austin, Tex.: Pacific Group, 2003.

Beal, Richard. *Highway 17: The Road to Santa Cruz*. Austin, Tex.: Pacific Group, 1990.

McCabe, Michael. "Santa Cruz's Timeless Boardwalk." *San Francisco Chronicle*, August 15, 1995.

O'Hare, Sheila, and Irene Berry. *Santa Cruz, California*. Charleston, S.C.: Arcadia Publishing, 2002.

Rubenstein, Steve. "Far from Sal's Last Laugh: Overhauled S.F. Carnival Icon Starts New Stint on Boardwalk." *San Francisco Chronicle*, May 28, 2005.

About the Author

JAMES LILLIEFORS IS A journalist and novelist whose work has appeared in the *Washington Post*, the *Miami Herald*, the *Boston Globe*, the *Baltimore Sun*, and elsewhere. He is author of the books *Highway 50* and *Bananaville* and was founding editor of the newspapers *Ocean City Today* and the *Maryland Coast Dispatch*, both in Ocean City, Maryland. Lilliefors lives in Florida, where he is senior writer/editor at the Philharmonic Center for the Arts, Naples.

A NOTE ON THE TYPE

This book was set in Goudy Oldstyle, a typeface originally designed by
Frederic Goudy for American Type Founders in 1915, and later adapted under
Goudy's supervision for use on the Monotype machine by Lanston Monotype
in 1930. The digital version used here utilizes OpenType technology, and was
released by the newly reorganized Lanston Type Company in 2005.

Book designed by Kevin Hanek
Typographic composition by Kevin Hanek and E. C. Graham
Printed and bound by C & C Offset Printing Company, Ltd., China